THE SONG
REMEMBERS WHEN

THE SONG REMEMBERS WHEN

hilary claire

DOUBLE
STOREY
a juta company

To the memory of my parents
and for my sister and brother,
Gay and Jon, who were part of all this.
For the next generation,
my children Thembi and Alexei and
my granddaughter Natasha.
— with love

Published 2006
by Double Storey Books,
a division of Juta & Co. Ltd,
Mercury Crescent, Wetton, Cape Town

© 2006 Hilary Claire

ISBN-10: 1 77013 041 1
ISBN-13: 978 1 77013 041 1

Editing by Henrietta Rose-Innes
Design and layout by Chalk Design
Printing by CTP Book Printers, Parow, Cape Town

| Contents |

Acknowledgements   6

Prologue: Johannesburg, 1964   9

Chapter 1: Coming Round The Mountain   16

Chapter 2: All The Bridges That You Burn   32

Chapter 3: Kol Nidrei   51

Chapter 4: Tula Baba   63

Chapter 5: Mona Lisa   75

Chapter 6: So Ver Van My Hart   94

Chapter 7: Goodbye, Clementine   133

Chapter 8: Ewige Gebergtes   151

Chapter 9: Coming In From The Cold   175

Chapter 10: But Who Knows Where Or When   196

Chapter 11: Mayibuye Afrika!   221

Epilogue: The Song Remembers When   259

| Acknowledgements |

A lot of people and even a horse were midwives to this book, and I want to acknowledge and thank them all:

The yearling who nearly kicked me into the next world – without him I would never have lain awake reconstructing my life.

My mother, Dorothy Blair – in the last weeks of her life, I promised that I would 'do something' with her autobiography, and chapters two and four are drawn from there.

My life partner, Jack Dowie, and my brother, Jon Blair, who patiently sought out websites and historical information and encouraged me to keep going.

My sister Gabrielle Blair-Maidan and my cousin Shirley Russ, who, along with Jon, read the manuscript in draft, encouraged me, picked up on details and made helpful suggestions.

Magnus Gunther, who sent me the draft manuscript of his research on the ARM, read the relevant sections of this book and offered constructive criticism.

Professor Milton Shain of the Kaplan Centre in Cape Town and Professor Aubrey Newman of the School of Historical Studies, Stanley Burton Centre, University of Leicester (UK), who helped with information about the nineteenth-century Jewish immigrants from Lithuania to South Africa.

Denis Judd, Emeritus Professor in History at our mutual place of work, London Metropolitan University, who answered questions about Jewish involvement in the South African War.

Russell Martin at Double Storey, who said Yes!

Henrietta Rose Innes – a meticulous and sensitive editor.

I am also grateful for information drawn from the following publications.

The extract from *Ha-Melitz* is taken from ND Hoffman (1860-1928), *Reminiscences of South African Jewry*, 1996, Jewish Publications, The Kaplan Centre for Jewish Studies and Research, University of Cape Town.

The quote from Sir Antony Sher is from his book *Beside Myself, An Autobiography*, 2001, Arrow Books, page 231.

I also made use of *The Boer War*, 2003, by Dennis Judd and Keith Surridge, Palgrave Macmillan.

Magnus Gunther wrote a history of the NCL/ARM as part of the 'Road to Democracy' project launched by Thabo Mbeki in 2001. For me, reading his research has been the first opportunity to get an overview, to understand the context, the history and the personalities involved; it is a powerful example of how history literally does not exist till it is researched and written.

The author wishes to thank the copyright holders for permission to quote from the following songs:
BMG Publishing (with thanks to Kim Hartogh)
    'The song remembers when' written by Hugh Prestwood
    © 1993 Careers-BMG Music Publishing (BMI)/Hugh Prestwood Music (BMI). All rights on behalf of Hugh Prestwood Music (BMI) administered by Careers-BMG Music Publishing (BMI). All rights reserved. Used by permission.
    'I started a joke' © the BeeGees
    'Mona Lisa smile' © Jay Livingstone and Ray Evans (with thanks to BMG for negotiating the rights with Hal Leonard Corporation)
Gallo Music Publishers (with thanks to Michaele Ceresato)
    'I started a joke' © the BeeGees (with BMG)
    'Gloomy Sunday' © Billie Holiday
    'Where or when' © Lorenz Hart
Peer Music Publishing (with thanks to Malcolm Burger)
    'You are my sunshine' © Jimmie Davis and Charles Mitchell
Universal/MCA Music Ltd (with thanks to Ryan Hill)
    'How much is that doggie in the window' © Bob Merrill
The author would also like to thank Consuelo Roland for the initial negotiation of the song rights.

I was standing at the counter
I was waiting for my change
When I heard that old familiar music start
It was like a lighted match
Had been tossed into my soul
It was like a dam had broken in my heart.

After taking every detour
Getting lost and losing track
So that even if I wanted
I could not find my way back

After driving out the memories
Of the way things might have been
After I'd forgotten all about us
The song remembers when.

I guess some things we bury
Are just bound to rise again
For even if the whole world has forgotten
The song remembers when.

– Trisha Yearwood –
The Song Remembers When

JOHANNESBURG, 1964

The judge said they were all rats. He was particularly unimpressed that some had ratted on their friends, had sold them down the river – he was good on mixed metaphors. They were a slur on genus *Rattus*. After they'd given evidence against their comrades, which led to long sentences for sabotage, these rats were given one-way tickets out of the country. The people they'd betrayed went to prison – like Eddie Daniels (photographer, age thirty, coloured, fifteen years), who joined Nelson Mandela on Robben Island; Hugh Lewin (journalist, twenty-four, white, seven years); and Stephanie Kemp (physiotherapist, twenty-three, white, five years with two years suspended). There were quite a lot more, most as young as Hugh and Stephanie, who worked out their sentences in Pretoria Central Prison. The judge patronised everybody:

he said he felt sorry for the students whom he was sentencing; he had taken into consideration their youth, the fact that they'd probably been influenced by older and more sinister characters, or had wanted to leave the organisation, or had already pulled out. For John Harris (teacher, twenty-seven, married with a baby), there was not patronisation but uncamouflaged hatred, the teeth-baring hatred reserved for those who have betrayed their own kind. Nobody had taken him seriously when he'd phoned the police and the press and said a bomb was going to go off, and they should clear the train station. A white woman had been killed. The defence failed to convince the judge that he was insane. John went to the gallows singing 'We shall overcome'.

Ronnie and I read the accounts of the trials in the newspapers sent to us in England. We were, it was reported, among the 'rats' who had abandoned the sinking ship, as was our friend Mike Schneider. We were intellectual rats, rats with attitude and some other surprisingly human attributes. Ronnie was completing his PhD in physical chemistry, Mike had a sensible grown-up job and wrote poetry. And as for me, I'd gone to one of the best schools in the country, achieved a good degree in history and politics, could type with all ten fingers, play the piano to Grade 7, speak three languages, swim and play tennis.

The judge's metaphor of abandoning the sinking ship sounded good but was confusing. Though we'd fled the country and become refugees, he couldn't have meant we'd abandoned the sinking Ship of State, since the South African regime wasn't sinking – it stayed afloat under the Nationalists for another twenty-seven years. Probably he meant that the group we were part of – the African Resistance Movement, ARM – was the ship that sank. But nearly forty years on, despite hitting a few ice floes, it is clear that the ship of resistance didn't sink at all. What we tried to do in the ARM was all part of something much bigger than us, continuing with Umkhonto weSizwe, Biko's Black Consciousness Movement, the 1976 Soweto riots, and then fifteen years in which violence, uprisings, funerals, sabotage and terror became daily occurrences. There was a civil war in South Africa and it led to liberation, finally, when Mandela walked free from Victor Verster Prison on 11 February 1990 and became one of the most respected statesmen in the world and elected president of the country where, twenty-seven years before, he had been branded a traitor and been lucky to escape the gallows.

I abandoned ship the year Nelson went to Robben Island. My parents had to deal with the Special Branch police. Their Peugeot was impounded, and my mother was questioned by a certain Lieutenant Swanepoel. They had found 'incriminating seeds and grasses' on the floor of the car, matching plants that grew round the site of one of the pylons we'd blown up. How could she explain this? She couldn't. All she could say was that I had borrowed her car.

In the months before leaving, when I had indeed borrowed her car, I had developed a painful, distressing plan to protect my parents, which depended on lies, pretence and ignorance. I fabricated arguments and stopped visiting my parents. I crossed the road when I saw my mother on the campus of Wits University, where we both worked. I wanted it to be public knowledge that she and I were not on speaking terms, so that if they took my parents in for interrogation they could truly say, 'Our daughter didn't even talk to us, everyone knew we were estranged, we certainly did not know what she was doing.' Under interrogation, my mother sincerely repeated the script that I had written for her in my imagination.

Swanepoel and his sidekicks came to her house and spent hours going through all our belongings, which she'd brought from our flat. They pawed over the books and the papers, photographs and letters. They confiscated a whole variety of 'incriminating' literature, including some of Ronnie's PhD notes, which they believed contained secret formulae. Ronnie was a physical chemist, and they became excited when they thought they'd turned up codes for making bombs. What they'd actually found were the results from his experiments on the chemistry of surface tension. They would have taken my copy of *Black Beauty* if it'd been in the flat, but they did find Bertrand Russell's *Why I am not a Christian* and they confiscated that.

Swanepoel demanded a formal interview with my mother. Dorothy insisted that he interview her in her office at the university, where she was a senior lecturer in French. She told me later that she'd wanted to put herself in a position of authority, behind her desk. She asked for her secretary to be present to record what was said, though the real reason was to have moral support. Attempting to maintain her superiority during this humiliating interrogation, she launched a counter-attack of intimidation, using high-falutin' phrases and correcting the policeman's spelling and grammar. She insisted that certain sentences in her statement, which, she said, had been put into her mouth, be changed.

But away from the Special Branch, she and my father raged at my deception. How dare I involve them, borrow their car and pretend we were just going for a drive in the country? My father was quick to suggest that I must have been Ronnie's dupe, under his thumb, doing what I was told. There were fearsome, accusatory rows between my father and my mother, with my little brother as silent witness. My father blamed my mother for my treachery, my selfishness, my lack of concern for his position as a government official, my putting everyone in the family at risk. They both slid into the established patterns of family war, the channels of which were cut into their lives like river beds waiting for flash floods. She rose to my defence, even though she too felt angry and betrayed. Things escalated quickly, so that both of them were soon tearing at each other's very identity.

When things got bad, my brother fled to friends, to his matchbox collection, to the far reaches of the garden beneath the old, old cedar trees, where once we'd had badminton parties. I'd kept rabbits in enormous hutches there, where they could tunnel into the earth and build their burrows.

Things which should never be said were said; the damage could not be undone. Eventually, my mother and father would fall into exhausted silence, refusing to speak to each other, until eventually it became necessary to communicate directly and not through a child or servants. But the strange thing is that, through it all, somewhere deep down, they were also proud of me. My brother told me so. Which I cannot explain, except that in their hearts they must have understood something of the principles and outrage that were behind our decisions and actions.

Songs and music have forever been the accompaniment to my life. I do not know how I could live without music, and I am bemused by people who tell me they are 'unmusical' or don't need or like music. I can be stony faced with self-control at funerals, apparently impassive in the face of jolly japes or tragic scenes on television; but when the music starts, my emotional wellsprings are unblocked and tears or laughter become irresistible. When I am old, I may no longer be able to hold a tune, but I want to go down singing.

The other week, at two in the morning, restless and sleepless, my leg shattered in an accident, cradled on soft cushions, my broken ribs making it impossible to move let alone muster the breath to sing, I went through part of my repertoire. First, over and over, without knowing why, I croaked out the Richie Havens version of the Bee Gees ballad:

I finally died
Which started the whole world living
Oh had I only known
The joke was on me ...

Perhaps my mind was playing verbal tricks, willing me to see the funny side of what had happened to me. Perhaps I was dead, or should be, or could have been. The joke was on me. But still, the song is not, I think, about jokes, but about the continuity and connections of generations, our failures to understand the past, atonement. When I'd lain crumpled and still on the grass after the accident – I'd been run over by a galloping horse – battling to breathe gently through the pain, my whole life had not flashed before me. Instead, afterwards, lying night after night unable to move, I lived through each year of my life, slowly reconstructing how I'd got from the smiling, innocent two-year-old child in the photo that had been on my parents' mantelpiece to who I am now.

It was a serial: each night I'd pick up where I'd left off the night before, fascinated by the detail of my memories – as if I were reading the life of someone I knew about, but did not know.

And, too, I looked for the key to my identity in the stories of those past generations who'd left everything behind – just as I'd done, nearly a century later. Whose names I no longer hold and did not pass on to my children, but who are still part of my and their identity. My flight from South Africa was the latest chapter in a family story that goes back to the nineteenth century, a story of exile and the creation of a diaspora. Lewis Green and Gumpert Woolf, my maternal great-grandparents, fled from Eastern Europe to England. Lewis Bledin and Esther Brody, my paternal grandparents, fled from Zhagare in Lithuania to South Africa.

Mostly, the Jews arrived in England, America or South Africa speaking only Yiddish. Their surnames got distorted: my grandfather became 'Bledin', but there are other descendants who spell their surnames Blieden, Bleadon, Bleaden and Bleeden. When Great-uncle Israel Blieden, the rabbi, who left Lithuania at the same time as my grandfather Lewis, realised that *bleedin* was a swearword in English, he changed his name to Bleehen. You trace your identity through your name; but the female line vanishes, and when the names change, it is hard to know just who and where you come from.

For those of us who come from Africa, memories are reignited by the smells of the crisply blackened, burnt veld, the sweat of people who have been labouring in the sun, the heat-soaked red earth, the pungency of seaweed and ozone that heralds the wide Atlantic Ocean miles before you catch the first glimpse of its misty horizon. And the pictures: remembered emotion animates the frozen figures set in their landscape of the past, gives them back their feelings. But the most powerful of all for me, the thing which ignites memory, is sound – words, music, where meaning, memory and emotion are entwined and inseparable. Beethoven, Bach, Monteverdi and Messaien, blues, jazz and rock, pop songs, hymns, ballads, political songs – all are part of a passionate language, 'the lighted match tossed into my soul'.

She' ll be coming round the mountain when she comes
Singing Yi Yi Yippee Yippee Yi!

| Chapter 1 |

COMING ROUND THE MOUNTAIN

They told me I sang 'Yi Yi Yippee Yippee Yi' at the top of my lungs (but in tune) as my parents wandered round the decks of the troop ship. We were anchored in the Freetown harbour, waiting for the next stage of the journey down the convex coast of Africa. It was early 1943. We were the only civilians on the ship; the other passengers, uniformed men and a few Quaker pacifists who were joining the Ambulance Corps, were going on to the Seychelles. I was the only child on board, a mascot for the troops. Eighteen months old, I rode on my father's back in a canvas bag specially made for me by the quartermaster, legs dangling, so that I would be safe with him if the ship went down – and singing.

Earlier, my parents and I had been sent from London up to Aberdeen in a blacked-out train, where we shivered and hung about for weeks waiting to be told we could finally be on the move. Eventually, the little ship left the British Isles and pottered down the northern Spanish coast, battered by wild weather in the Bay of Biscay, then round the huge curve of West Africa. Attacked by a blockade of U-boats, it limped into Freetown, burning. Wide-eyed, her first time out of Europe, my mother watched the boys diving for pennies in the warm West African sea; she bartered clothes for mangoes, avocados and bananas with the clamouring children who drew up alongside the ship in rickety rowing boats. When we were finally on the move again, our bodyguard as we crossed the equator into the southern hemisphere was made up of dolphins and flying fish. Now the heavens were upside down, the stars had lost their bearings and so had she ...

We disembarked at the Cape Town docks in May 1943. Dad was returning to his roots and my mother ... well, who knows what the future would bring for her, six thousand miles from home? There was no one to meet us. My parents had been forbidden by the British military authorities to give anyone any information about our possible arrival.

Dorothy was apprehensive about meeting her in-laws, whom we would stay with before starting the three-day train journey to Bulawayo in Southern Rhodesia. Grandpa Bledin emerged briefly from The Shop, gave his newly arrived daughter-in-law a polite, prickly kiss and vanished again behind the counter. Aunty Sheba, Uncle Solly's wife, hugged me in welcome, demanding 'come give your fat aunty a kiss'; and then bewildered my mother with the all-purpose South African expression of emotion – 'Ag shame hey!' – as she held me at arms' length, admiring me and my white coat of soft rabbit fur, a present from the Bleehen cousins in London.

Ouma Bledin was suspicious and apprehensive: Mum was blonde and blue-eyed, I was even blonder though my eyes were brown, the English accent was all wrong ... probably her son had committed the cardinal sin of marrying out, and this impostor was really a *shiksa* – despite the wedding in a shul, announced with a gold-rimmed invitation card sent all the way from Birmingham to the South African parents who would never ever go to England.

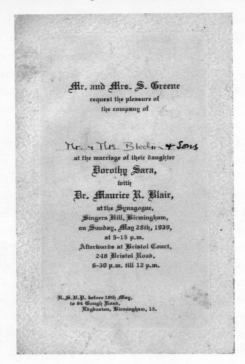

Mr. and Mrs. S. Greene
request the pleasure of
the company of

Mr. & Mrs. Bledin & Sons

at the marriage of their daughter
Dorothy Sara,
(with)
Dr. Maurice R. Blair,
at the Synagogue,
Singers Hill, Birmingham,
on Sunday, May 28th, 1939,
at 5-15 p.m.
Afterwards at Bristol Court,
248 Bristol Road,
6-30 p.m. till 12 p.m.

R.S.V.P. before 18th May,
to 54 Gough Road,
Edgbaston, Birmingham, 15.

The huge wooden crates containing the wedding presents of china, glass and silver, packed and shipped from England, sat on the docks at Cape Town, badly damaged by the fire on board. In due course, they would follow the little family into the heart of Africa.

We didn't really get to know our grandparents till we returned to live with them four years later. To us children, Pa, my grandfather, was a kind, quiet little man whose face lurked somewhere behind round-framed glasses and a grey beard, under a matching grey hat. He'd been kicked in the face by a horse, so they said; he was embarrassed by the dent in his jaw, and had grown the beard to conceal it. (Although I have been in the path of a galloping horse, which charged through me as if I were invisible, and I nearly lost my life; so I wonder about that kick in the face.)

He spoke heavily accented English, and was much easier to understand in Afrikaans, which he spoke to the coloured servants and clientele in his shop. No one knew why Lewis had left 'the old country' and come to South Africa. Lewis's older brother, Israel, had settled in the UK round the same time. They came from an observant Orthodox family and, though Israel kept the faith, Lewis was a very reluctant Jew.

It is hard to find out anything about this lost generation. The Nazis were pretty effective in wiping out the evidence, and they themselves left few papers, never talked about their own past. We have just one bit of information about Lewis's earlier years: the South African records show that Lewis Bliedin, dairyman, born in 1881 in Zhagare, Russia, arrived in Cape Town in 1898 aged seventeen and was naturalised in 1905. Imagine the triumphant smiles, the waving of papers as those who can read English scrutinise and translate the foreign words, a toast – *lechaim!* A citizen of somewhere ... at last.

Tantalisingly, that's it. That's all we know. Nothing more about the years before Lewis came to South Africa and little enough about the years after. But perhaps his story went like this ...

> The news went round Zhagare about the possibilities of a new life in ... South Africa? Where was that? Someone came with a map of the world. The family huddled round as a finger traced the long journey all the way down the west coast of Africa, round that huge bump first negotiated by the Portuguese four centuries earlier, and yes! There it was, at the bottom of the continent ... the tip ominously named the Cape of Storms. Someone knew someone who had gone there, and written home. Africa! There were many rumours, not just of storms and shipwrecks on a wild rocky shore, but of unimaginable wild animals and savages, people with skins as black as night, walking round almost naked in the heat of the sun blasting down on a shrivelled landscape.

Young Lewis and Israel Bliedin were Russian Jews living in the Pale of Settlement – the ghetto areas where Jews were allowed to live in all the countries under Russian domination (a bit like townships in apartheid South Africa). They were part of a huge exodus of Jews from Lithuania that started as a trickle in the 1880s, built up in the 1890s and continued until the First World War. Four million Jews left the Pale of Settlement during those years, people who were persecuted at every turn and restricted politically, geographically and economically by the Russian government, still reacting with brutality years after the murder of Tsar Alexander II.

Persecution of the Jews would be played out again in Europe in the next century. Some of them learned from their own history when another target in another continent, the black people of South Africa, were the victims. But unlike the people who left their countries in the late 1800s and the 1930s, the black population of South Africa had nowhere to go; there was no exodus; they created no diaspora.

By the time Grandpa made the journey south, Jews had been leaving Lithuania for the Cape for ten years already, creating a community that he would join. One of the established Jews in the Cape used to send articles to a Lithuanian newspaper, *Ha-Melitz*. In 1891, readers in Lithuania suffering under the Russians were awed and fired up to learn:

> The farmers in South Africa generally respect Jews very much and exalt them above all the nations under the sun. When a Jew comes to these farmers, they receive him with great hospitality. They immediately outspan his horses, then the Jewish guest is called inside, is honoured, given food and drink and a place to spend the night without payment. The snakes of anti-Semitism have not laid their poisonous eggs in this country.

Heady stuff, and not entirely romantic wishful thinking – the pious Dutch Reformed Afrikaners lived by the Old Testament. Good publicity like this must have filled young Lewis's heart with hope for his new life on the other side of the world.

His parents blessed him, sent messages of love to his brother,

and reminded him to keep the faith, make sure the rituals and festivals were properly observed, eat kosher and marry a nice Jewish
girl when the time came. No one else in the family that we know
of followed him from Zhagare to South Africa. Lewis, a mere boy,
was on his own. He never returned to Europe and he never saw
any member of his original birth family again.

The story went that Lewis walked all the way to the sea
from his home, with a bundle on a stick like Dick Whitting-
ton. Probably, he slipped over the border into Latvia, making for
Liepaja on the coast in Latvia, where the boats went straight to
London. He was one of the first to line up at the newly established offices of agents who organised the whole trip – from what
the travellers should do in London, to food and accommodation,
to berths on the ships that would take them to Cape Town.

When the ship docked in London, Israel came to find his
brother and took him up narrow stairs to his cramped little room
in a grimy alleyway near the main Whitechapel Road. There
wasn't room there for Lewis, so he slept for a couple of nights
on the bare wooden floors of the Jews' Temporary Shelter. Money
was short for both of them, so he queued at the soup kitchen for
a kosher meal. He spent most of the precious few days he had
in England with Israel, swapping news, or trying to find his way
round the back streets of Whitechapel. Surrounded by people
speaking Yiddish, with little shuls behind ordinary house doors
round every corner, shops selling kosher food and notices everywhere in Hebrew, it was a bit like being back home again. Except
that the English that the natives spoke was incomprehensible.

A few days later, Lewis was taken by train to Southampton
with the other emigrants to board one of the Union-Castle ships,
which would take them down to the Cape along with the Royal
Mail. For their ten-pound ticket (more than it cost to get to
America), they were packed into steerage or third class, in shared
berths. Safety, sanitation, health and modesty were not top priori-
ties for the people selling the tickets. The story goes that Grandpa
lived on hard-boiled eggs and cold toast for the entire six-week
voyage.

Lewis and Israel's decision to leave Lithuania when they did was timely. Less than ten years later, the pogroms slashing through the shtetls of the Pale had started up again. Perhaps they wouldn't have survived. And ten years later, Great-uncle Israel would have been kept out of Britain by the Aliens Act, the outcome of a campaign orchestrated by the 'British Brothers League', the forerunner of the fascist, anti-semitic British National Front.

My mother's family were also refugees from the Pale who settled in England. Great-grandfather Lewis Green and his huge family lived near Israel Blieden in Great Prescott Street in Whitechapel. But they were Polish refugees, not Lithuanians, and even though the Greens and the Bliedens passed one another in the streets, they never met and would not have talked. It would take another generation to bring together families from different shtetls, though they were all subject to the same huge historical imperatives.

Docking in Cape Town, Lewis got off the boat onto the wooden slatted quay, stretched his cramped legs and wandered around, looking for somewhere to sleep. How amazing and beautiful his new country seemed, even when the extraordinary flat-topped mountain looming over the peninsula, rising almost directly from the shoreline, was shrouded in mist. Coming as he did from the flat forested lands round Zhagare, he contemplated with awe the mountains spreading away into the distance. The sea sparkled in the sun, waves curled and stretched and crashed, spreading themselves on the sand, bubbling and fizzing. Quite unlike the grey leaden North Sea, reflecting an overcast sky and moving gently on a stony shore, which he'd seen for the first time when he'd stepped onto a boat to take him from Lithuania to England. This white sandy beach was extraordinary, strewn with monstrous black seaweeds – vegetable, but more like many-legged animals with bulbous blind eyes, the likes of which he'd never seen or imagined before. Lewis remembered the stories they'd told back home of this dangerous, unpredictable world which was now to be his home.

Checking a name and address written in Hebrew on a piece

of paper, which had been given to him by friends of the family a lifetime away in Zhagare and saved carefully through the long voyage, Lewis trudged up Adderley Street and down Longmarket Street. He walked past the grand Victorian civic buildings, the banks and import-export firms and houses with broekie-lace balconies, till he eventually came to the slummy quarters where the Jewish immigrants lived cheek by jowl with the coloureds. Initially, he sank with relief into the comforting warmth of people who had come before from the old country, speaking his own tongue, following customs that were instantly familiar. But there was the frisson of the unknown, of risks and adventures. People were talking about the goldfields, unbelievable wealth up in the Transvaal a thousand miles to the North; gold waiting to be gathered up, fortunes to be made. It was almost too good to be true – a young Jew from Zhagare could dream of being a millionaire!

So, shortly after his arrival in Cape Town, Lewis joined the gold rush in the Transvaal. When the young Lithuanians got to Johannesburg, whatever their dreams, they had to make do: huddling together, sharing the rent in tiny rooms in Berea, Fordsburg, often exploited by people who knew the ropes better than they did. The reality and the dream were a long way apart.

When the Anglo-Boer War (now more inclusively called the South African War) broke out in October of 1899, Lewis was still in the Transvaal. They say in the family that he joined the army – but which one? There was no formal conscription on either British or Boer side, though if you lived in an Afrikaner community you were obliged (more or less) to go along with your local commando groups, and apparently some Jewish immigrants to the Transvaal did go off to fight with the Boers. So, did Lewis wear a soft khaki hat and ride a horse – *could* he ride a horse? Did he carry a wonderful new Mauser supplied by the Kaiser? But it seems unlikely. He wasn't a sinewy farmer with land, wife and children to protect. He was just a skinny nineteen-year-old come to the goldfields to seek his fortune. I guess that he joined the British volunteers, that he had some sympathy with the grievances of the Uitlanders in the old Transvaal Republic – he and his family knew all about being denied citizenship. With the British, he would have had to make do with a much inferior Lee-Metford rifle, but ultimately, he would have been on the winning side.

After the war was over, Lewis returned to Cape Town. There was no fortune jingling in his pockets. He became a *smous*, a travelling salesman, peddling goods from door to door. His main clientele was the poor coloured community of the Cape, but he provided for the kosher needs of the Jewish community too. He established a regular round of people who took his milk, eggs, butter and cream. Some of his compatriots – smouses who traded in old clothes, haberdashery or shoes – carried their wares from door to door in sacks on their backs. Grandpa had a cart for his goods, for they were far too fragile to bang about in a sack. In the early days, he could not afford a horse so he pushed and pulled his cart manually up and down the unmade sandy roads of the Cape Flats, with the wind blowing the loose greyish-white sand in his eyes. But when he wrote home to his family and to his brother Israel in London, he talked not of the hardships and humiliations of his new life, but of the promising future, the opportunities. He'd made a good choice, he thought, coming all this way to the tip of the world. London was all very well, but here in Africa how much more freedom he had to build a life. And he was getting married – a beautiful girl, Esther, yes, Jewish, also from the old country, from Plungyan, not far from Zhagare as it happened, very devout, hard-working – everyone should be proud of him.

By the time my parents returned to the Cape in 1947 with me and my sister, my grandmother Esther – 'Ma' or 'Ouma' – was a small, thin-lipped, bad-tempered, disappointed woman already nearly seventy years old. I remember her striking face: high prominent cheekbones; firm round chin, which some of her sons, I and several of my cousins inherited; widely spaced black eyes. Years later, I saw a documentary about the Baltic States, and stared amazed at my grandmother's faces populating the screen. Esther never learned to read or write English to her dying day, and her spoken English was not easy to follow. She spoke Yiddish to

Oupa and Afrikaans to her coloured servants. With us, she spoke a mixture of broken English and Afrikaans.

Who was she, this girl, only eighteen or nineteen years old when she travelled across Lithuania from Plungyan to the coast, then to London, then six thousand miles to South Africa? She did not come out to the Cape to marry Oupa, and did not know him or his family till she arrived. Before her marriage, she lived for several years in Cape Town with people her family had known back in Plungyan; they had sponsored her to come out. Like Oupa, she came alone and knew she was not going back. She left behind everyone and everything she knew in a bid to make something of her life. We were told that her family were scholars and rabbis. The Plungyan records show a family called Braude, which was probably hers, though in South Africa she became Brody. Did something happen to persuade her to leave on her own, or was it just ambition for a new life?

When I was much younger, I daydreamed that I would somehow be able to research and write Ma's story, recreate and acknowledge a totally ordinary but moving life. The stories I told myself about Ma became part of my own identity, my sense that I was part of a line of women of steel, courage, ambition and determination. I was surely fantasising, inventing a history which I had no way of verifying. Even though I knew she was considered difficult and bad-tempered, that she bullied and fought with her daughters-in-law and intimidated her meek, low-key husband, when I thought about Ma my eyes would glint, my back would get straighter, my resolve firmer.

Ouma could make a man's suit. She'd been a tailor in Plungyan and had brought her skills with her. In the early days, she quickly found work among the immigrant Jews who had already settled in Cape Town. Round the end of the century, when she was in her early twenties, a marriage was arranged by the *shadgin* with young Lewis Blieden, also from Lithuania – a couple of years younger, but with good prospects, quiet, hard-working and trying to establish himself in the dairy business.

She was ambitious, orthodox, industrious; the engine that kept that family of wild boys grinding on. She threw tantrums to get her way, cried but never showed affection, either to her husband or her children. Still, her life was her family and their future was her reason for being. My semi-literate grandmother's energy and determination fired the family. She ensured that her sons went to an English-speaking school where they would get a good education, even though she couldn't understand much when they jabbered away in their new language. Two of her five sons became doctors, one a lawyer. Oupa might have been a washout in her eyes, but her sons fulfilled the dream.

Half a century after her death, I now realise how Esther impacted not just on my father's childhood and adolescence, but on his feelings and relationships with women all his life: on my mother, on me and my sister; which, in a chain through the generations, impacted on my relationship with my daughter. Esther inspired a heady mixture of awe, respect and resentment. She manipulated people through tantrums and tears and enforced her certainties about education and observance – all of which led to gratitude, guilt and rebellion, and also deep confusion.

Dad admired and valued intelligence and ambition in women; he was disarmingly proud of his wife's and his daughters' work and achievements. But Esther had marked him with ambivalence. He encouraged 'his' women in public life, but was also angry and bitter not to have a 'proper wife' who would keep the observant house his mother had kept. He backed my sister and me in our ambitions to have careers and to be financially independent, but found girls and women with opinions, who challenged his paternal authority or mocked his conventions, intolerable.

My grandparents' and indeed my parents' generation created networks of material and emotional support in strange lands. It's not an unique story, but told over and over again by Jews and Irish, by Caribbeans, Poles and Italians, Somalis and Rwandans, all through the nineteenth and twentieth century and into the twenty-first, and it is my link to the experience of millions of others trying to better themselves – sometimes faced, as were my grandparents in the old country, with hatred, racism and genocide.

My own immediate family survived, but we know what happened to the descendants of the Bliedens and Braudes left behind in Zhagare and Plungyan. Between 1923 and 1939, the Jewish population of Plungyan, which dated from the fifteenth century, went from 4 236 to 1 700. During the war itself, the whole Jewish community was wiped out. When the South African actor Sir Antony Sher, whose family also came from Plungyan, went there in 1992, he met the last Jew still living there, who told him 'Jewish history stopped here in June 1941'. The last Jew had created a monument to the Jews massacred in the forest just outside the town. Seventy-five Jewish school children were buried here – baptised by the local priest at the last minute in a desperate but hopeless attempt to save their lives.

In South Africa, Lewis and Esther Bledin set about building their new lives together. By the mid-1920s, they had moved up in the world, from Brooklyn to Main Road, Maitland. The shul was up the road, and they now had a house with five bedrooms and an inside bathroom. They owned 'The Shop' next door – and the police station across the road. Ouma, Oupa, Uncle Solly and his wife Aunty Sheba took up their positions behind the counters, though Ma was not always in her appointed place, since she also presided over The House next door, 'Leomor'.

The sun never seemed to penetrate The Shop, which was dimly lit with low-wattage bulbs. There were wooden counters running round three sides, with two flaps with brass hinges that you lifted to get to the back. Wooden shelves and little drawers on one side contained haberdashery – threads, needles, buttons, pins, snap fasteners, hooks and eyes in all sizes, sewed on to paper sheets. Opposite were clothes: adults' and children's vests (white, with or without short sleeves); socks – white, grey, long, short; underpants and grey shorts; shirts all neatly folded in labelled drawers with curved brass handles. People equipped their children for school from these counters. There were bolts of material kept under the counter; lengths were measured on a brass yardstick fixed to the counter, and ripped with a satisfying sound after being started off with enormous scissors. In the middle section, next to the door leading into the storeroom at the back, was food – raisins, cheese and dry goods like beans, sugar, samp and salt, all sold loose from huge sacks and measured in the brass balance that stood on the counter. The Shop even had bacon in the food section, since the customers were not all Jews. There were drawers full of screws, nails, nuts and bolts, and tools in one corner – spades and picks hanging from the ceiling, screwdrivers, saws and hammers: impor-tant equipment, essential to life in this raw new country, where people were still building their livelihood from scratch. Every-thing hanging from the wooden ceiling had to be hooked down while precariously balancing on the wooden stepladder. This was the Algemene Handelaar. You name it, they sold it, as Aunty Sheba said.

There was a vast and magical storeroom behind The Shop. A brooding grey cat lived there. This was special for us, since my mother claimed she was allergic to cats and we weren't allowed to have one. There were also mouse and rat traps, set with lumps of cheddar cheese, and occasionally we'd find a poor broken body, limp and bloody. Here were enormous yellow wheels of Edam and Gouda and, most delicious of all, the strong 'cooking' cheddar cheese, from which my Oupa would cut me a crumbly, tongue-biting sliver. Here were industrial-sized tins of Koo jam – apricot, watermelon and peach – and dried fruit in barrels: prunes, apricots and raisins. Here too was the konfyt and the mebos which my grandmother made herself: watermelon, apricot, ginger, pineapple and citrus. The Shop and its storeroom smelled dry and sweet. We were allowed to take a prune, a handful of raisins or some apricots from the barrels. There was sawdust on the floor, and we made patterns with our bare toes in summer sandals.

Oupa and Ouma set up all their children to the best of their ability. The eldest boy, Solly, was taken into The Shop and served behind the counter with his new wife, Sheba. The second son, Leopold, had been set up in his own business by the parents. But the third son, my father Morris, was ambitious, discontented with the narrow life of Cape Town, determined to do better than his brothers. Esther's hopes and dreams – doctors, lawyers, professional people of substance in the world – had penetrated his ambitions and his vision of his own future. He looked at the options in Cape Town, discovered that one of the few professions not taught at the University of Cape Town was dentistry, and announced that he would become a dentist – which would mean he had to go to England.

In 1930, nineteen-year-old Morris arrived at Southampton, off the boat from Cape Town. He was taken in by his cousin Zalman Bleehen, Israel's son. Morris Bledin was about to become Maurice Blair. Dorothy Greene, the grandchild of nineteenth-century Polish Jewish refugees, was about to enter his life. Hitler was about to squeeze Europe by the throat and, in my own family, the old certainties of Judaism would not survive.

Growing up under apartheid, that oppressive and heartless regime, has helped me understand my ancestors' past, as well as the world I grew into. But religious identity is something I still struggle with. Judaism dominated my father's childhood, but it did not dominate ours. We were defined by negatives – not Christian, not practising Jews. As the years went by, we were more and more alienated from the Jewish cousins, aunties and uncles that we visited from time to time. My cousins called us the 'hoity-toity Blairs', referring not just to our passage up the ladder of class and status, but to the secularity of our household. Thought ourselves too good for the Jewish family we came from, did we? The decision to send us to Christian-faith schools, to move into smart, mostly gentile suburbs of Cape Town and Johannesburg when we could afford it, and above all the influence of our English, secular, intellectual mother all turned me into a teenager who was mortified with embarrassment when cousin Beatie – vulgar and loud in purple and red, unmistakably Jewish – greeted me effusively one day when I was out in the street with non-Jewish friends. Ag shame hey.

Religion and ethnicity and identity were all tied together for my grandparents' generation, as they are for many, many people still. Religion gave them the rules to live by on a daily basis. The violent persecution of the pogroms was a part of their story. Treated as social problems and hated aliens in their own countries – as people who would devour babies, who were scarcely human – they kept a sense of pride in their identity through the very things which had marked them out as 'beyond the Pale': the rituals and certainties of Judaism. For intelligent young men with an intellectual bent, there was only talmudic study. For women, there was not even that. It is not surprising that, though German or French or English Jews would claim the national identity of the countries they lived in, with Jewish identity secondary to that, Jews from the Pale only thought of themselves as Jews and this is what they passed on. They really didn't have any choice.

Both my brother and I were sent to shul and went through bat or bar mitzvah ceremonies. Years later, my Dad tried and failed to get Ronnie, my non-Jewish husband-to-be, to convert to Judaism before we married. If only, he often said, trying to rationalise the unhappiness of his own personal life, he had married a woman who was prepared to be a proper Jewish wife and mother ... if only Dorothy had lived up to the wedding vows: 'And the said Bride has plighted her troth unto him in affection and with sincerity, and has thus taken upon herself the fulfilment of all the duties incumbent upon a Jewish wife.'

As for Dorothy, her main memory of the orthodox ceremony was 'disappointment and slight outrage at my passive role ... not even the opportunity to say "I will!" '

So we grew up with confused and confusing messages about ethnicity – outsiders 'passing' for Wasps, with no sense of our own history. The irony is that my ancestors were all refugees, fleeing discrimination, enforced conscription or persecution. My own parents lived through times when the odds were stacked against them, when their ethnicity might have destroyed them. But from my family members themselves, I learned nothing at all about any of this history – a history that would have given me some sense of who we were and why they were like they were. Only now do I have some sense of what their Judaism meant to them.

For me, the religious rituals were irrelevant. If I claim my identity as a Jew now, it's because of history, not religion: the nineteenth century, the tragedies of the twentieth. Through chance – call it serendipity – our family escaped; but a few decisions taken differently ... the realisation is with me always. I have also learned something from this history. Being a Jew is not an excuse or a refuge. One cannot inflict on other people, simply because of who they are, the evils that were perpetrated against the Jews.

In this ambiguous world one thing was certain: we were South Africans. But what did this mean? With our English mother and our South African father, who had both reinvented themselves in their twenties, we children also ended up inventing ourselves as we went along.

| Chapter 2 |

ALL THE BRIDGES THAT YOU BURN
COME BACK TO HAUNT YOU

Dorothy's grandfather was called Gus. He'd been born Gumput, an unsuitable, 'foreign'-sounding name which his English in-laws, the Samuels, quietly ignored. He'd fled from Poland to avoid conscription when he was still in his teens, like Lewis and Israel when they left Lithuania. The army – especially a conscripted army – was not an attractive option for an ambitious boy, brainy rather than brawny. Gumput's youth, shut up all day in a *cheder* with a *rebbe*, learning the holy words and interpretations of the Torah and the Talmud, did not prepare him for a soldier's life, and he had no intention of taking the risk of being forced into it. Gus was shrewd and he was not penniless. His papers were in order: he had an expensive 'passport' – not to enter a European country, but to leave Poland.

A hundred years later, my brother Jon was twenty-five and living in England when the South African Defence Force caught up with him. The SADF was pouring into Angola, where the Portuguese had left and the Cubans arrived. The army authorities required Jon to report at Middelburg, Transvaal, for his National Service. He did not bother to respond. A different continent, a different cause. *La diaspora continua.*

Once Gus reached England, his was a real rags-to-riches, immigrant-to-pillar-of-society story. His family had been lawyers in Poland; he was already an educated man, and as soon as he arrived he went to night school to learn to read, speak and write English. He met someone who knew someone and it all led to marriage (arranged by the rabbi) with wealthy, beautiful young Esther Samuel, whose family had been in the country for generations and were 'something in the clothing trade'.

The Samuels sponsored their son-in-law's first business, and by 1879, the ambitious young Polish immigrant, still only twenty-five years old, had joined the Freemasons. By 1886, he was Master of the Lodge. In the 1890s, he applied to be naturalised as a British citizen. No scrabbling about for 'three upright respectable citizens' to sponsor him: no less than fifteen masons offered to vouch for his good character.

Gumput brought with him from Poland little besides his rigid commitment to Orthodox Judaism and to education, his ambition to better himself and a good head for business. The established Jewish community – anxious that the new Ashkenazi arrivants might embarrass, make demands, stir up anti-Semitism and generally prove to be short on cultural know-how – didn't need to worry about Gumput. He observed their carefully prepared instructions, which gave newcomers helpful advice about talking quietly in the street, not pushing in and not drawing attention to themselves. He swiftly established himself in the middle class: he lived in a salubrious area in a large Edwardian house, sent his daughters to one of the best schools in Birmingham and was a founder member of his local Orthodox synagogue, Singers Hill, where in due course his daughters and his granddaughter would marry. By the time my mother was old enough to remember him, her grandfather Gus Woolf was a stocky, dour, laconic man with gold-rimmed spectacles and a toothbrush moustache, who did not waste words talking to children.

His pretty, loving wife Esther's story is hidden but not too hard to imagine. She had eleven brothers and sisters, most as successful and wealthy as her future husband was to become, but far more free-and-easy and fun-loving. One of them may have spotted young Gumput and, recognising a reliable potential husband, set up the marriage.

When he died, he left a fortune. Such a pillar of the community merited a decent-sized column in the *Birmingham Post,* announcing that his estate was valued at the huge sum of £10,191. He left his money to the hospital, the synagogue and various Jewish charities; he also endowed the Salvation Army ('because they were so kind to our boys in the Great War'). The remainder went to his sons-in-law, daughters and grandchildren, with the desire expressed that 'as far as possible this money shall be used for the Hebrew and religious education of my said grandchildren.' Gus dotted the *i*'s and crossed the *t*'s of his will with his own particular bit of blackmail: HUSBANDS MUST BE JEWS. 'Should his daughter Natalie [the only one who remained unmarried] or any of his grandchildren marry a person who shall not have been born of Jewish parents and who shall not at the time profess the Jewish religion, such daughter or grandchild shall forfeit all share and interest in his estate.' To 'marry out' in an Orthodox Jewish family is to commit familial suicide; your grieving family will sit *shiva*, as for a death, drape the mirrors in black, put out the special chairs left empty for close relatives; friends and family will come and sit through the week of mourning, nibbling on snacks and drinking the offered cups of tea or coffee.

Curiously, though the Bledins' commitment to Judaism flourished under the South African sun, in England great-grandfather

34

Gus's religious orthodoxy backfired. All his daughters turned away from Judaism. After she married and left home, my English grand-mother, Evaline, seldom set foot inside a synagogue, except for the High Holy Day services and weddings, which didn't count. She passed on to her children not a sense of important, mean-ingful rituals which defined their ethnicity, but bitterness about the restrictions and rigidity of her Orthodox upbringing. She did not care that two of her children married 'out', if only they were happy. And so, by the next generation, religious zealotry had died out. Not one of Eva's five children carried on the reli-gious traditions that their Orthodox Polish grandfather had been so determined to perpetuate. All the grandchildren inherited their hundred pounds from Gus's will, but by then Gus had been dead for years, and there was no one left to insist on the terms of his will.

Who cares now about these rigid old men, bringing their faith and their rituals with them from 'the old country', surrounding themselves with the signs of their religious identity – creating a ghetto in a new land? In a new century, where religious funda-mentalism, whether Jewish or any other, represents a threat to rationality and peace, I ask myself what my great-grandfather's religion must have meant to him. He was not part of that later generation for whom proud and unapologetic Judaism, obedi-ence to the biblical injunction to 'go forth and multiply', would be their answer to the Shoah. But in Russia and Poland, the Jews stuck together so that they could survive. Judaism was their identity. Judaism was a cloak to wrap around themselves in the hostile, gentile world – both in the old countries, and in the new countries where they sought asylum. More than that, religion and its injunctions – about how to be a good Jew, what to eat, what to do on Fridays and Saturdays and all the festive occasions – kept alive their connection with their past. 'We are what we remember,' someone once said; but perhaps, too, we are what we believe in, and perhaps in all these years of trying to understand this family I come from, I had been asking the wrong question about religion. Not 'How can these people believe all this?' but 'What does it mean to them?'

Not long ago, I met someone I had been to school with in South Africa. We talked about how each of us had tried to fight against the hypocrisy, itched and scratched and torn at the unchosen identity of oppressive white 'madams' which constrained us; how we looked for something to believe in. A secular political ideology which I believed might save us and our country had carried me through and stopped me going crazy. My friend had turned to fundamentalist Christianity.

For Jews in my great-grandfather's time – apart from those who embraced socialism, the only available alternative belief system offering a brighter future – being Jewish *was* their identity and provided meaning. To search for anything beyond this in the nineteenth and early twentieth century is to miss the point. For such people, religion was as taken for granted as the air they breathed, and to question them about their faith and its rituals would have been as peculiar and redundant as to ask why they got up in the morning.

Judaism failed in this family line, but belief in education didn't. In her miserable, doomed marriage, Gus's daughter Evie, my grandmother, held on to the belief that education would be the ticket to freedom for her children. She enrolled them at the Public Library, subscribed to the *Children's Encyclopaedia* and the *Children's Newspaper*; organised piano lessons when she could afford it; and sent my mother Dorothy to Saturday-morning concerts, with Sir Adrian Boult conducting the Birmingham Symphony Orchestra. A quarter of a century later, though I was completely unaware that I was following in the footsteps of her childhood, Dorothy sent me to Saturday-morning concerts in Cape Town, and once a week the *Children's Newspaper* would arrive through our letterbox, all the way from England, months out of date.

Mum's father, Sam Green, was born in Whitechapel in London. His father, Louis Green, was a tailor who had come in the 1880s from Konin in Poland – another refugee from the Tsar. In 1902, Great-grandfather Louis was naturalised a British subject, just ahead of the Aliens Act which was designed to keep people like him out.

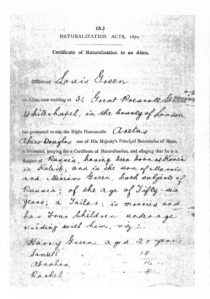

The Greens could hardly have been more different from the Woolf family, living out their repressed, assimilated, middle-class lives in smart Edgbaston, with servants, silver and cut glass to show their social status. There were thirteen Green children in this close-knit, gregarious, noisy family. Sam's father and mother only communicated in Yiddish. They never learned to speak English, were never anything other than working-class, Jewish, East End immigrants. His many brothers and sisters were a colour-ful lot – entrepreneurs, part-time musicians, artists, in show-biz; one, nicknamed the Duchess, set up a hotel in Hove (a cut above Brighton), where poor relations came from time to time for free holidays. None had any pretensions or ambitions to become pro-fessional people. These two families, who might well have had their origins in the same small Polish town, but at very different ends of the social scale, were about to meet.

In 1907 Gus's daughter, Eva Woolf, was in her late twenties. She was under five foot, slim, rather plain but with large beautiful blue eyes, which all her daughters and some of her granddaughters would inherit. She was a serious-minded, clever young woman who looked set to be left on the shelf. More worrying, in the eyes of her parents, was her liaison with a *goy* called William, whom she was meeting secretly in the park; they were exchanging loving messages on postcards and threatening to marry. To save her from a fate worse than death, Esther's friend Lil, who lived down the road, came up with a solution. Young Sam Green had recently come to Birmingham. He was twenty-three, poor but Jewish – and available. Ergo, he was an ideal husband for Eva. (Lil was married to Sam's brother, Maurice.) Gus declined to give a large dowry, but paid for a very grand wedding which was reported at length in the local paper. After a smart honeymoon, in which the new bride 'travelled in a dress of strawberry silk, and a hat of silk straw adorned with French flowers', Gus Woolf, a pawnbroker himself, set up his new son-in-law in his own pawnbroker's shop in Birmingham.

This was to be a marriage made in hell: Eva and Sam were incompatible long before they started life together. Eva had grown up in a middle-class household with several servants, books and music. Her father might have been a religious fanatic, but he believed that his daughters should have an education. Eva had matriculated at a girls' grammar school and worked as a secretary; she could speak French, produce a passable oil painting (my sister Gay inherited one of her pictures) and play the mandolin. She did not know how to cook, sew, or keep house and did not care to learn … and she was in love with someone else. Sam was a working-class cockney, a charming, presentable, happy-go-lucky chappie with no trade or prospects, who had left the Jewish Free School in Whitechapel when he was twelve. He was also a gambler, and for the first few years of the marriage, when my mother and her elder sister were little, was unable to hold down a job. Gus bailed him out, not once but twice, and so did Sam's elder brother Maurice; but when Sam went bankrupt a third time, they both washed their hands of him.

Sam did not get called up and sent to the front, but even though he was at home throughout the First World War and in the years after, the Greene family became increasingly hard up. With three little girls under eight, Eva struggled through the years of the Great War. Her mother tried to help. In a bizarre reversal of the Red Riding Hood story, Grandma Woolf would turn up at their rented house with baskets of goodies and bunches of flowers from her garden. But in 1918 Grandma died, and Gus withdrew into tight-lipped disapproval of his feckless son-in-law – and, by association, his daughter and her 'brood'. Uncle Maurice Green and Lil, who had acted as go-between in the doomed marriage, offered material help – hand-me-down clothes outgrown by their daughter, a bolt of cinnamon-coloured cloth from which two coats were made for the eldest girls, to be passed down from one sister to the next till they finally fell apart. Eva's younger sister Mabel passed on hand-knitted dresses for the poor-relation cousins. When these started to unravel, they were never to be fixed – Eva had no aptitude or interest in needlework. Dorothy and her sisters were spared the hand-knitted knickers.

The three little Greene girls were sickly and bronchitic, always undernourished, prey to every epidemic: mumps, measles, chicken pox, whooping cough, diphtheria, pneumonia. They suffered from chronic catarrh and agonising chilblains. Mum's brother, Uncle Victor, born in the year after the First World War ended, had rickets.

Eventually, after the Great War, when there was no work and no money coming in, one of Eva's many Samuel uncles came to the rescue. He owned and ran two cinemas, and he found Sam a job first as a projectionist, then as a distributor of films for Classic Cinemas. Family to the rescue again … and again … and again. This time, Sam found his niche and kept his job.

Sam came and went from the family home; sometimes he was there, mostly not. He was based away from Birmingham and returned for weekends. No one asked questions. I have also lived with a husband who was away all week, leaving me with young children, and I know how the tensions build, without time to resolve things before the man leaves again for his weekday world. When Sam came home, there were arguments and rows, but conducted in the manner of middle-class people. Eva never raised her voice: instead, there was that cold, tight-lipped anger which is so scary for children. One day, Dorothy came home from school to find the bailiffs sitting smoking by the fire. Eva had rushed off to find her father, Grandpa Woolf, to get proof that the furniture was all in her name.

They may have been living in poverty, but Eva still held on to her middle-class values. The mandolin hung on the wall in the parlour, untouched; there was a piano in the front room, though no one played it; wedding-present china was displayed in a glass-fronted cupboard in the 'dining room' (also unused). She did not associate with the 'lower-middle-class' neighbours down the road. Her wealthy parents and the Samuel uncles and aunts all lived near each other in grand detached Edwardian houses, with marble sundials in the gardens and conservatories – even electric bells under the carpets to summon the maids. Fallen on hard times, Eva held on fiercely to her ideas of middle-class propriety. When she could no longer afford a charwoman, she still refused to clean the house – servant's work – and did nothing when her children were being eaten alive by fleas. But she instilled in her children the notion that, poor as they were, they were a cut above 'common', working-class people. She was, after all, the woman who had added the '*e* at the end', turning Sam's original surname Green into the more genteel Greene.

Ten years after coming to Africa, when Dorothy could afford it, the proper ways of doing things all came back to her. In the heat of South Africa, Dorothy unpacked the heavy crystal and the cut glass, the silver-plated cake forks and grapefruit spoons which had been wedding presents from the wealthy Samuel uncles. She made special holders out of green felt, which kept the silver shiny inside its mahogany boxes. The ivory-handled knives were held in place with individual silver clips. We grew up using the correct knives for fruit, dipping our sticky fingers into glass bowls set out next to each place, unfolding our table napkins in their personalised rings (not serviettes – please!) and spreading butter curls – fashioned with ridged, wooden butter pats and set out in cut-glass containers – on the toast, which we took from a silver rack that had to be polished once a week. All this silver and glass was kept shiny and sparkling with Silvo and rags by a black maid sitting in the sun against the wall in the yard. And underneath the carpets in the dining rooms in our houses in Cape Town and in Johannesburg, Dorothy installed electric bells to summon the maid.

Underneath the surface, Dorothy carried the scars of childhood poverty, which time had not managed to obliterate. The memory of poverty clung like blackjacks. She'd been comfortably off for years, but my mother re-used envelopes, printed out the first draft of everything she wrote on the blank backs of old letters and circulars, glued every fragment of broken china back together with superglue, stuck pieces of soap together on a bottle-top to make a new bar. Decades before recycling, she saved tiny bits of string, rubber bands, glass jars, pots and pans that were chipped beyond redemption. She had jars of 'fresh herbs' years past their sell-by date, scraps of material that no one would ever use in a huge drawer underneath a bed, jars full of buttons that matched up with nothing. She could not bring herself to throw anything away. I'd always thought I was seeing in my mother the fallout from desperation dating back to the Depression years. But I was wrong. It was real poverty, long before the Depression. My parents' experience of poverty meant they were always frugal, never extravagant, and that's how they brought us up. My mother's bag of cleaning rags, the labelled jars of used screws, the stubs of sealing wax – these frugal habits link her children, of a generation which takes for granted the laden supermarket shelves, to the 1920s.

For a while in the late sixties, in England, living on social security with two small children and an out-of-work husband,

I would pick over the cheapest cuts in the self-serve section in the supermarket, blocking with my body what I was doing from critical eyes; calculating just how small a piece of scrag-end of lamb would stretch to feed the four of us, bulked out with lots of potatoes, onions and carrots; buying the broken biscuits sold loose in the market; waiting for the end-of-day reductions before the stallholders packed up and went home. Later, I could afford more, but it took me years to break free of that frugality and remember that I did not have to scrimp and save any more. Dorothy was like that too.

Even when Sam started to earn regularly, he was reluctant to support his family, and there was controlled anger, more devastating than shouting. Perhaps Eva never said it out loud, but Dorothy picked up this message: her father did not care enough for his children to be there for them. He did not care sufficiently about his wife, who felt she had given up her life. Dorothy believed that her father would rather throw his money away in the betting shop or watch dogs chasing a rabbit round a track than spend time with his young children; that he cared more about his card-sharp friends than about the girls' school fees. He expected Eva to have food on the table when he returned home, never saying where he'd been, and then complained that it was only leftovers. When Sam walked out, Eva would turn to her children and say bitterly, 'See what he's like? This is what marriage brings you. Take my advice. Don't get married.' A message which only one of them, the eldest, Vera, took to heart. She became a nurse – a bossy, jolly, hearty woman, a woman with plenty of woman friends. Always plain, she grew stout as she got older, and wore her thick, straight hair pinned to one side with a slide like a child. She was busy; she did good things in the community. She took physically handicapped children camping, ran the Guides. In due course, she took on the duties of an unmarried daughter, and cared for her ageing mother in the home they shared till Eva finally died, aged ninety-four.

Eva discovered the existence of Molly through a letter left in a pocket of a jacket to be taken to the drycleaners. The writer said how delighted he'd been to meet 'Mrs Greene' at a reception. The real Mrs Greene had been at home with her youngest children. This is how she found out that when Sam disappeared, he made a short journey to Bournville, where his girlfriend Molly – a gentle, roly-poly Irishwoman the same age as Vera, his eldest daughter – cooked him a nice meal, fussed over him and compensated for the misery of his marriage.

Sam's generation did not contemplate divorce. They remained locked together by vows that no longer meant anything. As she grew older, Eva played her trump card: she refused to turn on her hearing aid. So she sat out her days, deaf, sour and discontented, a woman who seemed never to smile, a sad hostage to an arranged marriage and middle-class morality. Finally, even her disappointment lost its sting in senility, the unaggressive absence and incomprehension of a woman who asked her adult grandchildren what they planned to do when they grew up, if she recognised them at all.

Molly was with Sam for nearly forty years. He never moved in 'properly', saying it would not be correct; in his nineties, when he was too old to drive, he would get Vera to drive him, or take two buses there and back between his own house and Bournville, where she still lived. Molly was at his funeral, standing quietly apart, a dumpy little figure of nearly seventy, in a not very well-cut coat and a frumpy hat. By then, all his surviving family, his children and grandchildren, knew of her existence. Not all had the grace to go and talk to her.

As well as the hundred pounds, Gus left us all another legacy. Passed on to my grandmother and my mother, it reverberated through their personal lives and in due course mine. It was not about education, faith, ritual or Jewish identity. My great-grand-father was cold and aloof, interested only in religion and his business. His daughter Eva grew up in a bleak household, where her father showed no affection to his daughters or his wife. Trapped in a loveless, arranged marriage, Eva in her turn would fail to give her second daughter, Dorothy, the loving warmth that would have helped her grow through her difficult childhood into confident adulthood. Reflecting on this sad heritage, *her* second daughter, my sister Gay, once said: 'Dorothy passed on this legacy to me. She did not know how to show her love, she did not know how to reach me as I was growing up. Not till the end of her life did she finally discover how to express her emotions. But she *was* a survivor – she survived through her intellect, she clung to her intellect to save her, even when she no longer needed saving.' Like the cancer which in the end claimed Dorothy, the experience of growing up without love may go into remission, but it comes back to destroy personal lives. Though she came to understand and empathise with her parents, she died without ever letting go of her bitter feelings of having been cheated and deprived as a child. With no other model to draw on, as she admitted herself, she fell back on familiar patterns of anger and resentment in her own marriage.

In 1930, the year Dad made his way towards the Northern hemisphere from Cape Town, reversing the journey taken by his father and his mother, Dorothy's school entered her for the entrance and scholarship exam to Somerville College in Oxford. After the interview, the telegram arrived saying she'd had been awarded an Exhibition – a minor scholarship, worth £40 per year. She couldn't possibly survive on this meagre amount, her father would not help her and Somerville did not agree to hold the place open. Oxford opened its doors, offering a tantalising glimpse of the life of the well-heeled, and then slammed them shut again. Thirty years later, in 1960, the same telegram arrived for me. I was not the daughter of a travelling salesman who'd gambled away his daughters' school fees, who would never support one of them through university. So I went up to St Hugh's, up the road from Somerville. But as it turned out, I could not make my mother's dreams come true.

Instead of Oxford, Dorothy went to read French at Royal Holloway College, in the country some miles outside London, on a full scholarship which covered everything. It was a claustrophobic, all-female world, but the day was saved when she became friends with Marie-Rose Martinet, a young French *assistante* at the College. In the Easter vacation, Dorothy went to France and stayed with Marie-Rose's parents and brother Daniel. A medical student, he went soon afterwards to Spain to join the Republicans in the Civil War.

Marie-Rose's father was Marcel Martinet, a published poet, a pacifist, a conscientious objector and a socialist. He knew all kinds of famous people: Trotsky had visited him before escaping to Mexico; Stefan Zweig and other radical artists and writers were his friends. But his pacifism and socialism were not popular in those days before World War Two. He'd been excluded from the literary elite of Paris because he spoke out against war and championed the voiceless and the oppressed, and since 1918 the family had been living quietly outside Paris.

In the Martinets' drawing room, Daniel and Marie-Rose, M. and Mme Martinet talked about the unfolding politics in Europe. Dorothy listened. In those brief days before Europe imploded again, Marie-Rose's politicised family gave her a new way of seeing and making sense of the world, even as it threatened to fall apart all around them. The Martinets talking about how poverty structured people's lives, and how power was with the wealthy and the privileged; Dorothy thought about her own family and how true that was, even on a very local scale.

Dorothy started to learn some very bitter truths in the years running up to the war. She stopped going home to Birmingham, and got jobs in her university holidays in different cities in Europe, mostly teaching children English and being an au pair. In one house, the Frenchwoman and her daughters openly mocked her hand-knitted swimsuit, which stretched ignominiously when she came out of the pool, drooping below her crotch and hardly hiding her breasts. As far as they were concerned, she was nothing more than a servant. There was another humiliating incident at a dance in Germany. An aristocratic Hungarian seemed to fancy her and, holding her close, said, 'I can smell if there is a Jew in the same room.' She froze but was too frightened to say anything. When the music ended, she quickly slipped away. Then there was the occasion in 1934, when she stayed for a while with the Witte family in Frankfurt. Herr Witte was a senior manager at I.G. Farben. Frau Witte didn't know she was Jewish and one day at table said, 'We don't like what is happening here, but it isn't safe any longer to entertain our Jewish friends. We have to pretend we don't know them in the street, and we sometimes even cross the road rather than meet them. We have to consider Herr Witte's post. We can't afford for him to have any unfortunate associations.' Dorothy kept silent. Even though she hadn't believed in Judaism for years and certainly wasn't a practising Jew, she felt she was living a lie.

After that, she didn't return to Germany, and found jobs in Hungary instead. In Budapest, she lived with a wealthy Jewish banking family, the Zweigs, talking English to their son Bela and his friends. They told her about the quotas preventing some of their Jewish friends from entering university. Bela kept urging his parents to make plans to leave, but they felt they had too much to lose to make themselves refugees; they couldn't accept that they stood to lose their lives. A young nephew, Karl, had come from Vienna to stay with them. He belonged to the Austrian Social Democratic Party, already forced to go underground. He was probably the first man that Dorothy was really serious about. When he asked her to marry him, she thought about it. He was very special, brave, interesting, committed. But how could she exile herself from her roots?

One day, back in London, she received a large album containing a valuable collection of postage stamps, with instructions from Bela to keep them safely till further notice. Then came a small carefully wrapped parcel. Inside was a glass jar – of tomato puree! Buried in the puree was a diamond ring. Dorothy had it valued and put it in the bank for safekeeping. The Second World War broke out and she lost touch with Bela. Some years later, she received a letter from Australia. It was Bela. He had survived. His parents and Karl had gone to the gas chambers. He asked Dorothy to send the ring and the stamp collection, which would give him some much-needed funds.

So Dorothy became a feminist and a pacifist, influenced by Vera Brittain's *Testament of Youth* and what she saw in Europe. But her real choices were much more personal. To take this job or that one, live in this flat or that, go out with this man or that one. Marry my father, or wait for something better to come along. If my mother had married Karl, and gone to live with him in Europe, she would have been another statistic in the Shoah. Instead, she married my father, and ended up on the other side of the world.

In May 1939, a few months before war was declared, at Singers Hill Orthodox Shul, the marriage was solemnised between Maurice R Blair and Dorothy S Greene, second daughter of Samuel Greene and Evaline (née Woolf). The bride wore a long white dress made of heavy guipure lace, a soft veil that spread to the ground and twirled round her ankles, and lace gloves that covered her arms modestly above the elbow, and she held a bouquet of fat white peonies. Lewis and Esther Bledin had not made the 6000-mile journey from South Africa for the wedding, so they never saw their third son's transformation from Brooklyn

boy to this elegant young man in top hat and tails and a white bow tie, carrying his white gloves with the confident, languid air of someone born and bred to this manner of dressing.

Neither of them wore their glasses, and in the photo they have the short-sighted, soft-focus half-smiles of people posing for the camera.

Dorothy and Maurice met through mutual friends. Unlike both their parents' marriages, this was not arranged, but their own choice. Years later, when my father was already dead, faced with the incontrovertible failure of either of them to be happy together, Mum told me with regretful hindsight that she had been naïve, insecure, romantic. In spite of the miserable example of her own mother and father, she arrogantly thought she knew where they had gone wrong and could do better. And deep down, she was desperately afraid of being a spinster, yearned to love and be loved.

Neither of my parents ever talked about the war when we were growing up in South Africa, and we never asked; it was very remote, a history that didn't concern us. My mother took me to England in 1952 when I was ten. I took in the unrepaired bomb damage, the sodden misery, the charmless suburbs, the pale, pasty relatives, the ugliness of it all. My aunt Beryl said, 'Put on your shoes when you go out the gate, people don't go round barefoot here. What will the neighbours think?' None of this was redeemed by the Jewels in the Tower, Hampton Court or the Changing of the Guard. Where was the sun? I knew I had been born here, but proudly claimed my South African identity. Still, I picked a leaf from a laurel growing next to St Paul's and pressed it in my diary, and decided that God existed when I realised how close to destruction the magnificent Cathedral had been.

By the end of 1941, when I was born, Dorothy and Maurice were in digs in Erith, on the south bank of the Thames, immediately opposite the docks. Dad was a locum, replacing a doctor who had gone to the war. Erith has no Underground, and we did not make the nightly trek to sleep with hundreds of others. When the sirens started, we crouched under the Morrison Shelter – a fortified table in the living room. Sometimes my parents used the precious petrol ration allowed to doctors and drove out of London, away from the bombing, and we all slept in the

second-hand Morris. All that was left in my own consciousness was a terror of sirens – fire engines, ambulances, police cars; well into my teens, I would go rigid at their hee-hawing screams.

My parents' marriage was already in trouble before I was born. One night, their road was air raided, and the whole of the neighbourhood was ablaze from the firebombs. Everyone rushed out to help put out the fires, but Dad chose this moment to smoke a cigar he'd been saving for a special occasion. For Mum, contempt grew slowly, but this was a significant incident: a mark of cowardice. He once told me that yes, he had been in Whitechapel during the Battle of Cable Street in 1936, when Jews and socialists together confronted the fascist Mosleyites. He'd been visiting his Uncle Israel Bleehen, but had hidden in an upstairs room, terrified out of his wits at the potential violence. He had peeped through the net curtains at the Jews and their non-Jewish allies holding up their banners with the famous slogan 'They shall not pass', blockading Cable Street and preventing the Blackshirts marching through. Years later, Dad still suffered huge anxiety about anything he thought was physically dangerous. When we were growing up in the Cape, my sister and I simply ignored his anxious cries of 'Be careful, Hila; don't go up there, Gay!' as we rushed recklessly around on the rocky beaches of Boulders or Clifton, climbing on the rocks and jumping into pools, or splashing fearlessly into the huge breakers that broke over the wall of the sea pool at St James.

Dad returned to Southern Africa in 1943 with me and Mum. He always told people that he'd served as a medical officer with the RAF in Southern Rhodesia during the war. Mum never contradicted his story, but after he died she told me the truth. Dad had never been in uniform and had never served with the armed forces. In 1942 his call-up papers came and he was terrified. He tried to return immediately with his new family to South Africa, but found that all boats had been requisitioned and it wasn't possible for civilians to get passages. Then there was one of those chance meetings that change the course of a life. Someone suggested that he apply for the Southern Rhodesian Health Service. They needed doctors to replace those who had volunteered for the military. Who knows now what anxieties my father felt about the news from the continent, what terror that mindless anti-Semitism would simply sweep him, his wife and child out of existence, what barely repressed pain from his experiences of anti-Semitism before the war? He was not a pacifist, but some barrier – whether in his own character or his experience – meant that he was terrified of physical risks. So, a chance meeting at a party, an introduction ... and our lives took a different turning. Throughout the war he would be thousands of miles from the line of fire, first in Southern Rhodesia and then Kimberley, and we would grow up as South Africans.

We left England at the moment when the Nazi threat was at its most extreme. My parents couldn't have known about the dangers from poisonous fascist groups within South Africa itself, friends and supporters of National Socialism in Germany, which already in 1937 were proposing that immigrants who could not be assimilated – 'such as among others the Jewish' – should be banned from entry. My father did not think to tell my mother about South Africa's own special version of race laws, and neither of them can be blamed for failing to consider that South Africa, already a divided society, would career into racial fascism within five years of their setting foot on the continent.

Yit'gadal, v'yit kadash, sh'mey rabbah, A-mein ...
V'hey sh'met rabbah m'varach l'alam ul'almey almahyah
Yit Barach, v'yish'tabach, v'tit pa'ar, v'yit rohmam, v'yit nasei
V'yit harar, v'yit'aleh, v'yit halal
Sh'mei d'kudshah, brich' hu
... A-mein.

May His great Name grow exalted and sanctified, Amen ...
May His great Name be blessed forever and ever
Blessed, praised, glorified, exalted, extolled
Mighty, upraised and lauded be the Name of the Holy One,
Blessed is He
... Amen.

| Chapter 3 |

KOL NIDREI

The Kaddish. Not really a song. But part of the music.

In the days when my Dad, his four brothers and their only sister were growing up in Brooklyn, a few miles from the centre of Cape Town, the place was a ghetto. Brooklyn was where the Jews coming off the boats, escaping persecution and pogroms well into the twentieth century, settled alongside the coloureds who had been there for centuries. The shul was within walking distance – Orthodox Jews could reach it easily on foot on the Sabbath. Horse-drawn carts threw up the dust – nobody in the area could afford a car. Dad and his brothers and their sister lived all their childhoods in Brooklyn-without-a-bathroom. They had an outside pail lavatory and a tin bath which they filled by hand, till Oupa built a lean-to shed with a bath and a wood-burning

geyser so that the children could prepare hot water on Sunday for bath night.

In 1928, they bought a big house on Main Road in Maitland, a few miles further towards town. This had five bedrooms, an inside bathroom and, wonder of wonders, a tennis court! The new house was named 'Leomor', for Dad (Morris, who became Maurice) and his older brother Leopold (who became James). When we moved in, in 1947, everything was pretty much as it had been in 1930 when Dad left for Europe: a gloomy place, with long, dark, uncarpeted corridors. Even the furnishings seemed to sit in disapproving judgement of jollity and raucousness. Dark brown curtains, faded at their edges, shut out the bright South African sunlight. On Friday nights, Ouma still lit the candles for the Shabbos meal. They flickered in the gloom. We sat round the stinkwood table on ugly, uncomfortable carved wooden chairs, with ball-and-claw feet and pale, cracked leather seats.

In 1947 Oupa and Ouma's coloured servants, Katie and her husband Johnny, were still there, living in rooms in the yard at the back of the house. By the late forties, the tennis court was over-grown with weeds, which had pushed through the tar surface and cracked it open. The wire fence was raggedy with holes children and cats and dogs could climb through. Gay and I played there with our older cousins, batting balls over the tattered net with our hands, but no one played proper tennis there anymore. Our cousins treated us like dolls. They put purple ribbons in our hair from the shop and pushed us around in a pushchair, even though I was already six and Gay four.

The original family of six children, Dad and his siblings, were an unruly bunch who squabbled all the time. Ouma would scream at them in Afrikaans or Yiddish, but it didn't do much good; only when she started to cry would they be ashamed and stop fighting for a bit. The children switched without thought between English and Afrikaans – English for school, Afrikaans – so like Yiddish – in deference to Ouma.

Leopold, the second brother, was one of the first young men in Brooklyn to get a driving licence, and even though Leopold was the only one who could drive, Oupa got a car. They all piled in – Ouma, Oupa, Solly, Dad, Benny, Lily and baby Max – and Leopold drove them round and round the streets, going nowhere, just showing off. The boys would squabble to be in the dicky seat at the back, and shout, 'Home, James, and don't spare the horses!' That's how Leopold got called James.

Solly, the oldest, was something of a lost soul. Ouma and Oupa couldn't help much; he was the first child, and they were both still finding their feet as immigrants when he came along – Ouma's English was minimal. So poor Solly struggled on alone. After three attempts at matric, he did not know what to do with himself, and so decided he'd be a farmer. No one in the family had the faintest idea about farming. They sent him off to an agricultural college, but never had the capital to help him buy a farm of his own. That ambition fizzled out. Solly came back to Cape Town disgruntled and frustrated, and ending up working alongside Ouma and Oupa in The Shop, together with his new wife, Aunty Sheba, who'd worked at Woolworths. Solomon and Sheba ... such regal names. When Ouma and Oupa both died, Solly and Sheba continued to manage the shop, and did so till the end of Solly's life.

Solly was eccentric, rather embarrassing but good for a laugh if you were a kid. His three-day beard prickled when he kissed us hello. Gay and I would wait for him to intone in his sing-song voice, 'Hey, Hilary, Gay! Time Marches On!', and snigger and give each other knowing glances, because he always said this. We'd mimic him behind his back and waggle our fingers just like he did. His shirt was dirty and hung out of his shabby brown trousers, held up by braces or a raggedy belt. He pronounced Dad's name *Morris* – not Maurice; you just knew he didn't hold with this fancy new French spelling. He made off-colour jokes about sex or smelly farts – jokes children love, and that have grown-ups turning pink-faced and saying, 'Please, not in front of the children.' He probably made jokes behind our backs about us having turned into Blairs, though he never did to our face. We didn't care that he argued and waved his arms about, and talked too loudly with embarrassing enthusiasm or passion, and lectured people, and didn't seem to notice that people were getting annoyed or embarrassed; but our folks cared, and they'd always comment about it when we got home. Dad said Solly read whatever he could lay hands on, even though he'd struggled at school. When he argued, he'd quote from books he'd read about politics – about how we needed a revolution like in Russia, and how capitalism was the root of all evil. I wonder how he squared this with being a small shopkeeper?

Many years after his death, Aunty Sheba confided, 'You know, Hilary, Solly was a communist. He liked to repeat this saying which he invented: "Religion is the opium of the people." Of course I didn't agree with him, but I didn't argue.'

Uncle Solly wasn't taken seriously in the family. He was openly contemptuous of Jewish rituals and religion generally; his mother tried to insist, but Solly just shrugged her off. Oupa didn't seem to care about religion either, but he didn't like confrontations, and when Ouma called him in from chatting with his friends, he'd get dressed and dutifully troop off to shul.

Solly was a teenager in 1922, when the mineworkers on the Rand declared a general strike. He would have known about its infamous contradictory slogan, 'Workers of the world, fight and unite for a white South Africa.' In the thirties, he attended meetings of a Trotskyite group who read the Marxist classics together. Ouma and Oupa were as distressed by Solly's political activities as by his disdain for Judaism. They had fled from Russian violence; their son's allegiance to a Communist faction with its roots in Russia was incomprehensible and unacceptable. He lectured his incomprehending and uncomplaining wife Sheba, trying to get her to understand. When the government made savage reprisals against dock workers attempting to organise for a living wage in 1942, Solly pontificated: 'Listen to me, Sheba. Do you understand what this is about? This is what the late lamented Trotsky (may he rest in peace) has explained to us. Workers' rights, workers leading the revolution. The proletariat must take the lead in defeating the capitalists. We must stand together. The miners and dock workers are the proletariat of our time and place, do you get my meaning, am I making myself clear?' Sheba responded sympathetically, 'Yes dear. It's so sad how Trotsky was stabbed in the head with a pick axe by that crazy person sent by Stalin. His poor wife.'

'Ice pick, Sheba, ice pick, how many times must I tell you!'

'Ice pick, schmice-pick, same difference. Shame, hey.'

Solly urged his indifferent family to take the international political situation seriously: 'It's so terrible, man, what has happened with the war. Are you listening? Are you paying attention? To think that it was just a few votes that saved us from going in on the German side! That Hertzog! That traitor!'

By then, Dad was gone, qualifying to be a doctor in England. He toured Europe during his holidays from medical school, a young man with a neat moustache; in photographs, he is posing in open cars with running boards, apparently oblivious to the political situation unfolding around him.

When Dad brought his little family back to South Africa, Solly was still waving his hands and spluttering about politics. He buttonholed and hectored people in the shop about the black mine workers, living on wages below starvation levels, their strike suppressed with police and batons. All they did was laugh at him – not always behind his back. But though no one else in the family cared about Solly's obsessions, little brother Maxie was listening. In his teens, Max was going with Solly to meetings and joining him in street corner leafleting to protest against the treatment of workers by the government.

Max was nineteen and thinking about his future as a lawyer when the sinister paramilitary organisation, the Ossewabrandwag, was set up in 1939 to 'reclaim the freedom of the Afrikaner nation'. It took its credo directly from Nazi propaganda, and its mission was to sabotage the war effort by blowing up telegraph wires and railways, and passing information to the Germans. It was banned by Smuts and the leaders were imprisoned. Maxie and his wife-to-be Marcia went out leafleting in protest against the new race laws, till this became increasingly difficult and dangerous; anyway, the family – meaning Ouma – disapproved and put a stop to it. Maxie's daughter remembered the way politics was discussed in her home when she was a child in the fifties – so different from what was happening in mine.

As communists, Solly and Max were labelled dangerous dissidents. By 1950, the Nationalist government was putting a Suppression of Communism Bill through parliament. As a strategic measure, the SACP disbanded, going underground long before the ANC and other political groups, who survived for another ten years. Maxie was 'gutted'. We hardly saw Uncle Solly in those years, for we had moved away from Cape Town. When we came down to the Cape on holiday, he still lectured and hectored the grown-ups, but with less passion. He left us kids alone, although he still intoned 'Time marches on' – ritualistically, without the giggle, without conviction, perhaps only because it was expected of him. After years behind the counters of the Algemene Handelaar, the fire had gone out of him.

Dad was only nineteen when he came alone to England on the Union-Castle boat from Cape Town, the daughter of the ships on which his parents had emigrated south thirty-five years earlier. Ouma raised the money for the trip. He docked at Southampton, but there were no Jewish Shelter officials to meet him; he made his own way to London. He'd never been beyond the Cape Province before, let alone out of South Africa. He went straight to Brick Lane to find Oupa's brother, Israel. Dad tracked Uncle Israel down in one of the small synagogues, where he was the *yeshiva* teacher. Israel was underwhelmed to see the nephew from the other side of the world, the first human connection with his brother in thirty-odd years: 'You come into a shul without a hat?' he asked, shocked. Dad went to live in Willesden with Israel's son, his ultra-orthodox cousin Zalman Bleehen. He fitted in with the family, going to shul every Sabbath and on festivals, at which times he wore a top hat, striped trousers and spats, and was introduced to all the nice Jewish girls of Brondesbury Park and Hampstead. During the Sabbath, nobody cooked or did anything that could be construed as work. The 'Shabbos-goy' came in and did all the forbidden tasks like switching on the lights and stoking the fire.

Dad became a dental and then a medical student at Guy's Hospital, the first person in his immediate family to return to Europe, the first to go into a profession, the first of the brothers to move into the middle classes. In 1933, the year that Hitler took power in Germany, Dad took a new surname and adapted the spelling of his first name. He would not discuss his transformation from Morris Bledin to Maurice Blair – an upper-crust, gentile-sounding name, with unmistakable Celtic connotations, which had been suggested by his gentile friend Roy. My mother told me about the anti-Semitism, the relentless teasing of Dad – 'bloody Bledin' – among the medical students. He did not choose to call himself Bleehen like his cousins; he went for broke. (The result was that we children not only had to put up with endless rhymes on our adopted surname, but deal with ironic questions about the family tartan.) Always so neat, trying so hard to learn the culture and acquire the attitudes which would take him out of the ghetto of his past, so ambitious to make something of his life ... did anyone then – or ever – believe he wasn't a Jew?

Dad was highly self-conscious and sensitive, not just about 'looking Jewish' but about all the subtleties of racism through which Jews can be put down and made to feel like outsiders. He taught us by example always to notice someone's ethnicity. We knew who was also a Jew – in the same way that, as white South Africans, we believed we only had to look at people's fingernails and the texture of their hair to gauge whether someone was 'really' white. We grew up with his throwaway comments about the shame of our identity: 'So-and-so looks Jewish,' or, 'You wouldn't know he was Jewish,' or 'She gave herself away as Jewish.'

When Gay and I were teenagers in the fifties, there was a fashion for rich Jewish girls to have 'nose jobs'. The girls we disparagingly called Jewish princesses would straighten and iron and back-comb their over-curly, unruly hair and have their Semitic noses bobbed into little round snubs. Dad thought he would have his nose done too. The Nationalist government was firmly in place, our lives, black and white alike, concreted in with the blocks of legislation which imposed apartheid. English-speaking South Africans were not popular in the Department of Health, where Dad was a reasonably senior official; Jews even less so. Did he really believe that, having changed his name, changing his nose would somehow obliterate his identity? Fortunately, in the face of our incredulity and mockery, he abandoned the nose job idea. And yet he remained deeply ambivalent all his life, anxious both to preserve his Jewish heritage and to deny it. When I was eight and Gay was six, still living in the Cape, he read to us every evening from a children's version of the Old Testament. He took us (and my reluctant mother) to the Orthodox shul where his family attended High Holy Day services. Here we sat separately, upstairs, while the men rocked and chanted below us; all around us, women in smart hats chatted and went in and out. Later, in Johannesburg, where he'd also joined a synagogue, we were kept off school for the High Holy Days. I fasted for Yom Kippur, just to see if I could, and went in and out of the synagogue like the other girls and boys, depending on what was going on; but I always made sure I was there for the blowing of the shofar and the unbearably tragic chords of the Kol Nidrei.

After Dad died, we went through the photograph albums. There were the sepia 2" x 3" Brownie photos from the thirties, when he came to Guy's Hospital to qualify, first as a dentist and then as a doctor and then in public health. It all took nine years. He has the look of someone trying to suss things out, unsure of how he is being judged. His thick, wiry black hair, which in the last weeks of his life stood up round his head like Einstein's grey halo, is smoothed back with Brylcreem. Dad wears tennis whites and holds a racket, or stands with one foot on the running board of a car with friends near a fjord in Norway. The photos record the transition from Morris Bledin to Maurice Blair. He was learning to be an Englishman: going to concerts, reading books, absorbing a culture that the folks back home in Maitland didn't even know existed. He hopefully pursued a variety of women, most importantly Hilary L, after whom I was named. I wondered how my mother could stand having her daughter named after her husband's ex-girlfriend, and when I finally met her when I was ten, her clumsy attempt to reassure me upset me instantly: 'I didn't really love your father,' she said. 'There was no danger I was going to marry him, rather than your mother, who was actually one of my friends.'

Dorothy – poor, no dowry, but Jewish. Cruelly, he wrote later that she really had nothing but her brains to commend her, which wasn't true. You can tell from the photos that she was attractive, with delicate bone structure, soft, silky blonde hair, big greenish-grey eyes framed by wire spectacles, a shy, wide smile and wonderful teeth that she was proud of till the end of her days. Did he perceive, even then, that Mum would provide the helping hand into the cultured world that he so longed to join, or was this cynical and self-serving thought nowhere in his consciousness? Wearing a cheap ring bought at Woolworths, they went off on holiday to France. In one black and white photo, Mum, in the wide-legged shorts of the thirties, rides a donkey on the beach of Pornichet in Brittany. She didn't like big animals, and she looks nervous, clasping the front of the saddle in a tight grip.

It was her very first holiday with a man; with her fluent French, she took charge of all arrangements. But despite that lovely

holiday, with the bitterness of hindsight and many years of a miserable marriage behind her, Dorothy said she never really loved my Dad. At twenty-five, with low self-esteem and no family backing, she was afraid of being left on the shelf. Maurice, she thought, was probably the best she could do.

Dorothy coached Dad through the interminable exams that gave him his qualifications as a doctor, and then in public health. She sat for hours with him, going through the quantities of facts he had to memorise, testing him, doing mock exams. She never acknowledged his determination, the hours of work he devoted to memorising chunks of medical texts – which, in that benighted age, was how doctors were trained. It was fatal to ask Dad anything about the body. Ask about a sore toe, and a trigger in his brain would switch on the whole section of *Gray's Anatomy* relating to feet, legs, muscles, bones, nerves. He was unstoppable.

Dad changed his name to Maurice Blair before he met my mother, but without her he would never have learned how to reinvent himself to fit the new name. He was never really comfortable with his identities, Morris Bledin/Maurice Blair. When he was seventy, he still avoided mentioning publicly that he was a Jew — while at the same time trying to find a suitable synagogue to join. 'Dad,' I would say in the 1980s, 'I can only guess at why you're embarrassed to admit you're Jewish. We must not be ashamed of who we are.' He understood, but was sheepish and apologetic, unable to escape the scars of anti-Semitism, incapable of living up to the proud ethnic identity I tried to foist upon him. Dad spent all his adult years trying to pin down the meaning of life. His favourite phrase was 'This has meaning for me.' Searching for meaning, he read biographies and history books; took on voluntary work with drug addicts; sat silently in Quaker meetings. He listened to classical music, tried to learn French, joined courses on the history of music and the history of art.

Dad died in 1991, a week after his eightieth birthday. He was a doctor. He'd known what was wrong with him, and had tried to explain to us, in medical terms, how his heart was failing. At the end of a secular ceremony — in which my sister and I paid tribute to Dad's sense of fun, his love of music, his pride in my mother's achievements, the almost embarrassing interest in other people's lives that led him to chat intimately with total strangers on trains — my brother put on a *kippah* and read the Kaddish.

Yit'gadal, v'yit kadash, sh'mey rabbah, A-mein ...
V'hey sh'met rabbah m'varach l'alam ul'almey almahyah
Yit Barach, v'yish'tabach, v'tit pa'ar, v'yit rohmam, v'yit nasei
V'yit harar, v'yit'aleh, v'yit halal
Sh'mei d'kudshah, brich' hu
... A-mein.

Once again, the rhythms of the ritual language rolled over me hypnotically, churning up memories from a rebellious childhood: of sullenly enduring the long Day of Atonement service, stomach rumbling; of waiting patiently through endless chanted prayers for the minor keys of the music of Kol Nidrei, the prayer for the dead. It used to reduce me to tears. Now I wept again, for us all. Many people in the congregation said they were stunned. They had not known he was a Jew. So Maurice Blair had succeeded, at least in part, in making himself over. His nostalgia for a happy Jewish family, one which had never even existed, served a role in his sense of identity and belonging that we never fully understood or appreciated.

Tula baba, tula sana

Hush, little baby, hush now

| Chapter 4 |

TULA BABA

Africa! And no warning or preparation for the heat, space, distance, silence, strangeness. For two years in London, Dorothy had lived with air-raid sirens, the dust and destruction of wrecked buildings, the buses driven by women struggling to get through the rubble, millions of people milling around. On the boat, it had been impossible to get away from people living all on top of one another. There was so little privacy you could hear the shuffling and soft sounds of talking through the partitions of the cabin. And then there was the constant sound of the sea and the wind and the hum of the engines as my parents lay in their narrow single bunk beds, with me breathing quietly in my cot. When we first came to Southern Rhodesia, Dorothy felt as if she'd been dumped down in a silent world. But then, tuning in, she realised that there was no silence. In the hour before nightfall, as the whole sky filled with birds collecting and preparing to settle, the sound of their beating wings and their calls of recognition to one another were briefly as strong as a symphony. As the sun went down, the chorus of cicadas became louder and louder, filling all the air. Dogs barked mournfully, echoing across the veld. The sound of villagers singing in the distance in languages she could not understand, playing the same melancholy guitar chords over and over, drifted across the empty air, sometimes joined by the distant rhythms of intricate drumming.

The odours of people's cooking drifted across the veld in the evening, mixed with the warm smells of red earth, open wood fires and people's sweat. The colours of Africa stunned Dorothy. Such contrasts, such vivid, startling brashness – the birds, the flowers ... cannas like nineteenth-century soldiers in uniform, in the brightest of yellow and red; purple bougainvillaea and exuberant bignonia cascading everywhere; hibiscuses with enormous pink trumpet-like flowers; heads of blue agapanthus lined up along a driveway. The bleached-out white skies, the pale brown and pink grasses, the reddish earth, the grey and white stones. The sunsets were overwhelming, as if a childlike giant were playfully streaking the canvas of the sky with reds, golds and pinks from his huge paintbox. Africa did not feel like England. There was little that was soft, gentle or caressing. Sharp, hostile stones and even the dry grass hurt her feet; plants with vicious thorns lunged as she walked by. The sun in the middle of the day was not just colour and heat; day after day it attacked her fair skin, burned her up, grilled her eyeballs. It was impossible to sit on the seat or touch the steering wheel of a car left in the sun at midday. She was homesick for cool, grey, drizzly skies, for plants that thrive in gentler climates: the subtle shades of anemones, sweet peas and pentstemons, for snapdragons and forget-me-nots.

As we came north from Cape Town, we stopped at the stations to stretch, buy cold drinks and use a toilet that was less cramped than the little cabins on the train. I was too little, but Mum noticed: 'native' people were doing all the manual work. Anyone who wore a uniform, blew a whistle, waved a flag, organised the luggage – anyone in authority – was white. Even on the train, the stewards in uniform were white. They waited on us for the meals we took in the special dining car, made up our bunk beds and brought us trays with Marie biscuits and strong tea in a silver pot, with another silver pot full of hot water at six thirty in the morning. Everyone seemed to wake up early in Africa.

It was the first time in her life that Mum had ever had servants. In France, when she'd been an au pair, she'd been the servant. Gladys had been hired to be my nanny before my parents even arrived in Bulawayo. Meeting her, Dorothy noticed her widely spaced, watchful eyes, the sheen of her skin. A short, too-small pink dress pulled tight over her new breasts; over this was a white apron. Her very short black hair was covered by a white cap gathered with elastic at the back, rather like nurses wore in the hospitals in London. She stepped forward, smiling and holding out her arms to me. Soon we were both crouched under a tree, poking sticks at a line of red ants that were marching-as-to-war towards and straight up the trunk of a tree with enormous, red, bell-like flowers. A lucky-bean tree. Like so much in Africa, beguiling, seductive and deadly.

And so began our new life in Africa. Dad was away at the hospital from early morning to early evening. Dorothy had no idea what to do with herself. There was nothing to read and no one to talk to, and she couldn't get used to the heat or the flies which were always round black children's eyes and mouths, on any open sore, droning round the heads of animals, settling on bowls of sugar and jam, laying their eggs in the meat. Many of the children had enormous tummies and reddish, softly curling hair. Dorothy thought this was because they belonged to a special tribal group, and that their tummies were a bit like the large bottoms of the Bushmen who lived in the Kalahari Desert. Dad put her right. These poor little kids were suffering from kwashiorkor, a dreadful disease of malnutrition which affected not only their bodies, but their brains at the most important period of their development

Together in the shade of the lucky-bean tree, Gladys and I

played and sang: 'Tula baba, tula, tula sana ...' Gladys was Christian and had been at the mission school, and now, as well as 'She'll be coming round the mountain' and 'Rock-a-bye baby', I would march round the verandah trumpeting a rousing new song she'd taught me:

> *Onward Christian soldiers*
> *Marching as to war*
> *With the cross of JEE-sus*
> *Marching on before.*

'Must she sing that?' Dad asked, pained.

If you walked out in the veld, round burrs and sticky blackjacks clung to every bit of your socks, the edge of your frock, your trousers. You had to pick them off laboriously, one by one. Huge, colourful birds alighted on the trees outside our bungalow, crying eerily and demoniacally. There were spiders in the outside toilet, lizards sunning themselves on the windowsills and, everywhere we walked, creepy-crawlies – songololos, scorpions, red ants and white ants, black dung beetles that struggled hopelessly if they fell on their backs. Mum tipped up her shoes every morning, checking for some creature which might have decided to make its bed there during the night. People told horror stories about snakes that curled up on your pillow, or returned to find their mate if you killed her, and lay in wait to take their revenge. Mambas, they said gloatingly, watching my mother's horrified expression with glee, could move faster than a car, and would slime their way into the engine and emerge at your feet as you drove, while cobras ... 'Rubbish,' said Dad, but Mum did not sleep easily till she had checked all the pillows and my cot. One strike by a cobra was all it took. My parents carried a little snake-bite first-aid kit, just in case.

The social life of Bulawayo revolved around cards at night and tennis in the day. Dorothy was a disaster at both, an embarrassment to herself and to my Dad, and pretty soon the invitations to join the bridge evenings or the tennis parties stopped coming. Then, before she'd had time to find something purposeful to do, they were on the move again, this time to Salisbury. There was a notice in the paper saying people with European languages were needed to read and censor the letters written by prisoners of war, who had been rounded up into camps. So Mum presented herself at the Central Post Office, offering her services as a linguist to the censorship office. No one checked on her degree and teaching certificates, and the next day she had a job, steaming open letters from families in Italy and Germany and the replies from soldiers captured in the North African campaigns, as well as correspondence from German civilians in South West Africa. How ordinary the enemy seemed, as she checked their children's school reports to make sure they didn't hide sinister encoded messages, and shuffled the photographs.

After a couple of months they were moved again; and then it seemed as if every two weeks they went somewhere new. It was hardly worth unpacking. All there was for Dorothy to do in these dorps in the bundu was wait for the train to come through once a day, hoping it would bring a letter from one of her friends at home; walk to the general store; or sit on the verandah of the hotel with a cold drink. I entertained myself with a stick in the sand, crooning a new song someone had taught me:

Little Black Sam across the sea
Goes to school like you and me
Makes his letters in the sand
With pieces of stick and little black hands.

Dorothy felt bored and useless. Africa was supposed to be an exciting adventure, but the reality was nothing to do, in a world where she felt like an alien. Then she found she was pregnant again, and feeling sick. There was no prospect of a permanent job for Dad in the Southern Rhodesia Health Service, and she happily helped him search the papers for a job in South Africa.

After just one year in Southern Rhodesia, we arrived with our crates and our cases in Kimberley, a city dominated by the biggest open-cast mine in the world. We signed in at the Savoy Hotel. It was a single-storey, iron-roofed building, with a bar and a stoep facing onto the dusty main street. A warm wind spun the leaves and sand into the eyes of people passing along the pavements with their heads down. Some soldiers from the nearby camp, out for a few hours, slouched drunkenly in the shade. Dorothy felt she'd been dumped in the Wild West. And to make things worse, the majority of white people didn't seem to speak English.

Her stomach cramping with dysentery that she'd picked up in the last weeks in Rhodesia, she sat down on the bed in that uncomfortable, inhospitable hotel room and wept. 'Don't cry, Mummy.' I put my ear against her taut belly, where my sister-to-be shifted and moved a leg. 'I'm going to sing to the baby, I can feel him move! I'll sing to help you feel better? Tula baba, tula, tula sana,' I sang.

Dorothy was eighty-five when she died in the winter of 1998, in a hospice down the road from rich Aunty Leah's (the Duchess) hotel in Hove, where she'd spent her childhood holidays. Drugged with morphine, almost unable to control her fingers, still she made lists of things she wanted to talk about when Jon and Gay and I came, things she'd like us to buy her – a last mango from the exotic-fruits counter in Sainsbury's to remind her of South Africa, some litchis. Towards the end, we couldn't make out the writing any more. We whispered to her, telling her we loved her, we were there, though we weren't sure what she heard. Jon chose classical music for the CD player, placing earphones by her bedside. We talked quietly to each other and made cups of tea in the hospice kitchen, waiting.

When I'd got through the numbness of the early days of loss, then the desolating depression which had me weeping in the streets, I started to talk to her in my head, remembering the conversations we'd had as she lived through her dying. I told her what I was doing with myself, asked the questions I'd not got round to or thought of when she was still here. Imaginary conversations – but with the advantage that I could allow her more compassion and understanding of my father than she ever showed in real life, more willingness to acknowledge the compromises she found herself drawn into. She'd left an unpublished autobiography, the final chapters written for us in that last heartbreaking year as the cancer spread, when, weakened by the chemo- and the radio-therapy which were worse than the disease itself, she had realised the pointlessness of trying to fight it any longer.

The autobiography filled in the years we spent in Kimberley and Pietermaritzburg, which I was too little to remember for myself. As in Bulawayo and Salisbury and Plumtree, every day in Kimberley seemed to stretch forever for Dorothy, even though she was quite busy with Gay, who was a sickly baby. She never found her feet in those dusty one-horse towns; perhaps we just never stayed long enough. In Kimberley, she started to get a sense of the hostility between Afrikaners and English, which she hadn't known about before she came to Africa. There was an army camp near Kimberley in 1944, and the soldiers used to come into town to drink. They had to be very careful, because they would get ambushed by supporters of the Ossewabrandwag, who sympathised with the Germans, and have bottles broken over their heads. Dad would be called in to mop up the blood.

We left Kimberley by car early one November morning, less than a year after our arrival there from Southern Rhodesia. I was just three. Under the wartime regulations, no one was permitted to travel more than seventy-five miles from their home, but Dad had a special permit and an extra supply of petrol coupons. We covered 350 of the 500-mile journey on the first day, with the maid Irene and Gay, who was only six months old, in the back, and me sitting between my parents on the wide front seat of the Studebaker. Dorothy had no taste for the harsh, bleak scenery of the Orange Free State, crawling with goggas, scorpions and snakes, or the burning, wide, white skies. It was all as alien and hostile to her as it must have been to the English tommies who had fought there for the great British Empire, forty years before.

We stayed the night in one of those hotels that you used to find in every little town in South Africa. In a vast, empty dining room we struggled through soup, meat and potatoes and vegetables, and some stodgy pudding with custard. The hotel had rooms in the servants' quarters for travellers' maids, rather like an eighteenth-century inn, where Irene stayed. (In Pietermaritzburg, Irene got homesick for her own people, and soon went back to Kimberley.)

I can remember our first house in Pietermaritzburg. It had high concrete steps leading into the front room. I sat in the sun on those steps, peeling the skin off the leathery leaves that fell there and sucking them, and popping jacaranda flowers in my fingers. We kept chickens, which Dad chased round the yard and beheaded for the pot. Once I watched a chicken running about, shaking blood from its headless neck into the dust. The head was lying separately next to the step with its eyes closed. I was fascinated and horrified.

Mum disappeared one day, and I was told she'd had to go into hospital. I found Dad sitting on the double bed crying, and I thought my mother must be going to die. It is the most terrible thing to see your father cry. In those days, they didn't allow children to visit, and even after Mum came home, Dad never told me what was wrong.

Later that year the family moved into a house in King Edward Avenue, opposite the fever hospital. The land that they built on was dirt cheap because people thought they might catch something contagious from the hospital, but Dad knew there wasn't any risk. Mum designed the house, as she'd always wanted to do; it had a red-tiled roof and rough plaster painted white, like the houses in the white towns of southern Spain.

Dad and the gardener, Charlie, dug a pool for us. Charlie put us in the wheelbarrow and gave us rides round the garden. Kleintjie, the little girl from up the road, used to roll down the grassy slope with me. Mum called her 'Klankie'. Although she was such a proficient linguist – French, German, Italian, a smattering of Spanish – Dorothy never got her tongue round Afrikaans.

Fifty years later, the Spanish House was still there. Jon and I went back there in 1992. The tiny bushes and cacti which Charlie and my Dad had planted were now enormous trees, the Christ thorn a huge, thick hedge blocking visibility from the road. The pool had gone. Charlie and Dad had lined it properly with concrete so it wouldn't leak, but they hadn't remembered a drain – so the water got slimy and stagnant and attracted mosquitoes. Perhaps the people who came later thought it was a health hazard. The house had become an orphanage, but only for white children. The woods opposite had been cleared to make way for a hideous housing estate. Here, when I was five, Kleintjie and I discovered a packet of marshmallows hidden in the crook of a tree, and forever after I have believed in good fairies; though now I am older, I call them serendipity.

For nearly two years, till I was four and a half, I wore irons on my legs from ankles to hips, strapped on with leather and buckles and attached to surgical boots. I even had to wear them in bed. The irons were supposed to straighten the limbs of polio victims, until the Salk vaccine eliminated the epidemic in the fifties. My little sister Gay contracted polio and many of my peers limped into their adult lives, or had memories of living for a while in isolation in an iron lung. But I didn't have polio. My bandy legs were part of the price of being an undernourished 'war baby', I was told, as well as starting to walk precociously. I sat with my rigid legs stuck out in front of me in the sandpit and learned to climb the monkey frame at my nursery school in the irons. Eventually my mother took me to a different specialist, who said, 'Good God, woman, who on earth advised this contraption? Completely unnecessary. Throw the whole lot away, and leave her little legs to sort themselves out.' Which they did!

Nearly sixty years later, as I pulled the Velcro firm round the 'moon boot' the London hospital had provided to support my leg, smashed when the horse galloped straight through me, or carefully nestled the vulnerable limb into a pillow for the night, I found I could still remember the irons I'd worn when I was four. The way the straps rubbed against my legs, the discomfort of the leather harness round the tops of my thighs, the way I wriggled to try and get comfortable. This time, the metal was invisible, buried in the bone; an armoury of pins, plates and screws protruded through the thin skin, sensitive and bluish. 'Horses never go for people,' everyone said. 'The sun must have been in his eyes. A freak accident. You could have died. His full weight hit you at god knows how many miles per hour, sent you flying across the field.' But I was lucky; serendipity. I was alive. All you can do with accidents is accept the challenge. Memory ... as with music, the wiring in the brain can trigger the actual physical sensations of early childhood, a half-century later, perhaps as people who have suffered an amputation can still feel tingling and aches in the limb that has gone. And so, in the long hours of stillness, remembering the life I nearly lost in a fraction of a second, I ended up with a book to write.

While I went to the nursery with irons on my legs and Gay was looked after by a Zulu nanny, Mum got a job at St Anne's girls' school, teaching French. She drove into the hills from Maritzburg, and one day the headmistress asked if she could give a lift to the new Afrikaans teacher, Mev. Greyling, who lived near us. She had perfect discipline and the girls liked her. She persuaded them to bring her their discarded, worn clothes and contributions from their pocket money to send to poor German children, survivors of the War. When the girls' parents got to hear of this, they were furious and objected directly to the Head. They were a patriotic lot, these descendants of English settlers, and Germans were still the enemy a year after the war.

For ages, Mev. Greyling and Mum kept up safe conversation in the car about school and students; and then one day she invited Mum in for coffee. Every wall of every room, including the narrow passage in their small house, was literally papered with newspaper cuttings and hung with framed photographs from the South African War. Some documented the fate of thousands of Boer women and children who'd died in the concentration camps set up by the British. By then, Mum knew about the Nazi death camps, and she tried to make sense of this hidden history of her newly adopted country, which was indelibly imprinted on so many Afrikaner minds.

Dad's new job in Maritzburg was with the Local Health Commission. It was a pioneering body, unique to South Africa. The director, Dr David Landau, was the son of the Chief Rabbi of South Africa; he was a man with a mission about preventive medicine for the black population, way ahead of his time. The patients came to the Health Commission clinics from miles around, and queued for hours and hours with babies who'd been coughing all night, or had diarrhoea or worms or bilharzia or TB ... all the diseases of Africa that Dad had learned about theoretically from books when he was doing his Public Health Diploma at the London School of Tropical Medicine. Now he was faced with them on a daily basis.

There were just two white doctors, including Dad; Zulu nurses and health officers worked alongside them in the clinics. The field workers went out to the kraals and spread health education, and tried to spot problems in advance. Speaking Zulu was essential, and David Landau and Dad couldn't do that. Some of the field workers must have been outstanding individuals. My father tended to assume automatically that black people, 'natives' as we called them then, were less intelligent than whites. Not just less educated, but actually less intelligent. Perhaps it was his South African up-bringing? But even he used to speak with respect about Kumalo, the chief field worker and member of the Zulu royal family. My mother later wrote that she wished she'd met Kumalo (never 'Mr' or 'Chief Kumalo'), but 'didn't have the opportunity'. The lines of social intercourse were already so clearly drawn that mixing socially with black colleagues was unthinkable. Did she consider breaking the taboos, I wonder, or was she so under the thumb of my father that the idea was inadmissible and unmanageable? Or was she so taken up with the new house, the new baby, the new job?

I was six when the Nationalists came to power in 1948, when we had already moved back to Cape Town. The radio was on in the bathroom, where I was cleaning my teeth. As the news came through, I had a sense of something terrible and doom-filled as my parents talked about the replacement of General Smuts's United Party by Dr Malan's National Party. Although they were anxious, they had no idea of the long-term significance of this election, no premonition of what was in store for the country: a half-century of tragedy.

'Got what was coming to them,' people said about Smuts's administration. 'Lost touch with the people's real feelings. Couldn't sort out the native problem.' And, much more ominously, 'The only ones who can deal with the *swart gevaar* are the Nats. We're going to get swamped. It will be the end of white civilisation, everything we've worked for – all down the plughole.' Smuts hadn't a hope against Afrikaner nationalism and the fear of a Black Peril whipped up by white, fascist supporters, who came out of jail and the woodwork after the war.

The Natal Local Health Commission was one of the first casualties of the election. In bleak, sparse language which conveys the inhumanity of what was to come and the sense of powerlessness of those who watched their dreams destroyed, Mum later reported in her memoirs: 'The new Minister of Health decided that the work of the Commission did not conform with government policy and consequently it had to be closed down.' Dad must have seen the end coming: he got a new job with the Government Health Department, which took us back to the Cape before he could be ignominiously paid off and told to go. It was left to Dr Landau and Chief Kumalo and the rest to perform the last rites for their progressive, short-lived project.

Mona Lisa, Mona Lisa, men have named you
You're so like the lady with the mystic smile...
Is it only 'cos you're lonely they have blamed you
For that Mona Lisa strangeness in your smile?
Do you smile to tempt a lover, Mona Lisa,
Or is this (mos) your way to hide a broken heart?

| Chapter 5 |

Mona Lisa

The journey by train from Pietermaritzburg to Cape Town took a couple of days. In the evenings, black men in uniforms arrived to lift the green leather backs of the seats in our compartment to create the upper bunk beds, where they unwrapped and laid out the parcels of immaculately starched and ironed bedding. They unhooked the wonderfully fashioned little wood and metal ladders and Gay and I clambered into the tiny spaces, flicking the personal reading lights on and off and giggling if one of us banged our heads on the ceiling, inches away. In the day, we had to open the windows because of the heat. The cool wind blew in but so did the soot from the steam engine, covering the foldaway table, the miniature metal basin and our faces and necks with tiny black smuts. We ate formally in the leather-seated dining car, served by black waiters in red sashes and white gloves; a world of sunlit, contrasting colours, so bright it hurt your eyes.

Dorothy hoped the endless wandering was over. Now that Dad was a civil servant employed by the Government, they imagined that they were secure. Actually, he had to be ready to up sticks and work in any of the main cities in South Africa. But we settled down, first with our grandparents in Maitland and later in one of the flats they owned, until my parents finally bought a small house near where Rondebosch East is now – then just a sandy, empty space with pine trees nearby. They called it 'l'Avenir', 'the future'. Mum planted calendulas in the grey sand; Dad dug holes for the poplar trees, which would quickly grow tall and become a windbreak against that spinning wind, the 'Cape doctor'. In the yard opposite us, two lean and scary Dobermann pinscher dogs went round and round in circles on their short chains. Imprisonment had made them mad, Mum said. They barked incessantly, and if you came near the high fence round their compound they bared sharp, terrifying teeth. At night they were let loose and we had nightmares about them coming to attack us.

The change in government did not affect our lives and probably had nothing to do with my Dad's decision that we should learn Afrikaans. In the first winter holidays after we moved into the little house, and then every year after that till we left the Cape, I was sent to stay with the Afrikaans-speaking Van Jaarsvelds on their farm about a hundred miles into the interior. The first time, the folks took me by car, but after that I travelled on my own on the steam train. I was excited about my adventure away from my family, not anxious. The Van Jaarsvelds were warm, comfortable, welcoming. They did things differently, but Mum and Dad had explained to me that I should expect this and fit in. When I was nine, Gay came too. I was in charge, being older. On our own, we pushed the train windows down and hung out – forbidden when we'd travelled with the folks. The cold winter wind blew our hair back and stung our eyes. As we came through Sir Lowry's Pass, we watched the long train chuffing slowly up the steep and winding track behind us, smoke curling across the sky from the two engines. Far below us, we could see a second engine pushing from behind. We were a giant pushmepullyou, straight out of Dr Dolittle. 'Please God,' I prayed silently to whichever God was listening, holding my breath in sympathy with the effort of the engines to get us up and through the pass, 'don't let the train fall off the mountain.' Once we were through, the train no longer depending on our willpower to stay on track and keep going, we cruised downhill into the Overberg, leaning back in the green leather seats with our sandwiches and fruit. There was fresh water in the glass bottles with stiff brass taps at the end of each coach, held into their little alcoves with leather straps.

Dad was fully bilingual and spoke fluent, idiomatic Afrikaans. This was not just because he'd been brought up among Afrikaans-speaking coloured people in Brooklyn and Maitland, and because his mother spoke better Afrikaans than English, but because he'd made an effort to learn the language properly. He was like that, a persevering man who would make lists of useful phrases, carry them around and practise them. Both English and Afrikaans were compulsory at our school, and Dad was determined that we should be competent in both the official languages, not just get by. Of course, not a single indigenous black language was an option in the white children's curriculum, let alone compulsory. I had no idea that our fluent Afrikaans was anything special till it became obvious that none of my English-speaking classmates could speak 'die taal' as well as I could. I don't know what Mum thought about it – she refused to learn Afrikaans herself. When Dad sent us to a farm to learn Afrikaans among Afrikaans speakers, he pragmatically thought that he was merely smoothing our path in life. He didn't appreciate the ramifications of the gift he was giving us. Nor did I, till years later, working with young bilingual children in London. Then I learned about the advantages of being multilingual, and appreciated how one's understanding of one's own language is deepened, and how one is tuned in to the subtleties of another culture through the language.

The Van Jaarsveld family had been on The Farm (like The Shop, spoken with capital letters) for generations. The farmhouse had a white gable and wooden floors made from oak planks eighteen inches wide, indented at the doorways from so many feet over the last century. Oak trees planted in the middle of the nineteenth century, when the family first built the farm, protected the house from the African sun. There were eucalyptus trees lining the dusty avenue that led to the main road, their long grey leaves whispering in the hot berg wind that blew between the koppies and across the veld. The rooms were connected by long shady corridors and stoeps. The smooth, shiny lino which had been laid in the kitchen and over the concrete of the stoeps was polished on hands and knees by the servants; the smell of the red polish clung to their hands and to the cloths that protected their knees. We raced and charged and skidded on the shiny surfaces. There was a pianola in the front room which played Brahms's 'Lullaby', over and over. The delicate paper roll patterned with tiny holes turned, producing tinkly music as ghost fingers depressed the yellowing ivory keys.

One cold night, I crept next door from the bedroom I shared with Gay and Petrina, the only daughter in the family, and into bed with eight-year-old Johan. He was the one I fancied, the one who'd given me a decent strip of rubber and a piece of leather to make a catapult and showed me how to shoot. So much for Freudian latency theories. Tant Anna found us and was angry and horrified and gave us both a serious lecture about her shame and our/my unacceptable behaviour. But she did not send me home in disgrace, and I returned the following year.

The Van Jaarsvelds were United Party supporters, knew Jan Smuts personally and called him Oom Jannie, and were so openly dismissive about the new Nationalist government that even we children picked it up. Every evening, there were long prayers before dinner, with the coloured servants standing round the edge of the dining room. For the first few days, till I'd learned the ropes, I watched the other children – bowed my head like them, said 'Amen' at the right moments and sat down swiftly when they did. On Sundays, we went to the old, unadorned, whitewashed Dutch Reformed Church in Riviersonderend and sat in the family pews, the coloured workers standing in their places at the back. A chameleon child, I enthusiastically joined in, singing the powerful hymns and repeating the prayers in Afrikaans. The rhythms and the music carried me on their currents. *Our Father which art in heaven ...*

> *Onse Vader wat in die Hemel is*
> *Laat U Naam geheilig word*
> *Laat U Koninkryk kom*
> *Laat U wil geskied*
> *Soos in die Hemel*
> *Net so ook op die aarde ...*

Back home in Cape Town, kicking oak leaves around outside our house, I would whisper the powerful mantra:

> *En die heerlikheid tot in ewigheid,*
> *En die heerlikheid tot in ewigheid.*

The power and the glory, forever and ever, forever and ever.

On the cold winter mornings at The Farm, we huddled barefoot round a paraffin stove or the Aga with mugs of coffee, bowls of reddish-brown mabela porridge with brown sugar, and slabs of bread with homemade apricot jam. When the day warmed up and the sun dried the dew, we ran still barefoot over the prickly grass to the vlei, where we stripped off and swam.

There were six children in the Van Jaarsveld family: five boys, one girl. We were left almost entirely to our own devices throughout the day, and only expected to turn up for meals and be ready to go to church. Johan taught me how to shoot down a bird with my catapult. The soles of my feet toughened, and I ran with Johan and his brothers over the stones without hobbling or even slowing down.

In the farmyard, Meneer Van Jaarsveld – Oom Piet – shot pigs and the coloured farmworkers skinned them, hung them up and later carved them into joints. Mev. Van Jaarsveld – Tant Anna – supervised the making of boerewors: the minced meat was stuffed through a machine with a handle, into slimy, translucent guts threaded over an opening at the other end. The milk in the churns was thick, warm and creamy. When a black calf was born one autumn, it was 'given' to me and called 'Hilary'. In the dairy, the coloured women churned butter by hand, slapped it into huge yellow slabs and then carved it into smaller chunks for the table. Butter we bought in the shops in Cape Town didn't taste like this at all. The Van Jaarsveld children, working alongside the coloured labourers, sheared sheep and boiled sheep fat in huge vats to make soap. In the kitchen, Tant Anna made enormous, sweet pumpkin pies and melktert dusted with nutmeg, and served vast meals: roast meat and potatoes; vegetables grown in the garden and sprinkled with brown sugar; bobotie and bredie. Oom Piet ate steaks for breakfast along with his eggs, fried tomatoes and boerewors. We drank Braganza and rooibos tea with our homemade scones, buns and fruit cakes. Bobotie – I learned then how it should taste. For bredie, the secret is to have lots and lots of fresh tomatoes and good lamb. And melktert – it's the nutmeg. The nutmeg.

When I was six and we'd moved into our own house on the Cape Flats, my parents bought a shiny upright piano and I started piano lessons. It was a miniature piano without a full keyboard, not because it was meant for a child but because the dining room where it lived was too small to fit a bigger one, along with the dining table and chairs. Dad started learning the piano too, and practised the same scales and Grade 1 pieces in the mornings, before we both went to school and work. Dad always wanted to learn something new, and he put the same effort into learning the piano as he had into his tennis lessons and speaking pure Afrikaans. He was mortified that he wasn't immediately a brilliant pianist. He found it hard to do things for their own sake, but he perse-vered with the piano lessons. Years later, when I was a teenager and thinking about doing music for matric, he was still practising the studies by Mozart and Czerny, struggling to make his fingers do what his brain and his patient young teacher, a music student who came to the house in the evenings, asked of him. I was entered for Eisteddfods and the English 'Associated Board of the Royal

Academy and the Royal College of Music' exams. The grey music books had to be ordered specially from London. Grade 3, Grade 4 ... I learnt Haydn, a Beethoven bagatelle, peculiar modern stuff that I didn't like.

At my junior school, which was close enough to ride to along the pavement on my bicycle, I was required to play the morning hymn. All the little girls in their pink dresses would stand up to sing while I alone sat rooted to the piano stool. It wasn't that the music was too hard for me, but that I was terrified by this public ordeal. I never got over my stage fright. I knew before I began that once again I would be humiliated, so nervous that I'd find it impossible to keep time; I'd speed up and soon be completely out of sync with the singers. I would thump out the introductory chords of 'All things bright and beautiful' or 'Gentle Jesus sweetly sleep', then launch into the main tune, repeating it however many times there were verses. One of the two head teachers – Buzz, who was short and stout, unlike Willy, who was tall and thin – stood next to me, tapping out the time on my shoulder like a human metronome and singing loudly to try and force me to keep time, hissing 'Slow down, slow down' between verses. All to no avail. My piano teacher was in the Cape Town orchestra, and took me to the children's concerts on Saturday mornings. I sat next to her in the pit among the musicians, with the violins tuning up all around me, the great shiny brass instruments close enough to touch. Once I watched the whole of a pantomime version of *Alice in Wonderland* from the pit. All I could see from my impossible blocked angle next to the piano, where I turned the piano teacher's pages, were the white rabbit's legs and Alice's shiny black-buttoned boots.

Other things happened as the forties drew to a close. Gay got polio, and when she recovered someone suggested ballet to strengthen her legs. When Mum took her to the dancing class down the road to enrol, it turned out that she'd already been going unofficially with the children who lived three doors down from us. The dancing teacher, who'd tolerated her presence with amusement, was pleased that now she'd be paying properly and wearing her own ballet slippers. That was the beginning of Gay's career in dancing. She became a professional, leaving South Africa when she was sixteen to enter the Royal Ballet School in London.

In 1949, my Mum's sister Aunty Mirrie arrived from England. She'd worked in the Ministry of Defence in the War, and though no one explained this at the time, I now know she'd suffered a nervous breakdown. The family hoped that emigration to the sunny south would pull her round. She came to live with us in our tiny house, taking my bedroom; I moved in with Gay. She was unbelievably skinny, spoke with a strange English accent and was kind and funny. My father resented her and undermined her fragile self-esteem, so my mother told me later, but we loved her: she told us stories and taught us songs. 'How much is that doggie in the window (wuff wuff!),' she would trill.

The one with the waggledy tail
How much is that doggie in the window (wuff wuff)
I do hope that doggie's for sale.

...

I read in the paper there are robbers (wuff wuff)
With flashlights that shine in the dark
My love needs a doggie to protect her
And scare them away with one bark!

But the Dobermanns chained in their tiny hutch across the road didn't protect us like the doggie in the song. They rushed and leapt against their thick wire fence, snarling and barking, revealing sharply pointed teeth, whenever anyone passed by. At night, when their owners let them loose, they'd roam around the streets, depositing enormous turds which we had to step over as we went to school. After a while, Aunty Mirrie moved out. Her marriage had been arranged through the *shadgin* with a German Jew who'd escaped to France, fought with the Allies against the Germans and emigrated to South Africa after the war. He hadn't been in South Africa all that long, and spoke English with a strong German accent. He was plump and jolly and won our hearts because he could read people's characters in their handwriting. Scrutinising my school report, he announced that my teacher at the convent – Sister Thekla, who put herself over as saintly and sweet natured – was concerned about money, rather inclined to bear grudges and had a fierce temper. He was a handwriting expert for the courts, and could tell if signatures were forgeries. He taught me how to forge a signature by turning it upside down and copying all the strokes and angles, ignoring what the letters were meant to be. This was useful later on, particularly for forging notes to school from my and my schoolfriends' mothers to get us out of Physical Education. (You said you had your 'monthlies'.)

Mary Henry, our coloured 'maid', didn't live with us like other people's maids. She stayed with her husband and her own children in District Six and came every day. She also sang as she worked round the house:

You are my sunshine, my only sunshine,
You make me happy when skies are grey
You'll never know dear how much I love you
Please don't take my sunshine away.

I believed this song was all about Cape Town – the lovely sun and the grey skies when the great mists came off the sea, submerging the city in a drizzly fog, and the Devil (who lived on Devil's Peak) spread his tablecloth, ready for a special feast.

At home, Dad installed speakers in all rooms, including the bathroom, and our musical education continued. First, the morning exercises boomed into our bedroom at 6.30 a.m., with a tinkly piano accompaniment: 'HOLD two three, STRETCH two three, LIFT two three, BREATHE two three ... AND REST.' The commentator urged us to throw open our windows and take deep breaths of fresh, cold air, to start the day the healthy way. In the bedroom next door, we could hear a light thumping as my Dad did the exercises: running on the spot, scissor jumps, clapping your hands above your head; but we didn't jump out of bed to join in. Still, it was the signal that it was time to get up. The morning concert would follow, and he'd come in to check on us and make sure we realised we were listening to Mozart, Beethoven or Tchaikovsky. It all came in handy a few years later, when I had to take an exam in the history of music and could recognise the main composers from a few bars.

In the Cape, I moved schools three times in four years, skipping two classes in the process. It was all part of the folks' determination to ensure that we had a good start in life through education – the key to their own status, their launch into middle-class acceptance and security. The first move was from the only government school I ever attended, Rustenburg. I was six and could read when I joined the class of seven-year-olds, but was not supposed to be able to do so. When she caught me turning over to the next page in my *Janet and John* reader when we were all supposed to be reading aloud together – all fifty of us – my teacher was outraged. I went home and told my Mum. Within a couple of weeks, I was out of there and in a small class in a private school, Micklefield. I swapped my royal-blue uniform (blue was my favourite colour) for a pink uniform with a grey jersey and a grey felt hat. This was where I played the piano for morning prayers, learned Latin and all about the Ancient Egyptians and their shadufs, where I was good at handstands but struggled at netball, being a good half a head shorter than my classmates. But two years later, we moved again.

By 1951, Gay and I were at Springfield Convent, run by Dominican nuns. My mother had been the French teacher at Springfield, but soon after we started there, she moved to the University to take up a lectureship. I rode my bike to school up the steepest hills I'd ever tackled – nothing like riding on the pavement to the pink prep school. I got a new, bigger bike and set myself daily challenges: reach that lamppost, then you can get off and walk; no, today you have to get further, to the next one ... I gave myself special personal brownie points for making it to the top without getting off at all. I'd been kicked out of the Brownies by then, not having been a good elf, so I had to make do with private tests and acknowledgements of my improving character and stamina.

I don't remember why I skipped a class when I moved to Springfield, but I was just nine while the rest of the kids in my class were nearly eleven. For the first time in my life, I came bottom of my class, struggling to make sense of work I'd never encountered before. I made friends with girls who were outsiders like me – Helen, who couldn't read very well, and Margaret, who was just a bit odd and lisped and believed in fairies, and Alice… what was it with Alice? I loved her name. If only I could be called Alice. We were all on the edge of the social scene – too small, too young, not pretty enough, no sign of budding breasts; although, unlike me, Helen and Margaret and Alice were at least Catholic. We didn't get bullied, but we hadn't a hope socially, except with each other. We watched the girls in the in-crowd carefully, trying to learn what it was that we needed to do to be accepted. We admired them and hung around the edges of their groups, hoping they would draw us into the secret talks, the shared giggling confidences. But they never did.

I spent hours on the roneo'd maps handed out for geography homework, using a thin-tipped paintbrush to outline the oceans in dark blue and then, carefully washing my brush in between, painting a dark-red border around the countries of the Commonwealth. Then, with a thicker sable brush, I'd paint a pink watercolour wash over all those red-rimmed lands, including our own right at the bottom of Africa, showing just how great and important Great Britain was. I filled in the names of capital cities, rivers, continents and oceans with a dip pen and black Indian ink, which smudged hopelessly in my clumsy hands and didn't wash off.

I learned to drop everything and jump to my feet for the Angelus, announced by the tolling of bells at midday in the Convent gardens:

Hail Mary, full of grace, the Lord is with thee.
Blessed art thou among women, and blessed is the fruit of
*   thy womb, Jesus.*
Holy Mary, mother of God,
Pray for us sinners now, and at the hour of our death,
Ay-men.

There were no other non-Catholics in my class of fifty-two girls, and I was told that I should not stay during Religious Education. So every day, I wandered alone round the beautiful grounds, lingering in front of the statue of the Virgin, surrounded by blue agapanthus which matched her soft, blue, carved robe. Her head bent so sadly and graciously, but she was not aware of us – her mind was elsewhere, on more important things.

Gay was also at the Convent, in the junior school, but her RE non-sessions were never at the same time as mine and our paths hardly crossed at school. She also hovered near the chapel, where the sounds of beautiful unaccompanied choral singing in Latin floated out through the trees. Gay used to slip into the chapel and pray there alone, till the folks heard about this and she was made to do extra Afrikaans during the religious classes. Who was responsible for this? My father, pointlessly protesting his Judaism in the face of our total immersion in Catholic Christianity? The nuns, erecting barriers against the infidel?

I peeked through the hedge round the vegetable garden, where nuns worked silently in the summer heat with hoes, their white robes tucked up to reveal heavy shoes and white stockings. The story went that the nuns were never allowed to get undressed, and me and my friends giggled wickedly, outdoing each other with outrageous suggestions about how they washed. We never thought about the nuns and sex, though the story was passed around that pretty, young Sister Mary Magdalene had decided to become a nun because her boyfriend had gone off with someone else. We knew they had to shave their heads when they were received into the Order, and we wondered what they looked like under their tight, starched wimples, which pressed into their foreheads and squeezed the flesh of their cheeks so they bulged unnaturally. We wondered if the nuns had to shave every day like our daddies, or was it a once-a-week thing, or even less often, like going to the hairdresser? One girl passed round a rude picture of Sister Thekla with a bald head and no wimple.

But mostly, what got passed round and collected and swapped were religious cards. These had gold borders and pastel pictures of the saints, Our Lady, or a blue-eyed Jesus in a shapeless long dress, with long fair hair, a fair beard and a very unrealistic heart with gold spokes on the outside of his robe. At home, we ate ox- and sheep-heart sometimes for dinner, and I knew that hearts were a dark purply-brown, not this colour at all. The people on the holy cards all either looked meekly at the ground with bent heads, like the statue of the Virgin in the grounds, or gazed upwards at something they could see in the clouds which was invisible to us ordinary mortals. Uplifting sayings on the backs of the cards helped us to think about being good.

When I was nine and we moved schools, we went to live in a house right on the mountain, on the old Boshof Estate. Not wishing to tempt fate with another name like 'L'Avenir', this new house was named 'Milestones'. We each had our own bedroom now, even my new baby brother, Jonny.

Gay and I had Dolly Varden dressing tables with kidney-shaped tops and flowery curtains which my mother had sewn, and little stools with matching flowery frills round their bases, so that we could sit and look at our faces from all angles in our three-wing mirrors and get our back partings straight and in the middle before we did our plaits. We each had a bookcase; mine was full of Arthur Ransome, E.E. Nesbitt, Elizabeth Goudge, Angela Brazil. I didn't read Enid Blyton anymore because my friend Margaret, who wrote stories herself, had told me they were rubbish. The Alison Utleys and Beatrix Potters and A.A. Milnes were next door, in Gay's bookcase. I had outgrown them.

At the end of Boshof Avenue, which was a cul-de-sac, lived an elderly couple whose children had grown up. These kind old people generously allowed the children in the neighbourhood to come and swim in their private swimming bath, as long as we announced ourselves — and as long as we were white. My preoccupied parents seldom checked where I was, as long as I turned up on time for meals — easier now that I had my own watch. One day, after my swim, instead of going back home, I crossed the road and started to make my way through the undergrowth growing up the mountainside. I pushed back the scratchy branches, hardly noticing the arum lilies growing wild on the banks of a stream that bubbled down between the rocks, or the huge, stiff, pink proteas. Underfoot I trampled the sweet, acrid fynbos.

I went on for a while, till I came upon open, flat ground shaded by a few pine trees. The stream trickled nearby. The open space was filled with windowless pondoks made of corrugated iron, flattened petrol cans and pieces of wood rescued from god knows where. The doorways had sacking across the openings. Small babies and children played in the pine needles, wearing shirts but no broekies. A few coloured women wearing doeks and shapeless dresses or overalls moved between the shacks or sat on rocks, calling to each other or their children in Afrikaans, hung out washing on the bushes, got water in tin paraffin cans, pushed twigs onto a small fire glowing between large stones. I stood silently, hidden in the undergrowth. After a while I turned and went quietly back the way I'd come. I told no one. But this was what I remembered when I went to England eighteen months later, and my cousin Sholom Bleehen told me I should be ashamed of being South African.

My Dad taught me to swim in the University of Cape Town baths when I was seven, in our second year back in Cape Town. He taught me with dedication and an expertise that would serve me well; a few years later, when I went to high school, I was quickly selected for the swimming team. First I held on to the rail at the edge, just beyond the shallow end, so that he could stand but the water was way above my head. I learned to keep my bottom in the air, my knees together and kick my feet as hard and fast as possible. I learned to hold my face in the water and swing my head sideways, taking great gulps of air and blowing huge bubbles as I breathed out. He supported me gently under my belly with one hand as I learned to kick and breathe and use my hands. My body still remembers the security and the safety as he held me. I could not sink. Nothing could happen to me. When I finally struck out across the width of the Olympic-sized baths, I didn't realise that he was no longer supporting me. A man with so little physical courage himself, he managed to transmit confidence so that I could swim way out of my depth.

Later, Gay and I started to play in the deep end of the pool, as comfortable and confident in water as racing around on the lawns. We did handstands, fingers just touching the blue-tiled bottom; we did the splits upside down, wiggled our toes in the air, looped under again and emerged suddenly right next to someone who hadn't seen us approaching. Then – when my Dad wasn't there – we dive-bombed from the highest diving board, a terrifying drop but an unavoidable test of courage. You couldn't hold your head up in front of your friends and say 'I'm frightened', even if your heart was beating like a terrified bird in your chest as you climbed up the long ladder leading up and up. If you misjudged when you jumped, you might hit a swimmer below; you or the other person might be badly injured, even killed. I know this because it really happened. There is a terrible inchoate memory of blood spewing red in the pool, two silent bodies lying on the grass, horrified people crowding round, and the ambulance men rushing up with their stretchers.

Although I loved swimming, my fingers and toes would turn quite white and numb when I stayed in the water for too long – I've had Raynaud's disease, a circulatory problem, for as long as I can remember. Cycling when I was a child was a nightmare, especially later on in the Transvaal winters, not just because my fingers and toes went numb, but because it was excruciatingly painful when they came to life again.

Most weekends, we crossed the Peninsula to get to the beach. Our identical wooden surfboards with our initials stencilled on them (even the nicest of sisters quarrel about possessions), our towels, picnic lunch, umbrella, wind shield, sunhats and grass mats were all packed into big bags which we would lug across the hot white sand — so hot we kept our sandals on to prevent the soles of our feet being burnt. We did not go to the 'Snake Pit' — the enclosed, protected part of Muizenberg where all the Jews hung out, greasy with oil in the burning sun (and where we might have bumped into our Maitland cousins), but to the windy, exposed 'Christian beach' further along. Exclusively Christian it clearly was not, given our presence, and in those days, before the Separate Amenities Act and the 'Slegs Blankes/Whites Only' notices, it was not completely white. Some families brought their children's maids to watch over their offspring on the sand, and the sea itself was not yet reserved for us — a brown body might be seen jumping the enormous breakers. There were never any black people, and we were told that 'natives' didn't like swimming anyway.

Mum wasn't much of a swimmer. She bobbed about with her head above the water, without her glasses and wearing a tight, unbecoming rubber cap, and never went out of her depth. We understood that this was because she was English, from England; not like us, who spoke English of course but were South African. Dad jumped about in the waves with us, dived through the breakers however big, taught us how to ride the waves on our surfboards and surfed himself with a manic gleam in his eye, determined to beat us as we cruised ashore and tumbled off onto the sand in the shallows. He raced us up and down the hard sand. He did funny little dances, complete with finger dancing, to songs about our friends that he'd invented himself — 'I'm a little PISH, PISH, PISH,' he'd warble, and we'd collapse in giggles.

On the long journeys to our holiday destinations on the Cape coast — Stilbaai, Port St Johns, Hermanus, Qolora; names that carry the magic of my memories — we took two cars. I usually travelled with my Dad. The car wound slowly up and over Sir Lowry's Pass, and we'd see the vineyards and orchards below us. Conspiratorially warning me that I shouldn't sing this in front of Mum, Dad taught me: 'Mam'oiselle from Marmentears, parlay-VOO, she aint be kissed for donkey's ears, inky pinky parlay-VOO!' And 'Molly Malone', 'Danny Boy', 'Tipperary', 'Clementine' ...

> *Light she was and like a fairy*
> *And her shoes were number nine*
> *Herring boxes, without topses*
> *Sandals were for Clementine*
> *Oh my darling, oh my darling, oh my darling Clementine*
> *thou art lost and gone forever, dreadful SARIE, Clementine.*

He taught me *boeremusiek*, some tunes dating from the Boer War, as we all called it then. 'Sarie Marais' would segue into a loud and energetic rendering of songs he had sung with his brothers when he was a boy, nonsense words and allusions to the war all mixed together:

> *We are marching to Pretoria, Pretoria, PRETORIA*
> *Oh we are marching to Pretoria,*
> *PRETORIA RULES THE WAVES!*
> *O, vat jou goed en trek Ferreira*
> *Vat jou goed en trek ...*

And then, like a record which inevitably takes you to the next track, we'd finish off with a swooping version of 'Alibama', sung as a round:

> *Daar kom die Alibama*
> *Die Alibama hy kom oor die see ...*

Which I later learned referred to a famous Confederacy warship, which entered Table Bay in 1863.

Once I was told by a family friend that I was driving her crazy with my singing, and was ordered to stop. Until then, I had not realised that some people didn't think singing at the top of one's voice was a delightful way to pass long car journeys.

The sea, the singing. 1951 was a very good year. As 1951 ended and we rolled through the New Year celebrations (watermelon on the beach, fireworks in our garden), we started to pack up the house on the mountain, which we'd lived in for only one year. Our leaving was marked, as every New Year had been since we lived at the Cape, by an enormous festival. But this year we didn't have to go into town and stand in the crowds by the side of the road, pushing between grown-ups' legs to try and see the parade. For the 'Coon Carnival' – as the Cape minstrels were known – came to us. We stood enchanted next to the old oak as they danced between the Cape Dutch gates and then right up Boshof Avenue. Dressed in shiny bright costumes of red and yellow satin, their faces painted white in a parody of black-face, they sang and bent towards us, shaking tambourines and collection boxes right under our chins. 'Mona Lisa,' they crooned with unforgettable poignancy. Their voices carried all the sorrow of unrequited love as they drew out the vowels and hissed the consonants, appealing to us with mocking, liquid eyes to look behind the veneer of Mona Lisa's façade, and pity and understand the brave pretence of a lonely woman.

> *Mona Lisa, Mona Lisa, men have named you*
> *You're so like the lady with the mystic smile ...*
> *Is it only 'cos you're lonely they have blamed you*
> *For that Mona Lisa strangeness in your smile?*

So I knew that Mona Lisa lived sorrowfully in District Six, hiding her true feelings behind a stony face when her heart was about to break. Like Mona Lisa, our hearts were about to break too. We were going to lose everything we loved: the Cape, the coloured children collecting acorns round the huge oak tree outside our house to sell for pig food, the empty swimming pool in the garden full of frogs and slippery leaves, the parents who talked to one another without anger, our Dad dancing and surfing and singing at the seaside... our innocence.

My Sarie Marais is so ver van my hart,
Maar'k hoop om haar weer to sien
Sy het in the wyk van die Mooirivier gewoon,
Nog voor die oorlog het begin.

O bring my trug na die ou Transvaal,
Daar waar my Sarie woon,
Daar onder in die mielies by die groen doringboom,
Daar woon my Sarie Marais.

Ek was so bang dat die kakies my sou vang,
En ver oor die see wegstuur;
Toe vlug ek na die kant
Van die Upington se sand
Daar onder langs die Grootrivier.

My Sarie Marais is so far from my heart
I long to see her again
She lived in the valley of the Mooi River
Before the war began

Oh take me back to the old Transvaal
That's where my Sarie lives
Down by the mielies and the green thorn tree
That's where my Sarie lives

I was so afraid that the Khakis would capture me
And send me far across the sea
So I fled to the banks
Of Upington sands
Down there by the Great River.

| Chapter 6 |

So Ver Van My Hart

Goodbye, Cape Town. Totsiens – till we see you again.

We didn't know it then, of course, but 1951 was not just the end of the idyllic years in the Cape; it marked a seismic shift in family relationships ...

'We have to leave here,' Dad told the family over supper one evening. He had obviously discussed it all with Mum already. She sat silently fiddling with cutlery, her eyes down. The maid Gertrude served us our soup. Jonny was in his high chair, banging a spoon.

'Stop that, Jonny,' said my Dad. 'I've been trying hard to avoid this, but I'm pretty much under orders now. Move or get out, they've told me.' He put on a different voice: 'They said, "You work for the Department of Health of the *Union of South Africa*,

Blair, not the Department of Health of the Cape Peninsula. There are *four* provinces here, Blair. Do you plan to be here till you're sixty, with all the younger men overtaking you, stuck in a lowly post?" ' Changing back to his ordinary voice, he continued: 'Even if I'd said that's just what I did plan to do, no one was going to let me. I'm sorry.'

'What about us? Will we have to change schools *again*?' Gay and I asked pretty much in unison. I was just ten and already at my fourth school, counting the nursery where I'd climbed the jungle gym in my irons.

Stupid question.

'Mum'll have to give up her job.'

'Yep.'

'So where are we supposed to go now?'

'Orange Free State. Bloemfontein,' said my Dad.

'Flower fountain,' my Mum said softly and sadly.

'*What?* We can't go there. It's *miles* from the sea. It's the middle of the bundu. We won't know *anyone*. They don't even speak English there. We'll have to go to Afrikaans schools. Mum, Dad … please?'

Mum entered the one-way conversation. 'We've thought about that. We think we'll send you to an English-speaking boarding school, back in Maritzburg. It's not that far from Bloemfontein.'

Well, that might be alright then.

So they sold the house in Boshof Avenue. We cleared the pictures from under the glass on the Dolly Varden dressing tables, packed all our toys and our books. Gay and I stood respectfully by the grave we'd made next to our own little flower gardens and said goodbye to Monty the Scottie dog, who'd got crushed to death in a horrible accident. Gay thought we ought to say the Angelus, but I wasn't sure. At school, all the girls in our class swore to remember us for ever. Even the ones who'd hardly ever spoken to us drew pictures of Minnie Mouse or daisies, signed our autograph books and wrote messages: 'Roses are red, violets are blue, if you can't be good, you're squashed tomatoes and stew.' The rude version, which tactfully no one actually wrote in our books, went,

'Roses are red, violets are blue, if you can't be a Christian, you must be a Jew.'

My mother packed up to move to the seventh town in eight years, with at least two moves in each town. Even Gay, who was only seven and a half, could do the arithmetic. Fourteen different places we'd lived in since coming to South Africa during the war. Dad went ahead to find a house. Mum put my one-year-old little brother Jonny in the Studebaker and they drove on their own all the way through the Karoo to Bloemfontein, stopping only when smoke started to pour from the engine somewhere in the middle of the veld outside Colesberg. There was a hole in the radiator. Mum struggled without Afrikaans in a one-horse dorp and finally found someone to fix it. On they went in the heat to live in a house with a tin roof Dad had rented in Bloemfontein, the dry and dusty 'flower fountain', capital of the Orange Free State.

Before she went, she put Gay and me on the train at Cape Town station. We were going back the same way we'd come less than five years before. She'd found someone to keep an eye on us on the train, a woman also travelling all the way to Natal, and someone from the school would meet us in Pietermaritzburg – it was all arranged. It never occurred to us to imagine that anything might go wrong, so we didn't worry. When Mum arranged things, all the details were seen to. Anyway, we were used to doing things like this on our own. It was just another adventure. Boarding school! Gay and I were over the moon with excitement.

We'd ticked off the items on the long, intimidating list of compulsory requirements from the Girls' Collegiate School. We'd packed our matching new white suitcases, onto which Mum had stencilled our initials: G.E.B (Gabrielle Eve Blair, named for Eva, my grandmother) and H.A.B. (Hilary Anne). She'd used the same stencils and indelible ink that she'd used for our surfboards. Every single item had been duly marked with a special indelible pen or with a tag from the long rolls of name tape, home made, with my mother's neat capital letters repeated over and over again. The Cash name tapes that you got through mail-order were too expensive – and how we would yearn for their delicate embroidered lower-case elegance. We each had the required number of regulation vests and broekies, homemade with elastic round the legs and the waist: black satin for wearing under winter uniforms and for PE, white for wearing under our summer school uniform. Green dresses for Saturday, white dresses for Sunday, navy pleated skirts buttoned to a white undershirt for winter, white pleated skirts for tennis, towels, flannels, tackies for sports, white square-necked blouses, summer panama hat and winter felt hat, both with the school hat band and badge, black swimming costume, black rubber bathing cap, summer pyjamas, winter pyjamas, summer and winter dressing gowns, slippers. We even had our own clothes hangers, padded and covered with material from the scraps box. More than fifty years later, I still have the hangers, all marked *H.A. Blair* in unfaded indelible ink. We each had a sewing kit for doing our own mending, including a wooden mushroom for darning our socks, and leather writing cases with pads and envelopes and special holders for propelling pencil and fountain pen. We were each given a supply of sweets, on the list of requirements for boarders, which were confiscated as soon as we arrived at school. Later, we discovered what had happened. Our sweets had been added to a large communal Quality Street tin. During our compulsory lunchtime rest (shoes off, blankets rolled back), the junior and senior school matrons doled out our sweets to us one at a time. My first lesson in socialism.

Although I'd spurned Enid Blyton, I knew all about boarding schools from reading Angela Brazil. 'You know what,' I told Gay authoritatively. 'We'll stay in a dorm.'

'A *what?*'

'A dorm. It's got lots of beds in one big room.'

'Oh.'

'And you know what else? After lights out …'

'What's lights out?'

'Oh for Pete's sake. When the matron comes round and switches out the lights. What do you think, dummy?'

'Okay, sorry Hila.'

'Anyway, after lights out we'll have midnight feasts in the

middle of the dorm, with torches 'cos we can't turn on the lights again 'cos matron will come.'

'Wow, really? Who's matron?'

'She'll be in charge of us. Sort of like our mother. Matrons are usually a bit fat, but they're good natured. They choose them for boarding schools because they like being with lots of children.'

'Oh. Okay then. What about the midnight feasts?'

'Yup. Chocolate biscuits and cooldrink and … anything we like.'

'Where will we get all this stuff for the feast?' Gay asked pragmatically.

'Oh, it's easy. The girls get it from their parents when they visit. We'll have tuck, it's called tuck. It's sweets and things. And then,' I went on enthusiastically, 'we'll climb out of the dorm and take our torches, and have adventures in the grounds. It'll be good that we know some French. Because boarding schools always have a French teacher who's really French, from France you know. It won't be like Mum teaching us on Saturday mornings round the dining-room table, it'll be real school lessons. I expect she'll have a strong French accent. It's good that we learned from Mum, 'cos her accent's good so we'll be used to it. We'll have to call her Mamselle. The French teachers are always young and they're the nicest teachers in the school. She may be in some sort of trouble, and probably we'll know about it and help, because you and me know a bit of French already.'

'Oh,' Gay said dubiously. 'Are you sure I can help? Really, Hila, all I can do is sing "Frère Jacques" and "Quand trois poules vont aux champs" that Mum taught us.'

'It'll be fine. I'll be there, anyway.'

I was already deeply into my role as the solver of major mysteries, the new girl in the school, Mamselle's friend and rescuer, talented, adventurous, ready to meet a challenge.

The long train journey from Cape Town to Pietermaritzburg on our own wasn't really all that different from going by ourselves to the Van Jaarsvelds' farm — it just took longer, and meant sleeping in the bunk beds, which were made up at night by a black or coloured man in a white uniform. At Maritzburg Railway Station, we stood with the lady who'd been asked to keep an eye on us. Our suitcases had been unloaded for us and were on a trolley, guarded by a Zulu guard. Soon someone came to meet us, just as Mum had organised, and we were taken straight to school.

So much for Angela Brazil. In the early 1950s, Girls' Collegiate School was not modelled on best-selling school stories. There was no glamour and little kindness. We found ourselves in a vicious, cynical, closed world, at the mercy of a sadistic head, Miss Williams, whom we called 'Bill', and her henchwoman Miss Holmes, 'Homer', the four-foot-nothing matron of the senior boarders. Between them they terrorised us all. There wasn't a kind, young French teacher called Mamselle or anything else. Bill was shapeless except for a large, droopy bust. She wore her thin hair in a bun at the back of her short, fat neck. Spectacles hung on a chain, resting on the ledge of her bosoms. Her cotton frocks, buttoned up the front and loosely tied in her middle (she had no waist), were the nameless, splodgy colours of the three different porridges we ate for breakfast in rotation — mabela, lumpy oatmeal, and mielie meal. A fat, spoilt dachshund (Marmaduke? Maupassant? — some forgotten, pretentious name) waddled round, attached to Bill by its lead. 'Heel, Marmaduke, good doggie,' — pat, pat, pat, grimacing as she strained to bend. Marmaduke too grimaced, baring pointy teeth at any of us who dared to approach too close.

Collegiate was all female and all white. Men and boys were quite excluded, except for a few black men, 'native boys', who worked quietly in the grounds, sweeping up leaves and talking to one another in Zulu, or cleaning the floors on their knees in their unbleached calico uniforms, a cruder version of the shortie pyjamas we wore to bed in the summer. They kept their eyes averted if we went by. Black women in white aprons came into the dormitories with buckets and brooms in the mornings to clean after us as we lined up to brush our teeth. They brought our food to the long tables in the dining hall and cleared everything away. They had no names and we knew absolutely nothing about them. They might as well have been invisible; no one referred to them and we never thought about them or their lives. When I went to university in England in 1960 and lived in college, I could not get used to being waited on by white women. So deeply ingrained was the sense that white people could never be servants that, breaking convention, I attempted to take my own plates to the hatch and serve myself – till I was firmly told how to behave properly, and squirmed with embarrassment in my seat.

Back in the fifties, Girls' Collegiate seemed modelled on Dotheboys Hall. Every move was wrapped round with mindless rules, which gave the more sadistic members of staff the opportunity to bully and punish us. Seniors and juniors were segregated – cruel for sisters who'd come from far away and knew nobody except each other – and no child could go into the front rooms or the front gardens without permission. Many years later, in England, I had to visit a mental hospital set in the grounds of a fine old country house which had been converted. Something struck a chord. The sweeping drive and wide lawns, the beautiful reception area with its elegant vase of lilies. The receptionist in a pink uniform. Not a single patient. You had to go through many doors to the back, which was where the patients lived out their time. Enclosed, imprisoned.

There were strict rules for the boarders about how many personal items we might keep in or on our lockers; how often we changed our underclothes; what we might wear on different days of the week; how to fill in the forms when we sorted our dirty laundry every Saturday morning into calico bags with our names on them. We learned to do hospital corners, and pull the bedcover as taut as a sail in the wind, with never a wrinkle. We stood at the ends of our beds for daily inspections. Homer would happily rip the bedclothes off and make us do everything again if she was not satisfied.

Mixing with 'daybugs' and juniors (even if they were your sister) was regulated. There were rules like biblical injunctions about the times when we might speak and when we must be silent; when we could have a bath, how deep it might be and for how long we might soak; at what time in the evening we would cease to use the lavatories and start to use the enamel pots under our beds, into which your pee thundered and which you had to carry without spilling to empty in the lavatories the next morning.

I was ten, in Standard 7, and so I was a senior. Gay was in the junior corridor. Sometimes we'd linger at the top of the stairs, where the junior and senior corridors met at right angles, hoping to glimpse each other. On Saturday mornings, the senior boarders sat in silence, doing our darning and mending, presided over by Homer. I learned to darn on my fist, since Homer believed that using a darning mushroom was effete. Boarders wrote letters home once a week, in silence, in our classroom. The envelopes had to be addressed but left unsealed, and the letters were read by a member of staff before they were posted. We lined up once a week for disgusting, slimy cod-liver oil doled out by Homer, and were required to report on the movements of our bowels and swallow a spoonful of castor oil if we were foolish enough to confess that we hadn't 'been'. Homer had decreed that girls with long hair were responsible for blocking the drains, so we were forbidden to wash our hair in the school basins. Two or three of us with long hair were sent once a week to Maison Vogler, the hairdressers, where we took out the elastic bands and Kirby grips, undid our plaits and were forced to pay out of our precious weekly pocket money to have our hair washed for us.

When I first arrived at Collegiate, I was put in one of the senior dormitories with seven other girls, not all from my year. Sometimes, just like the school stories had promised, there actually were midnight feasts, with chocolate biscuits and tinned condensed milk, when one of the boarders came back from Sunday out with her parents, loaded with goodies. I was not part of these festive occasions. As a new girl, I was bullied and victimised in the time-honoured way of girls – through exclusion and mockery and endless doggerel about my surname, rather than anything physical. Once, all my clothes were moved out of the communal cupboard and dumped on the floor. When I came into the dormitory, the girls all stood smiling conspiratorially, and one explained that my clothes were smelly. It works well – how do you know you don't smell? Maybe you do. How can you complain when people aren't speaking to you? How do you object to rhymes on your name without appearing to have no sense of humour?

> *Hilary Blair*
> *Sat on a chair*
> *Please don't stare*
> *She's not all there …*
> *She's really queer*

Still, it was probably better than being Hilary Bledin.

Once again, I was an outsider. Part of the problem this time was my failure to speak Zulu. Most of the girls were bilingual, not in Afrikaans and English like me, but in Zulu and English. Almost without exception, they'd been brought up by Zulu nannies on sugar plantations in places with the singing names of Natal and Zululand – Eshowe, Ulundi, Amanzimtoti, Gingingdlovu – and they would deliberately exclude me by talking Zulu with one another. My vocabulary in Zulu was stuck at 'sawubona', 'sala kahle' and 'hamba kahle', which didn't get me very far. They treated me with the casual snobbery of wealthy farmers' daughters for the town girls who came from outside Natal. Contempt exuded for people who lived in a small house with perhaps only quarter of an acre in a city, as they shared their stories about their farms in Zululand, Howick, Mooi River or Pinetown, their horses, their helicopters. Stories about the Van Jaarsvelds' farm at Riviersonderend would not have done me any favours ('She's friends with hairybacks, sis, man'), and I didn't even have a home to talk about. My Mum hadn't been able to cope with Bloemfontein. Dad's boss had taken pity on them and they'd been moved again, going to live in a hotel in Johannesburg. So far, Gay and I had not visited them there.

On top of my failure to speak Zulu, I now reaped the whirl-wind of being fluent in Afrikaans. I was 'shown up' in my first Afrikaans lesson at my new school, with an Afrikaans teacher who was herself despised and tormented. How much they knew or cared that I was Jewish, I do not know. My parents had arranged for Gay and me to go to synagogue with another Jewish girl in the school who'd come down from Johannesburg. So on Saturday mornings, Gay and I and Rosanne went off together, reluctantly forced to do things differently from everyone else. All the same, we also joined the crocodile to church on Sundays, wearing our white dresses (exactly two inches above the knee when you kneeled down). At morning prayers in the school hall and in church on Sundays we sang along with the rest of the school:

Eternal father, strong to save,
Whose arm doth bind the restless wave,
Who bids the mighty ocean deep
Its own appointed limits keep:
O hear us when we cry to thee
For those in peril on the sea.

Its melancholy chords would bring tears to my eyes and a lump to my throat, even though I did not know a single person who had perished at sea. But I remembered the icy sea at Milnerton, and the spring tides, and the wild waves that crashed against the wall of the sea pool at St James, and shivered.

There is a green hill far away,
Without a city wall,
Where our dear Lord was crucified,
Who died to save us all.

We may not know, we cannot tell,
What pains he had to bear,
But we believe it was for us
He hung and suffered there.

Like the crucifixes everywhere at Springfield Convent, the frightening and brutal imagery of Christ's suffering on the cross in many of the hymns made me anxious. I would pretend to sing but actually just mouth the words, uncertain of my loyalty. I knew that the Jews had killed Christ, and feared that my classmates might hold me personally responsible if they put two and two together and realised I was a Jew. No one actually accused me of this crime, though open mockery of Rosanne, who had a foreign-sounding Jewish surname, left me uncertain about whether I should come to her defence and draw attention to myself, or stay silent. Was this why, I wondered, we were now Blairs and not Bledins?

Some Sunday evenings, Bill called the senior boarders into her drawing room, where she read to us from Jane Austen or *Pilgrim's Progress*. We sat uncomfortably on the floor, watched by the weasel-faced Marmaduke (Maupassant?), who shared a wide armchair with Bill. In enforced silence, we improvised ways to survive our boredom — watching ants, picking at fingernails, day-dreaming, shifting on our bottoms.

By the second term, I had settled into a *modus vivendi* with the other boarders, who'd probably just lost interest in tormenting me; but now I spent as much time outside Bill's office as in lessons, disgraced and excluded from class for some rudeness or misde-meanour. I found the work easy — Springfield had been much tougher intellectually — but I'd become a problem pupil, cheeky, difficult, always answering back. On the long Sundays, dressed in white, with no family nearby and unable to find my place in any of the cliques that dominated the class, I hung around the grounds on my own, avoiding the parts of the garden which were out of bounds, playing dangerous games on the swings that involved jumping on and off when they were at their highest point. Some-times my eccentric friend Louise — a day girl whose parents were musicians — asked me back to her house. Gay would come too. It was the only break from institutional living for either of us for months on end, the only reminder of an ordinary world in which mummies and daddies and little brothers sat round a kitchen table and music played on the radio; in which we wore ordinary clothes, took our shoes and socks off, and were asked what we would like to do.

In the first half-term, when we were still very much new girls, it seemed that we'd be left alone at school, unable to go home because it was too far away. But someone took pity on us and Gay and I went home with two cousins in my class, who lived on the coast near Port Shepstone. And so, freed from the white dresses and the lace-up shoes, we gallivanted and rolled barefoot on the soft sand dunes with Libby and her sisters and cousins, accepted, it seemed. Normal. But when we got back to school, it was as if the week had never happened. Did Paula and Lisa avoid eye contact, move subtly away when I approached? Was there really something wrong with me, or was it the power of peer pressure that kept up the barriers against girls like me, girls who were not part of the in-crowd?

I did make one friend among the boarders, another outsider. Carola was openly indifferent to sport and passionate about horses, which she drew quite brilliantly. Carola and I cried over *My Friend Flicka* and *Green Grass of Wyoming*. We swapped *Little Boy Lost* and *The Three Musketeers*. Carola sat in the library literally reading through the encyclopaedia, volume by volume. I wished I could be like her, living in an enclosed world. She didn't care what the snobs and the sugar farmers' daughters thought of her, and I wasn't sure she really cared much about me either. I also tried to draw horses and read the encyclopaedia, but I could not wrap myself in a cocoon like her. Her parents were in India and she lived with an uncle near Greytown. The whole set-up was secretive and mysterious; she never explained it and never invited me to her uncle's home, where she went on Sundays. Once, her mother came from India to visit her, and after she left again, Carola was even more remote and silent. I heard that she went to Cambridge, and when I was at Oxford I tried to find her, but failed.

Halfway through my first year at Collegiate, my mother arranged to take me with her to France. She had a scholarship to the Sorbonne, to complete her PhD research. Her Royal Holloway College friend, Marie-Rose Paupy (who had been Marie-Rose Martinet) was happy for me to come and live with her family in the Auvergne and go to school in Clermont-Ferrand. A period of unparalleled happiness and excitement for me and my mother, it was a catastrophe for all the other members of our family, one which none of them ever forgot. This was the other side of the coin of the folks' hands-off mode of childrearing, in which Gay and I were entrusted to take train journeys halfway across South Africa on our own. Sent back on her own to boarding school after Mum and I boarded the *Cape Town Castle* in Durban, Gay was miserable, abandoned. My brother Jonny was two and he was left in my father's charge in a hotel in Johannesburg. Dad, of course, went to work during the day, and Jonny was farmed out to a sort of nursery, which sounded more like a Dickensian orphanage when we heard about it afterwards. Theories of maternal deprivation were still in the future, and in her determination to revive her flagging intellectual life and not be trapped into wife- and motherhood, Mum seemed to have no idea of the potential fallout from her leaving. Dad only let Mum know about the series of disasters which had befallen them when we returned at Christmas time. Dad himself knew virtually no one in Jo'burg. Jonny had become ill and the nursery wouldn't keep him. Dad had stayed in the hotel room with him, making excuses at work, trying to keep his new job going. He couldn't find anyone to look after the sick little boy: the sort of thing which countless women, mainly black, were faced with every day. Eventually, when Jonny got better, Dad's solution had been to board him all week in the nursery, which may have been nothing more than a children's home.

As for me, the lucky one, the privileged child who went overseas, I won first prize in the fancy-dress parties on the Union-Castle boat to Southampton. I was dressed as an Auvergne peasant in an elaborate costume, which my clever artistic mother made out of paper. I visited my English aunties and uncles, went to Windsor Castle, Hampton Court and the Louvre, and then moved in with the Paupy family, where I shared a bed and a small writing table with Marie-Rose's twelve-year-old daughter. I learned to eat a piece of bitter dark chocolate and a *fromage frais* for my tea, wore a *tablier* to my *lycée* and soon had sufficient everyday French to make friends and cope with learning Latin and maths in French.

The following January, when I came back from France, I was kept back a year because I'd missed so much school. Now, though there was less hassle with the other boarders – I think I'd gained a little glamour from going to France – I was even more rebellious. Finally, there was a confrontation with Homer which brought everything to a head.

It was the evening of my twelfth birthday, and I was faced with Hobson's choice. If I left my presents on my locker, I risked getting into serious trouble for exceeding the number of allowed objects; if I got up to put them away after the bell had rung for lights out, I would be in equally serious hot water. I chose to get up and put them away, and ran into Homer advancing down the corridor to switch off our lights.

'I'm sorry, Matron,' I tried to explain. 'I know I'm not supposed to be out of bed, but I hadn't realised it was nearly lights-out, and I haven't put my presents away.'

'You rude and cheeky girl. How dare you disregard the rules. I am not interested in your ifs and buts. Give me those, I'm confiscating them.'

'But Matron, please, it's my birthday. I was just trying to put them away like I'm supposed to.'

'Be quiet, you rude and insolent child. Give them to me. Now.' She held out her hand.

'But it's not fair.'

'Now. I'm warning you.' Her voice was ominously cold.

'No, I won't. It's unfair. You're always trying to get at me. I ...'

She grabbed at me. A mistake, since we were about the same size and I was probably stronger. I shook her free and took a swing at the tiny tyrant. I certainly didn't knock her off her feet, but I knocked her dignity for six, and this was unforgivable. I knew I'd gone too far, and just stood there, waiting for Armageddon.

'Oh God, what now?' I said to myself, and then a completely irreverent thought went through my head: supposing she'd had a wig on and it had fallen off when I swiped at her?

The girls in the other seven beds – sheets tucked up under their arms, blankets folded down tidily because it was summer, as per regulations – could hardly suppress gasps of amazement and horror. Someone giggled, as if they'd read my mind.

'You wicked, wicked girl,' Homer hissed when she'd recovered her equilibrium. 'Dressing gown and slippers on, now. You are coming with me. Miss Williams will deal with you.'

She held on to the sleeve of my dressing gown and I was dragged downstairs. In sorrowful tones, oozing with hypocrisy, Bill made it clear that my wickedness was beyond redemption, and put me in solitary confinement for the next twenty-four hours in the sick room, in disgrace. I was locked in, and if I wanted to go to the lavatory, I had to use a potty under the bed. The sickroom had a high, barred window through which I could hear but not see the other girls playing at break times. The only person allowed near me was a black servant; she brought my meals on a tray but did not communicate. Time seemed interminable. Most of the time, I lay on the sick-room bed in my shortie pyjamas and dressing gown, staring at the stains on the ceiling and trying to turn the patterns into recognisable objects. I hummed listlessly and for a while sang a few songs, but this did not cheer me.

Meanwhile, Bill phoned my parents, explaining that I was to be expelled and asking them to come and take me away. I was worried that the folks would be furious or ashamed or both, but I did not care that life at boarding school was coming to an end. Anyway, unbeknown to Bill, during the winter holidays I had written the scholarship entrance exams for Roedean in Johannesburg, where my mother now taught. About the time of my expulsion from Collegiate, the news came through that I'd won the scholarship. Farcically, realising that she was about to lose one of the few pupils who might boost the school's academic reputation and achieve a decent result in the public examinations the following year, Bill then tried to keep me, and rescinded my expulsion. But by now my parents were settled in Johannesburg and really didn't need to send us away to boarding school any longer. Thankfully, barely able to hide our relief, Gay and I left at the end of the term.

I never saw Girls' Collegiate School again, until in 1992 Jon and I, with little help from the Tourist Office, who directed us towards the school's grand new buildings in the hills above the town, finally found the familiar old red-brick building on Burger

Street. It was now a community college; all its students were black, and mainly in their late teens and early twenties. A Headstart reading project for the remote areas of Natal and KwaZulu was housed next to Bill's old drawing room; piles of puppets and props and boxes for the colour-coded reading books, waiting to be packed up, filled the floor space. Bill's drawing room, where we'd sat uncomfortably on the floor being edified and morally uplifted with readings from the classics, was now the meeting room, the heart of the community college. At the corner of the junior and senior corridors upstairs, I stood and listened for the ghosts from forty years before. I remembered how Gay and I had waited for each other as we lined up to go downstairs for breakfast or supper, touching hands as we passed. Anne Marie, the dark-eyed French girl from Maseru, who gladly spoke French with me when I came back from France; long-legged, brown-eyed Meryl, swinging her tennis racquet; Diana, so beautiful, silent and remote, and in retrospect so brainless; Belinda, who had diabetes and sat on her bed with her back to us every morning and injected herself with insulin. The old classrooms were now filled with wood-working benches, lathes and metal-working tools. Here we'd sat in twos, according to the alphabet, at wooden desks on which we carved our initials, with fixed seats always a little too far or too close to write comfortably, ink pots in round holes next to the groove for pencils and pens, and lids which we'd bang down in classes where teachers could not keep control. Now, there was a new kitchen where domestic-science training took place. Everywhere, we were greeted by young black students, the women in berets, some working with the equipment, some lolling in groups against the walls – even sitting on the grass of the forbidden D lawn. I laughed out loud with joy. The New South Africa!

Trying now to make sense of Collegiate, I am struck by how everything and everyone colluded to ensure that apartheid was accepted without question, and how we were socialised smoothly into our appointed roles as white English-speaking women. The girls were openly contemptuous of Afrikaners – 'hairybacks' – who might be good at rugby and were superior to anyone of colour, but were unquestionably our social and intellectual inferiors. Un-challenged racism pervaded everything, from the overt way in which black people were treated and we were expected to relate to them, through to the curriculum and the assumptions which all the girls had apparently bought into. The lone exception was Anne Marie, the child of French Protestant missionaries in Basutoland (now Lesotho), who went silent when dismissive racist comments about blacks were casually bandied about. As for the curriculum – private schools were not officially signed up to Christian National Education, but Girls' Collegiate wrote exams set by the national exam board, which would be marked by officials from the Department of Education. Pre-ordained interpretations were expected.

And then, suddenly, the nightmare ended, and Gay and I were back in Johannesburg, at home with our parents and our little brother. We were living not in a hotel room in Hillbrow, or a rented house in Roosevelt Park, but in an old house in Parktown, not far from the university. Mum had already started on her project to mould the wilderness round our house into a garden. English flowers, pentstemons and sweet peas, were planted outside the window of the kitchen, where they struggled in the South African sun. Daily, the 'boy' laboured to dig beds in the rock, transporting quantities of soil which had to be ordered specially. He made paths winding round the natural rock gardens, where slabs of paving would be cemented into place. A rose garden was created below our bedroom window, just beyond the sweet chestnut tree. A few years later, my dog would be buried there, and as its carcass bloated, it would burst the ground open again. The lower branches of the cedars at the edge of what would be our badminton court were trimmed, and the lantana, which had gone wild and woody, was cut back – although we could still climb behind it to hide.

I was twelve, and now my new term began at Roedean. All these transitions were much easier than they might have been because the curriculum just seemed to go round and round over the same ground. For History, throughout my three different secondary schools, we worked chapter by chapter through the

English version of the same official textbook (often repeating the same bits in a different year). Its hardback cover was mustard yellow, a colour I still loathe. It told a long and dismal story of white racial superiority, from the time of Van Riebeeck's arrival in 1652. Obviously, South Africa had no history before that. The conflict between the Afrikaners and the English, dating back to the British occupation of the Cape at the time of the Napoleonic wars, seemed unremitting. My teacher in Natal subtly emphasised the recalcitrance and unreasonableness of the Voortrekkers, their obstinate refusal to knuckle down under British rule, their insistence on living in backward independent republics. Nobody questioned the received wisdom about primitive, half-naked Bushmen and Hottentots roaming the Cape, till the fortunate arrival of Dutch and later British settlers brought civilisation and Christianity. Slavery was only mentioned in noting the date of its abolition in 1838, the same time it was abolished in Britain. We listed this as one of the causes of the Great Trek, but never discussed it further. There were so many parallels in history with the situation in South Africa as we were growing up, but not one of our history teachers had the courage or took the opportunity to help us understand the present through the past. They didn't get us to question the newly introduced Pass Laws and the removal of voting rights for coloureds and blacks. We listed the attempts at liberal reforms by some of the governors at the Cape, but it was history without a heart or a soul, just lists and dates, which we copied off the board and learned off by heart, hardly understanding what the concepts meant and never discussing them. There were a lot of gaps. We knew that the London Missionary Society had made a fuss about some things, but we didn't learn about the erosion of the few rights which black people still had in the late nineteenth century. This might have introduced an unacceptable discussion about the legitimacy of the world in which we found ourselves.

As for a history through the eyes of the majority black population – it didn't take Christian National Education to abolish this; it had never existed in white schools anyway. The official history required that we memorise names and dates of innumerable 'Kaffir' and Zulu wars and battles in the mid- and late-nineteenth century, in which barbaric natives attacked white people without rhyme or reason, or to steal cattle or land. They were mostly brutal murderers, justly punished and defeated by brave whites (often but not always English). Distorted by negative stereotypes and caricatures of the indigenous people, our history books taught us that 'the Zulu' were brave but barbaric, having driven part of their own tribe, now the Ndebele, north into Matabeleland in Rhodesia. 'The Basuto' were cunning, unreliable and inclined to attack surreptiously and without reason from their mountain hideouts. 'The Xhosa' were the naïve victims of their own superstitions, most impressively when under the influence of the cattle-killing prophetess Nongqawuse.

There were big names aplenty, mostly white and male; there was Lady Anne Barnard, the wife of one of the British officials, but otherwise it was the men who made history. Van Riebeeck, Piet Retief, Rhodes – whose statue stood in the Gardens in Cape Town, his arm pointing north over a continent which was to be British all the way to Cairo, but whose vision had unfortunately been curtailed by his early death. We learned about mad Paul Kruger, in the pocket of the Germans; Jameson, Rhodes's henchman, whose raid was justified in the light of Kruger's anti-democratic machinations. There were even a few black people with real names: Shaka, Dingaan, Dinuzulu, Mzilikazi – and that lone Xhosa woman, Nongqawuse.

We were force-fed a particular interpretation of the South African War – which was still, in those days of the mustard history book, viewed as a 'white man's war'. Although we might bellow out 'Sarie Marais' around the braaivleis campfires with our friends, most of us didn't know the words of the second verse; even if we had, we wouldn't have had the faintest idea what they meant: 'I was so scared that the Khakis would catch me / and send me far across the sea' (to Ceylon, St Helena or even Bermuda)/ 'So I fled away... Down there, by the Great River' ... and the Khakis burnt my farm, and rounded up my wife and my children, and all the black people living roundabout, and imprisoned them in tents surrounded by wire, where they died by the thousand. Important people from England came and inspected the concentration camps, making bad publicity for the English government. But no one in authority seemed to care much about the black people.

We never learned anything about reasonable, educated or politicised blacks. In our history book, non-Europeans were all savage or stupid, stuck in a time warp when the rest of the world moved on to civilisation. It was years before I started to consider the meaning of the African proverb, 'Until the lions have their historians, history will always glorify the hunters'.

So, despite the mixed messages about Afrikaners and English, we white children were learning to understand that we were the rightful rulers, while everyone else was doomed, endorsed by the Bible to be hewers of wood and drawers of water. Forever and ever. Tot in ewigheid. Amen.

Why, I ask myself now, did school history, which was dominated by South African history, effectively stop with the Act of Union in 1910? We did not learn about either the First or the Second World Wars, though South Africa was involved in both. We didn't hear about the League of Nations, the slide into fascism in parts of Europe, the persecution of minorities in Germany after Hitler took power in 1933. That South Africa had avoided neutrality during the Second World War by thirteen votes. We 'studied' the French Revolution and the Napoleonic Wars by listing (in order of importance) the ten causes of the Revolution – copied off the board – and reproducing essays which were dictated to us. This guaranteed a good grade in the public examinations. I did achieve this, but only after a conversation with my history teacher which went like this:

Me: Madam (we called our teachers 'Madam' at Roedean), I was talking to one of my parents' friends who teaches history at Wits, and she was suggesting that the real reason the British got involved in the Boer War was not because Kruger was denying the Uitlanders the vote, but because they wanted to gain control over the goldfields.

Madam: She may well be right there. But let me give you some good advice. You want a distinction for history, don't you? You're even thinking of doing history at university, if I've understood you right. Well, don't even think of putting those ideas into your matric paper. It won't do you the slightest good with the people who'll mark your answers. Stick to what I've dictated to you in my notes.

Lesson learned: we might be the master race (or anyway, their wives and daughters), born to rule, but that didn't imply we should question authority or think for ourselves.

Our history teacher was from England, and like several of our teachers had come from our famous big-sister school, Roedean in Brighton. Our maths teacher was also English, but she had married Eddie Roux, the professor of botany at Wits, and was deeply committed to the South African political struggle. The Rouxs were self-confessed former members of the Communist Party and, by the time I was in Win Roux's maths class, both actively involved with the Liberal Party. The book Eddie wrote about his life made clear that they were freethinkers, believers in human rights and universal suffrage. Nothing special, you might think, except that these ideas guaranteed that one would be harassed and under constant surveillance in apartheid South Africa. Though Eddie Roux had resigned from the Communist Party in 1936, twenty years later their house was searched by the Special Branch and many books confiscated. So, in the year I was in ante-matric, 1956, the first year of the Treason Trial, Win was sometimes attending court in the Johannesburg Drill Hall; many of her friends were in the dock. However, so circumspect was she that I didn't even realise what her political stance was till I was at university; only when I read the book she co-wrote with Eddie Roux, published in 1970, did I appreciate what they'd been living through every day as she appeared before us in class: mild mannered, sometimes distracted, always respectful.

The saddest thing about this is that the one teacher who might have got us to question what was happening in our country was probably doing her best to be invisible and uncontentious. There is a curious mismatch between my experience as a pupil and what Win herself wrote about teaching at Roedean. She does talk of the Anglo-Catholic ethos which Ella LeMaître, the Head, brought to the school, the emphasis on chapel and prayers; she hints that this might be why her own daughter, also a scholarship girl, openly a freethinker and, like me, not a practising Anglican, never became a prefect. But Win says that she enjoyed the freedom of views and lively conversations in the staff common room. My mother was also a teacher at Roedean, and she never mentioned any of this. The one thing she did pass on to me, circumspect though she had to be, was to beware of Ella's anti-Semitism.

So, none of this staffroom freedom of thought – if indeed it existed – seeped through to us pupils, not through Mrs Roux nor anyone else. In my final three years in Roedean Senior School, some of the most significant laws of apartheid were passed and some of the most important campaigns against apartheid waged. Roedean was the sort of school where it *would* have been possible, when the trig. lessons were over, to talk to senior pupils in a serious, adult way. But none of my teachers ever raised questions or asked us to debate the issues. The Senate Bill passed into law, taking away the voting rights of coloureds; the Tomlinson Report, the blueprint for the Bantustans, was published; women marched against the Pass Laws; the Treason Trial began; Sophiatown was bulldozed ... the list goes on and on. Mrs Roux confined herself to teaching us trigonometry, how to solve quadratic equations and the proof of geometry theorems. Was this a terrible testimony to the power of conformity and repression, or just a testimony to the low expectations our teachers had of their pupils?

So here is the question. Suppose that you are a white girl, fourteen or fifteen years old. Your parents are not involved in any way in the anti-apartheid movement. Unlike some whose stories you will learn later, nobody political, white or black, Indian or coloured, comes to your house. Nobody in your house goes on demonstrations. There are no mind-blowing conversations in the flickering light of the braaivleis with people who will suffer house arrest, be part of the Treason Trial, go to jail under the Ninety

Days law. You only learn the names of activists years later. Your father is not open-minded and your mother seems permanently pre-occupied with her job, finishing her PhD and her private students, who are bringing in a little extra to help pay for your school. In fact, you live in a family who discuss nothing. Your teachers and the curriculum keep you blind and deaf to what is happening, and the powers of segregation and censorship between them ensure that you really have little idea of what is going on. Suppose  that alongside your normal adolescent obsessions with boys, music, outbreaks of pimples, having a good time and being popular, you actually do care about wider issues. How do you break out of the bubble?

In the mid-fifties, I was a teenager, living in Johannesburg and trying to make sense of an increasingly insane personal and public world. And then – serendipity! In the year after we left boarding school in Pietermaritzburg and came to Johannesburg, Mum introduced us to the children of her new friend, Phyllis Lewsen. Phyllis was the historian who talked to me about alternative explanations of the South African War. She worked at the university where my mother now also had a job, and their three children matched us exactly in age and sex. Her husband Jack was a lawyer and a Liberal Party councillor. He and my apolitical father had little in common; our two families seldom met up, and when they did social relations were strained. Dad dropped political bricks and Jack sometimes bothered to argue, but sometimes just clammed up. But my mother and Phyllis liked one another, and we children got on reasonably well.

Public transport in Johannesburg was impossibly difficult. Black people would wait in long queues at the 'Natives only' bus stops along the highway. The blacks-only trains out to the townships were dangerously overcrowded; people hung on to the doors and windows from the outside, morning and evening, needing to get to work on time, desperate to get home. But public transport was also impossible for white people. Once, waiting forever at a 'Europeans-only' bus stop, a bus for Africans came by and stopped just up the road. Infuriated at the official madness that forbade me to board it, I decided I would try anyway – a reverse Rosa Parks gesture. But it pulled away just before I could get there, and so I never found out whether I would have been allowed on. All the white girls that I knew were driven everywhere – either by their parents' chauffeurs or by their mothers. But my mother worked full time, and we did not have a chauffeur.

'Mum, Dad, I've been thinking about the problem of getting to school. Now I'm fourteen, couldn't I get a buzz bike? It's legal now for me to ride one. I'm getting absolutely exhausted riding up all those hills to get to school,' I pleaded. 'What do you think? I could pay for it out of my own money.' (That should clinch it!)

By then, I was working on Saturday mornings (illegally) in a crafts shop where the owner didn't care that I was underage. I was saving every penny (though I did buy the 45rpm record of Frankie Lyman singing, 'Why do fools fall in love?' with 'I'm not a juvenile delinquent' on the B-side).

Done. The man at the bike shop replaced the back wheel of my ordinary bike with one with a little motor and showed me how to clean the carburettor and check the spark plug gap. I bought a can of the mixture of oil and petrol that the bike ran on, and yay! I was independent. Now I could ride all the way up and down hilly Jan Smuts Avenue to Melrose to visit my new friend Muriel Lewsen – eight miles there and back.

It was good to get away from the rows that blighted our house. I started to spend more and more time at the Lewsens. Afternoon turned to night without the interruption of twilight, so I would stay over rather than ride home in the dark. In the Lewsens' house, I learned that there were alternative colour schemes to the pastel tones that my parents had chosen for our sitting room – dawn pink on one wall, pale green next to it, then primrose yellow, dove grey meeting the pink at the corner. For the first time, I saw original art and sculpture on the walls of someone's house and not in a gallery. For the first time, I sat at a table where the adults were insiders and where politics were openly discussed, without the acrimony of people ready to kill each other over their differences.

At the Lewsens' dinner table, I first heard the slogan 'Azikwelwa!' (We will not ride!) Jack Lewsen would get up at dawn and, before going to his own office, drove their large car back and forth between the city and Alexandra Township. Along the road, he picked up men and women who were walking nine miles each way between Alex and the city centre, in protest against the fare rise of one penny imposed by PUTCO bus company. A trivial amount, but the straw that broke the camel's back for people already living below starvation wages. I heard about the Black Sash – the white women who stood outside the City Hall and the Public Library and the courts in silent protest against the new apartheid laws. And from Phyllis I heard that black women were protesting against the hated passes, and that thousands of white women too had marched, and camped in the grounds of the Union Buildings in Pretoria. And that she had been among them. Phyllis was writing a book about John X Merriman, one of the Prime Ministers of the Cape at the turn of the twentieth century, a liberal who had tried to protect the rights of coloureds and blacks. I picked up the message that you interpreted history, that what I was being taught in the mustard book was biased and selective, that history was not a set of facts that you just learned off by heart. Now I wish I had asked more, been more interested, for what I got wasn't much. But it is not easy to be a teenager in someone else's house, and I was uncertain of the boundaries, preferring to listen rather than initiate. But still, the Lewsens gave me first-hand knowledge, for the very first time, of protest and dissent by white people against the government.

Despite my parents, I was being politicised. At school, the girls in ante-matric had been invited to submit our names to go and spend four days at St Peter's School, Rosettenville, with tours of the townships and various charitable institutions. The high point was to be our visit to Ekuteleni, a charity which cared for young blind black people. Two girls would go to St Peter's, names drawn out of a hat. I was not chosen. Then one of the girls dropped out at the last moment, and mine was the next name. Serendipity: my good fairy who'd put the marshmallows in the fork of the thorn tree when I was five was there for me again.

The girls' private schools in Joburg had a three-term year, not four like all the other schools. So there would be no pupils at St Peter's and we would stay in their dormitories. We left the Northern suburbs in a VW Kombi, ten or fifteen teenage girls from posh girls' private schools. We crossed Jo'burg into the Southern suburbs, to Rosettenville – foreign territory. St Peter's School was next to the Church of Christ the King, Father Trevor Huddleston's old church.

Next day, we were driven through the sad ashes of Sophiatown, where Father Huddleston had ministered. The Group Areas Act had wreaked its terrible damage. Bricks and rubble were all that remained of the old houses which had been smashed by bulldozers even as the people were rounded at gunpoint in to lorries to be taken to Meadowlands. A new song entered the litany –

Utla, utlao maquoa arieng,
Arieng ko Meadowlands!
Meadowlands, Meadowlands, Meadowlands
Sithandwa sam

The white man says
We must move to Meadowlands,
Meadowlands it's so lovely!
Utla utlao Batotsi bareng
Ons dak nie ons pola hier
Utla utlao Batotsi bareng
Ons dak nie ons pola hier.

But the tsotsis sing
We're not going anywhere,
We're staying right here.

The brand-new township of Triomf, which would spring up in Sophiatown's place, was not yet complete. We drove around through Pimville, Jabavu, Orlando, Moroka. The names of these places were familiar. After all, our servants and sometimes their children lived there, if they were not away in the reserves with elderly parents. I was silent as I absorbed the tiny shacks made of corrugated iron, sacking and broken bits of glass, all crushed together and propped up in defiance of gravity. We bumped over the flat, stony ground on potholed, untarred roads, past barefoot and often bare-bottomed children in rags, playing in the dust and dry grass of the Highveld among discarded cars and rubbish, the detritus of their lives. There were no words to express my horror and my guilt. At fourteen, this shocking vision of apartheid confronted me not just with how people lived a bare twenty miles from my home, but with what was being hidden from us. Apartheid worked. Designed to keep black people out of our white lives, except as servants and workers, it ensured that children like me truly had no idea how black people had to live. The self-built little villas of wealthier black people in Dube, the rows and rows of identical new breeze-block houses in Meadowlands, raw and undecorated in the treeless, bare veld, the lines of lavatories on open plots waiting for the houses to come, did nothing to reassure me that somehow there was justice at the heart of the system.

On the Sunday, I loitered round the Church of Christ the King and finally slipped into a back row. A white priest who had replaced Father Huddleston was leading the service for a black congregation, with a sprinkling of young white visitors. I recognised a boy from St John's School, on the other side of the koppie from Roedean: Hugh Lewin, whose life was to cross mine in ways we could not predict. The soaring singing, the intricate interweavings and harmonies of sopranos, contraltos, tenors and bass in the congregation, took my breath away – an insight into the capacity of the human spirit to survive, clashing with the shocking images of the people's lives outside.

Meanwhile, at Roedean, we got mixed messages about our future role; it was not to ask uncomfortable questions about the ethics of our society. Ella, our imposing headmistress, rook-like in her Cambridge gown with her thick pebble glasses and wild grey hair, pronounced: 'Your destiny, gels, is to be the wives of leaders.' (But apparently not leaders ourselves.) Like the British Constitution, the rules for Roedean gels in the fifties were not written down, but known through case law. They ranged from very simple to understand and obey, to extremely difficult, if not impossible.

(1) Roedean gels are well mannered; they do not talk too loudly in public. They may cheer the team at the inter-school galas and so forth (which they usually win hands down), but in a genteel, couth manner. They wear their hats in the street at all times, a panama in summer and a navy felt in winter, with a badge on the green and navy hat band and a piece of matching elastic under the chin.

(2) Roedean gells do not do rude things with boys, even at the matric dance, to which they will invite nice boys from St John's or brothers who also go to nice public schools further afield. They will stay in the light and not stray out of sight into the bushes beyond the gym hall. (Corollary: if you are a boarder and are caught with a boy in the bushes, you will probably get expelled.)

(3) Roedean gells are expected to show their personal worth and uphold the honour of the school through being extremely good at sport – at least one sport will do, though several are even better. The choice is: swimming or diving (Olympic standard), tennis (good enough for Wimbledon), hockey or lacrosse (even though only one other school in the whole country plays the latter, which somewhat restricts the competition).

(4) Roedean gels may put darts in their summer djibbah (a corruption of 'djellabah') so that it fits at the waist, but it is forbidden to interfere with the maternity-smock shape of the winter djibbah, which shall hang from the bust and make you look like a sack of potatoes.

(5) The school song for Roedean gels shall be the Harrow School Song – with a few words changed here and there, since we are gels not chaps. They shall not ask why they sing this song, what on earth it means to have bases to guard or beleaguer; meantime, it

will be quite fun to bellow out 'FLOP FLOP FLOP!' in the rousing chorus.

Forty years on, growing older and older,
Shorter in wind, as in memory long,
Feeble of foot, and rheumatic of shoulder,
What will it help you that once you were strong?
God give us bases to guard or beleaguer,
Games to play out, whether earnest or fun;
Fights for the fearless, and goals for the eager,
Twenty, and thirty, and forty years on ...

Follow up! Flop, flop, flop — FLOP
Till the field ring again and again
With the tramp of the hockey team!

(6) Intelligence will be tolerated — and even rewarded through having your name read out in assembly; but the come-uppance will be that you will feel a total prat in front of your classmates, who will have noticed an important omission, namely that you weren't in one of the first sports teams, whose names are also read out, along with their victories.

(7) Roedean gels are expected to have the qualities to be made prefects during their final two years, so that younger gels will look up to them, obey them, generally admire them and have crushes on them. They will have all sorts of privileges, and it will be humiliating not to be chosen and walk up on the platform to have your shiny badge pinned to your summer or winter djibbah. The prefect system will be divisive and reinforce the hierarchy under which the school operates. The qualities for being a prefect will not be printed out anywhere, and the teachers and the headmistress will decide if you have them. If you are fortunate, you will move from being sub-prefect, through bronze and copper to silver prefect (gold is for the head girl). You may have your badge taken away; like a soldier stripped of rank, this will happen publicly (for instance if you are caught smoking or cheating in a test).

(8) Roedean gels shall be Christians, preferably of the Anglican

variety. Three (or exceptionally four) gels of the Jewish faith shall be permitted to be in the senior school at any one time, thus keeping the quota to one per cent, but they are expected to fit in with all Christian ceremonies and not draw attention to their difference in any way. Jewish girls shall not be silver or gold prefects, though they may attain the rank of bronze.

(9) Roedean gels should have the good taste not to talk politics at any time or raise any contentious issues in public. It will also be bad form to talk about politics in private, and you may find yourself jeopardising your popularity by any hint of nonconformity with the white, English, pro-YewPee official line. This will mean that those of you who do actually share common concerns, won't find out till years later.

(10) It is not clear what Roedean gels are supposed to do with their lives, other than be the wives of leaders. As a Roedean gel, you will not receive any career guidance, or particular encouragement to go on to university or train for anything. It will be up to your parents to sort this out for you. Fortunately for most Roedean gels, your fathers are mainly the aforesaid leaders, wealthy, with enough pull in high places or *nous* to know how to work the system. Many Roedean gels will prepare appropriately for their future by going to a finishing school in Switzerland or to a secretarial college. Since there are no entrance requirements other than money to attend university, some gels will actually go away to one of the English-speaking universities, Rhodes or UCT, though probably not Wits, which is considered somewhat disreputable and 'political'. They will do BAs, choosing subjects like Sociology, Psychology and History of Art, and wait to meet a husband.

Roedean in the fifties was an inclusive environment, as long as you didn't count class, wealth, race or sex. Those few girls who did not come from seriously wealthy families recognised each other. On a scholarship, living in a house without a swimming pool or tennis court, my father a mere civil servant and my mother a working woman, a teacher, I tried to hold my own. My mother did her best to help keep up the necessary social façade. We could not hold swimming parties since we didn't have a pool, or tennis parties since we didn't have a court, but we did have space for badminton at the bottom of the garden next to the giant cedar trees, so we had one or two badminton parties instead. Poor-relation stuff. It was pointless to try and compete in the social world in which most of the day girls moved – their fathers the chief executives of this and the other corporation, their mothers who did lunch – and the best thing to do was to be content with a decent short white dress for tennis parties and hope that your game would improve sufficiently not to disgrace you completely.

Luckily, being a good swimmer counted for something in the social stakes, though with a number of Olympic swimmers in the senior school, there was no chance of being selected for the team. But I earned the life-savers' certificates and medals, swimming miles in my sodden pyjamas to prove I could swim with clothes on if forced to do so during an emergency. I practised the extraordinary life-saving back stroke, knees together, an inverted version of breast stroke. Remember to kick downwards – your feet must be well below the body of the drowning person, whose chin you held cupped in one hand, her inert body sprawled across yours. There were stories that drowning people could pull their rescuers under in their frantic battle for air. Drowning became my worst fear – 'Oh hear us when we cry to thee, for those in peril on the sea …' (A fear I would remember when I started to find out about the horrific torture of suspected 'terrorists'. A suspect's head would be covered with a wet canvas bag, which clamped itself against their nose and mouth as they fought for breath.) Back then, learning came easy, but I was again setting myself difficult physical tests, testing myself against god knows what targets, for god knows what end. I practised swimming the width of the pool underwater, coming up for air at the end and then beating straight off again, to test how long my lungs would hold out in the unfortunate event of drowning. I would totter out of the school pool and collapse on the grass, barely able to breathe. And I still had to cycle home.

A few years later, when we had escaped and were in England, we heard about how our comrades had been tortured in jail. Not the near-drowning, I didn't know about that till the Truth and

Reconciliation Commission started to tell us more of what had happened, but the calculated sadism of attempting to break the will through the suffering of the frail human body. Then I was at it again, testing myself, trying to find the limits of my endurance. I held my breath till my face turned purple, imagining a sack had been put over my head. I stood on the crowded rush-hour train with someone's umbrella point piercing my foot: you have to be able to take this, you *have* to. They did. *You* never got tested. Would you have broken? Could you have held out against physical pain?

Back in 1957, for daily assembly Ella stood at a dais on the stage in her black Cambridge MA gown, with the rest of the staff sitting in a semicircle behind her. We filed into the hall, smallest girls in every class leading the way (that's me and little Jud Fry and the other Judy who'd come to St Peter's) and sat on benches according to our year group. We stood for prayers and hymns. 'And did those feet in ancient times …' – the soaring sounds of Blake's 'Jerusalem' never failed to move and to confuse me. There was something false about it – I was an imposter, despite the references to Jerusalem. But no one else seemed to mind the contradictions, the Christian iconography, the assumption that we were somewhere in the Home Counties, in cool, green, misty countryside – not on a rocky promontory in the Highveld, perspiring in our djibbahs, in a school which was trying to be a clone of its celebrated sister in England.

Forty years on, I attended a small reunion of Roedean old girls in a restaurant in London. Over glasses of wine and diet-conscious salads, we reminisced. It appeared that all my former classmates had really and truly been liberals underneath and had never been taken in by the propaganda of apartheid, or done anything to allow it to continue. The conversation turned to the joys of the chapel, the serene and soothing atmosphere. 'I never ever went into the chapel,' I said, almost to myself. My erstwhile classmates turned to me in surprise.

'You didn't go to chapel? How come?'

'I'm Jewish, I'm a Jew, didn't you know?'

'No! Are you? But not your mother?' (That would let them off

– Jews should have a Jewish mother, even they knew that.) 'Her too? No!'

They remembered her – a wonderful teacher, they said appreciatively, my fair-haired, English-accented mother who'd taught them French before she moved to the university.

What they also didn't know was the journey I'd made to say those words out loud. Throughout my teens I never used the word 'Jew', or the one with even worse connotations, 'Jewess' – not about myself or any member of my family, not about anyone. 'My Mum says you're only clever and come top because you're a Jew,' a girl had once told me, quite innocently, when I was eight, at my pink-uniformed private school in Cape Town. Sometimes I might say someone was Jewish, an adjective which was somehow less abrasive, less contemptuous. As if I could protect myself from the implicit distancing, otherness, contempt which curled in the knowing half-smiles of people who talked about 'the Jews' as if they'd remembered they mustn't say 'Yids'.

Would Morris Bledin/Maurice Blair have been proud, finally? He tried to have it both ways, for us as well as for himself. For three years in Johannesburg, I went to Roedean Mondays to Fridays and to shul every Saturday. I wore a little white crescent of a hat, with an artificial flower and a tiny veil, and stockings with a suspender belt in winter. At least it was the Reform Synagogue and the service was mainly in English. Boys and girls sat together. I joined the choir and, though I don't remember any of the words anymore, the music in minor keys stayed with me. When I was thirteen, I took the service for my bat mitzvah with pride and enthusiasm, revelling in the power of holding an audience in my hands, of allowing my voice to resonate across the congregation. Guided by the silver pointer held by the rabbi, I read a great screed from the Torah. I wasn't really reading, though I recognised some of the words. I was reciting off by heart.

And then, aged fifteen, I rebelled. I refused to stay off school to go to the Yom Kippur service. I refused to fast, refused to give up my Saturday mornings any longer, even though it was now too late to join the Additional Maths class, where Win Roux was teaching calculus to the lucky few. My brief flirtation with Judaism had run its course. The Kol Nidrei music was not enough to get me into a synagogue, and on the morning of Yom Kippur there was a shouting match in our garden. Gay was already waiting in the car with her best clothes on. I was also wearing my best, pale-coloured clothes and nylon stockings. It was hot and a school day, and I wanted to be out of these clothes and in school. It wasn't that I didn't want to be a Jew, or that I wanted to join myself to Christianity or be like everyone else. It was all much simpler. I didn't believe in any of it. It didn't seem to have anything to do with my real life, my school and my friends and the awful atmosphere in our house. Trying to sit through a religious service seemed completely hypocritical, and I'd passed the stage when I would do things to please my father.

'She is old enough to make her own choice!' my Mum shouted. 'She's got a right. She doesn't have to go just because you want her to.'

'Yes, that's right. Take her part. Undermine me!' yelled my father. 'It's always like this, isn't it? You don't have any idea how important this all is to me. You and your daughter don't respect my values. Or perhaps you do and just want to hurt and upset me.'

'No one should be forced into a religion,' my mother shouted back. 'She's fifteen. What do you think you'll achieve by trying to bully her into going to the service? Don't lay the blame on me.'

'You don't support me. She gets it from you. You don't care if I'm shamed by you and my children in front of my Jewish colleagues.'

'Is that all you care about? What the Jewish doctors and the Jewish colleagues at the bowls club think of you? It's pitiful!'

'What's pitiful and shameful is that you would do anything rather than please me. What kind of wife are you?'

This was pretty familiar territory. I didn't stay to listen to any more. Mum was probably thinking, 'It's not as if I believe in any of it either,' but perhaps this once she decided to just let it go.

They probably hadn't notice that I'd slipped away inside, where I'd rolled down the stockings and taken the suspender belt off and was quickly changing back into my summer djibbah. I came back out with my school bag and my panama hat and wheeled my bike out of the yard. I would be late for school, and I hadn't a clue how I was going to explain it away; but too bad, I'd think of something.

Dad was still standing in the garden. Mum was already sitting tight-lipped in the passenger seat of the car.

'Goodbye, I'm going,' I said to him, getting on the bike and freewheeling down the path without starting the engine. There wasn't much Dad could do. No one ever tried to suggest that I go to shul again.

I have only ever been to a service in a synagogue once since then, in England, taken by the family friend who got us into England when we were refugees. I could not insult her with a refusal. Nevertheless, although he'd had to accept that he couldn't force me into a synagogue against my will, as I moved into adolescence Dad persisted hopelessly in trying to ensure that my social life would connect to Judaism. His anxiety that I would not meet and go out with nice Jewish boys was very real as he absorbed the inevitable outcome of their choices about schooling and the resultant total immersion in Christianity. Roedean had a quota on Jews. The St John's boys with whom we fraternised at dances and tennis and swimming parties were even more exclusive. When my parents enquired about enrolling my brother Jon at St John's, the Head tried to make them sign an undertaking not only that Jon attend all Christian prayers and ceremonies, but that they would not stand in the way if he wished to convert. Incredibly, this proposal was seriously discussed over the dinner table. Already well into my new role as family troublemaker, I expressed my horror at this hypocrisy, loudly and insistently and with little finesse. Jon went to St Martin's instead – a new Anglican boys' private school – which occupied the buildings and grounds of Father Huddleston's old school, St Peter's. St Peter's had been closed down not long after I stayed there. There was no quota at St Martin's or requirements about conversion.

Roedean and St John's between them ensured that I simply didn't meet any Jewish boys, nice or otherwise. Dad tried to set up meetings with the sons of his friends or Jewish people he met through his bowls club (only Jews were members; they were excluded from all the other clubs in the city). These were dismal failures. I had nothing in common with the young men who arrived in our drive in their parents' borrowed cars, mostly a little overweight, wearing ties and suits. All considerably older than me and already out of school, they were studying accounting or taking a B.Com. at night and working in their father's firms, or possibly in their first or second year at medical or dental school. They took me to nightclubs and danced too close, to syrupy Frank Sinatra songs. I bought a fluffy pink angora top, chosen from the rails of the up-town second-hand shop run by Mum's friend Isabel, where rich Johannesburg women passed on the designer clothes that they'd worn just once. It didn't suit me. I was not the fluffy pink angora type and I already needed a size 36C bra, though it seemed my periods would never start.

Mum sat up for hours making me my first evening dress for a formal dance at a club – I'd been invited by one of these nameless, forgotten young Jewish trainee accountants. It couldn't have been the Country Club, because they didn't allow Jews to be members (though I did go once, as a guest at a classmate's birthday party). The party dress was a surprise for my sixteenth birthday and Mum was extremely circumspect about getting the measurements right, using the ruse of needing me to try on something else she was also making. The frock was white, with an excruciatingly tight waist and little pink ribbons and rosebuds sewn on looping net skirts over a sateen petticoat. It was strapless, with whalebones and a zip all the way up the back, which, like the corsets of yore, seriously hampered breathing. I realise now that she was trying to make sure I would never have to share her painful, bitter memories of adolescence, feeling skinny and ugly in her wire-rimmed spectacles, always in hand-me-downs. She was far more thrilled and excited than I was at the thought of the dances, the young men arriving in open sports cars with smoothed-down hair, the chiffon scarf she lent me, which I tied under my chin to keep my own wild hair tidy in the wind. Through me, she would rewrite her own history, fulfil the lost dreams, make up for the poverty.

The dress was a disaster and she and I both knew it. I looked ridiculous, like an iced cake, not at all sexy or glamorous. But still I wore it, suffering miserably from being too fat, too short, too busty. The whalebones in my strapless bra bit into my waist and the soft flesh under my arms, and I tried to remember to smooth down the layers of net, starched with sugar, which stood up round my legs like a tutu when I sat down and scratched the backs of my thighs, despite the underskirt. I squeezed my feet into white satin, kitten-heel shoes, which pinched my toes and rubbed my heels. All those childhood years of running barefoot had ensured that I had broad, flat feet, and in those luckless days, they didn't make shoes in wide fittings. Under the table, I kicked them off and rubbed the reddened toes against each other, trying not to grimace. Then there was the agony of trying to get the shoes back on when I was invited to dance.

Sometimes, the first-year medics, second-year dentistry students, trainee solicitors took me to the drive-in, turning to smooch when James Dean's beautiful, sad face filled the enormous open-air screen before us, one hand slipping under my home-made, roll-neck blue-and-white cotton top and expertly undoing my bra. None of this was sexy, none of this turned me on. This dutiful necking could not compare with the ache in my stomach, the physical yearning I'd felt one night when I went on holiday to Plettenberg Bay with the Lewsens, lying entangled on the beach with a dark-haired, dark-eyed Afrikaans boy called Andries. But, trying to appease my father, I sat around with the Jewish boys in the new coffee bars, drinking double-malted chocolate milk-shakes, engaged in unbelievably tedious conversations, mostly about business and sport. Only one of these young men was worth seeing again, because he introduced me to jazz – Ella Fitzgerald, Louis Armstrong – but he was intelligent and perceptive enough to realise I was a no-hoper and he never phoned back.

Back at school, Ella would read from the Bible, Old Testament as well as New. 'Let us now praise famous men,' she would intone sonorously from Ecclesiasticus 44;

And our fathers who begat us ...
Leaders of the people by their counsels and by their
    knowledge
Such as found out musical tunes and recited verses in
    writing

All these were honoured in their generation and were the
    glory of their times.
And some there be which have no memorial
Who are perished as though they had never been.
Their bodies are buried in peace
But their name liveth for evermore.

I pondered on the meaning of these familiar verses and eventually concluded that just as Gray's 'Elegy', which we read in English
class, celebrated those ordinary people who might have become
famous if their class background and their luck had worked out
differently, what was critical in the scheme of things was to be
male.

How I missed her, how I missed her,
How I missed my Clementine.
But I kissed her little sister, and forgot my Clementine

| Chapter 7 |

GOODBYE, CLEMENTINE

One day, the song we sang at the tops of our voices in the back of
the Studebaker came true. Clementine sank beneath the waters.
When she drowned, the memory of the loveable elder daughter
was lost and forgotten. She was replaced by a monster – an unpredictable, opinionated, argumentative and unhappy monster.
Fortunately for the monster's father, though Clementine had disappeared, her little sister remained, quiet, beautiful and graceful.
The silly finger games – 'I'm a little pish-pish-pish'; 'Here's the
church and here's the steeple, open up the door and here's the
people' – childish dancing on the beach, the games, the races on
the sea shore, splashing and ducking in the waves together ... all
this vanished too, though just sometimes there would be a little
hint of the good times that had passed. Before we left the Cape,

before we were sent to boarding school, before France, before Dad was left with Jon in a hotel room in Hillbrow while my mother researched her PhD in Paris, before Hila turned into Hil.

Hil was a troublemaker, a wicked child, the cause of family disharmony. Hil didn't seem to appreciate the basic rule that you don't discuss religion or politics around the dinner table if you want to keep the peace. Later, of course, I realised that it was all more complicated than this, and that though I'd surely been a tactless and troublesome teenager, the anger and resentment I'd seemed to stir up simply by walking in the door had had more to do with my parents' failing marriage than my antagonistic personality.

For my friends, there were other catalysts for trouble with their parents as they grew into turbulent adolescence – boys, staying out late, what they wore, not doing school work … just growing up. In my family, it was the 'little p' politics of our shaky family dynamics, compounded by the 'big P' Politics of the country we lived in. Despite censorship and rigid segregation, information about the world outside our protected and privileged neighbourhood did seep through. There was no television and the SABC fed us carefully doctored versions of official news, but we did get the papers. There were still honest journalists on the *Rand Daily Mail,* a courageous editor at *The Star.* It must have been through them, as well as listening in the Lewsens' house, that I knew about the huge bus boycott. I heard about the destruction of District Six, just down the road from my Aunty Mirrie and Uncle Felix's shop in Woodstock, where I once believed Mona Lisa, dressed in red satin, had her home. Before I went there and saw what the government had done, I knew about the plans to bulldoze Sophiatown.

It is so hard to grasp at memories from childhood … all the ordinary, daily details seem to vanish, leaving only frozen snapshots of special moments. I suppose I must have read the papers, because my parents certainly didn't discuss much of this in front of us. Their political positions differed so much that, as time went on, silence became safer than talking about such contentious things. But Dad couldn't really keep quiet: he was loquacious and had opinions on pretty much everything, so I suppose he did hold forth, even if Mum didn't always retaliate. There are small clues that some discussion must have taken place in our house, for how else could the names of certain Nationalist architects of apartheid – Eiselen, Dönges – be so familiar?

But the awful possibility is that if I don't remember discussion, appalled anger or a sense of resistance as the last vestiges of democracy were dismantled, it is because my parents had blocked their hearts, eyes and minds. Did the trivial, ordinary management of their everyday lives – my brother's birth seven years after Gay, moving house yet again, Gay's serious illness, my aunt's marriage, changes of job, my father's difficulties in the Health Department – leave no space for other concerns? Perhaps I should tell myself that, though the black population was certainly organising and demonstrating, only the most politicised whites were doing so. Perhaps the effects of those early laws were not yet apparent. Until the first enforced removals started, perhaps it was not obvious how Group Areas would destroy black people's livelihoods. Perhaps few whites understood how the Immorality Act would blight relationships, how the Population Registration Act would lead to the travesty and personal tragedy of people 'passing for white'. Once, coming home by train after a holiday at the sea, Gay, who is naturally darker than me and was deeply suntanned, was questioned by a railway official who believed she should be in the 'non-Europeans' compartment. We really *were* white, and the incident was easily forgotten. But I find that much larger questions will not simply lie down and die. These doubts are not about the people who voted for the Nationalists, believed that segregation was right and proper, that 'natives' were as children not yet ready for equality. Rather, uncomfortable questions insist on pushing themselves into my consciousness about ordinary white people, like my parents, who did not claim to support the regime, and who did not speak out at a time when it was still safe to do so. They might not have made any difference – but where were they? Perhaps the terrible, irresistible lesson from South Africa in the fifties is that the majority of people, however reasonable, cultured and decent, prefer to get on with their own lives, rather than become embroiled with the troubles or unjust treatment of others.

My parents were like thousands of other reasonably well-off white professionals. They dressed up and supported the theatre and concerts. They went to dinner parties. Mum collected interesting new recipes, featuring pineapple with chicken or litchis with pork (yes, we ate pork) and served these up to guests, properly waited on by their servants. As they became better off, they started to collect original art and sculpture. In a huge effort to join Mum's cultural world, Dad went to a French class at the Alliance Française. They went to Europe, they both read widely, they prided themselves on being cultured. And they were.

Race was the litmus test. There were many contradictions and anomalies in Dad's attitudes to race – he was patronising and insensitive about anyone of colour; he made us cringe by talking about 'munts'. Just as our one and only history book referred to 'the Zulu' and 'the Xhosa', Dad would talk about 'the native' in the masculine singular – stereotyping all blacks as men, or rather boys, and as childish, not ready to be given authority, lazy, dishonest and unreliable.

'The native', he would pronounce, 'cannot be trusted to follow through with the proper measures with regard to his health care. The native believes in superstitious practices which make it difficult for us doctors to prevent serious epidemics. The native won't bring his children into the clinic, even when we lay on free services. The native can't be persuaded to eat healthy brown bread, even though we have fortified it with vitamins.' This was when he wasn't berating our individual black servants for their failures.

I remember challenging him rudely: 'Just which native are we talking about today, Dad?' He would get furious at my cheekiness. He never, to my knowledge, made a connection between the racism suffered by Jews and that inflicted on the black population of South Africa. He seemed completely indoctrinated with the ideas of white superiority, and certainly in his daily life he contributed, like most white people, to helping petty apartheid run smoothly. And yet I have memories of small kindnesses, which no one forced on him and which were not to be taken for granted in the increasing madness of South Africa. The fisherman husband of our coloured maid in Cape Town, Mary Henry, was hurt in an accident: Mary came to Dad for help, and he took me with him when he drove out to their house on the other side of the mountain in District Six, Mary sitting in the back of the car with his black medical bag. A coloured man sitting in our kitchen in Cape Town with a deep cut inside his mouth, and Dad, drawing on his original profession of dentistry, carefully swabbing and stitching. I think the man was a stranger, hurt in a fight in the street.

A bit later, when he was Medical Officer of Health in the Transvaal, he used to visit the notorious farm jails, especially at Bethel. When Ruth First was a journalist, she wrote about them; the scandal became public knowledge. She reported how the unlucky victims of pass offences were sent to do hard labour on the potato farms for Afrikaners who treated them like slaves. Dad pushed for small improvements; he told me he'd insisted that they be provided with straw mattresses to protect them during the freezing Highveld nights. He was proud of himself because when he visited political prisoners in jail, he insisted on small, humane changes. At least he was never responsible for criminal cover-ups, like the doctors in Port Elizabeth who were supposed to check that Steve Biko was being treated properly in prison. But he never seemed to see how the inhumanity of petty apartheid connected to the bigger picture. I don't think he ever questioned that black people's role was to be workers in the white State – allowed in, registered, moved around and endorsed out when they became surplus to requirements.

Within five years of the Nationalists coming to power, the framework of Acts creating petty and grand apartheid went speedily through Parliament, efficiently bulldozing constitutional obstacles with ruthless indifference to the human cost. At the time, perhaps, it was not easy to see the bigger strategy being implemented – but does this mean that my parents' generation really didn't know what was happening? Germans also later said they hadn't known what was going on in the Führer's Germany, but we know now that the disappearance of Jewish business people, professionals and children from the shops, the offices, the schools and the streets was not invisible. We have become accustomed to asking questions about the responsibility of such people, who must have been aware of the consequences for those who found themselves forced to wear the yellow star.

The parallels are not precise, for if the 1950s of South Africa was in so many respects the 1930s of Germany, there were no SA storm troopers, no screaming, fanatical Führer, no concentration camps. But parallels there were all the same. As an adult, wanting to understand the complicity, ignorance and perhaps failure of courage of my parents' generation, I sat for hours in Colindale Library in London, rolling microfiche of fifties newspapers from South Africa through the lens, looking at reports on the issues of the time. This question – did they know? – was of the utmost importance for me; generation after generation, the collusion of 'ordinary' people gives permission to the perpetrators of inhumanity, whether through laws or direct acts of violence.

What I found confirmed what I'd suspected. Throughout the

fifties, the English-speaking papers did report the new Acts, the demonstrations, the bannings. On a smaller scale, South Africa's own special, racialised version of McCarthyism took root. Sam Kahn, a member of Parliament and 'Native Representative', was one of the first to be 'named' as a communist, and when he failed to prove his innocence he was forced out of his job.

'I was at school with Sam Kahn,' Dad told us proudly. 'Year above me at SACS.'

'So what do you think of what's happened to him? He can't be in Parliament any more because he's been named.'

'Well yes. But if he's a communist, then he can't be a good Native Representative. The communists want the natives to take over the country. This cannot be allowed,' he said with impeccable logic.

You could see where he got it from – the anti-red rhetoric was everywhere. Speaking at the Transvaal Congress of the National Party, Prime Minister Malan whipped up his audience. 'Communism', he cried, 'is already within our gates. The non-Europeans are susceptible to communism and the communists know this.'

As the laws came through that altered the constitution to remove the franchise from coloureds ('Challenge to Rule of Law in Parliament', a headline read), there were rallies and demonstrations, attended by thousands of whites. ('Demonstrate at Zoo Lake. June 8th. DEMOCRACY DEPENDS ON YOU. Only YOU can save South Africa,' a boxed advert urged readers.) Making a point about growing official censorship, an editorial noted that the SABC had failed to report a rally of 35 000 people protesting against constitutional changes.

The papers kept on reporting as the Group Areas Act established the basis for forced removals. The Pass Laws were put in place. They also reported the hostility and concern of the British press, just in case their readers wanted to check on the attitudes of a wider world.

When the non-violent 'Defiance Against Unjust Laws Campaign' started in June 1952, the headlines read, 'Non-Europeans in Open Defiance Bid.' In Johannesburg, readers were informed, Indians had been arrested for entering a native area without permits, and natives arrested for defying the curfew regulations. In Port Elizabeth, thirty blacks were arrested for entering the station through the Europeans-only entrance. It took a lot to displace sport on the front page, but there they were – the speeches by the Minister of Defence 'inviting all English-speaking South Africans to come forward and strengthen the hand of the present government and to face facts and to try and keep this country a white man's land.' Prime Minister Malan explained apartheid to an English-speaking audience in Durban; there were rousing cheers and roars of approval as he reminded them that his government had withdrawn legislation which might have enfranchised the Indians in the House of Assembly.

The meetings organised by the opposition, with the support of the war veterans of the Torch Commando, to protest against the destruction of the constitution were dutifully reported. In June 1955, a large group of women – Phyllis Lewsen among them – marched on Pretoria; many of them camped all night in the grounds of the Union Buildings. Next morning, they presented their petition demanding withdrawal of the Senate Bill, which reduced the already meagre voting rights of coloureds. Pictures of women in their tents filled the front page of the *Rand Daily Mail*.

In a smaller box on the same page, without pictures, was an item about a meeting that same day at Kliptown, of the 'Congress of the People'. Our reporter noted that *Nkosi Sikelel' iAfrika* was chanted between each clause as the Freedom Charter was ratified by delegates representing radical groups, white and black. Messages of goodwill were read from the author Howard Fast and the American singer Paul Robeson. Throughout the conference, members of the Special Branch stood watch at the gates of the enclosed area, taking notes and photographing people going to the meeting. They also confiscated the signs showing where you should queue for 'soup with meat' and 'soup without meat', and brought them as evidence of coded messages to the Treason Trial the following year.

I don't think Mum knew about all of these developments or

realised their significance. If my parents were taking any notice of political events at all, their eyes were on what the white government was doing, and what whites were doing to protest. I don't think they looked wider than that. If the papers mentioned radical organisations, it was usually just to report that people had been arrested; what readers got was a picture of sedition. In another country with a free press, they would have had the arguments clearly put to them, but as it was, when the papers talked about the death of democracy, it was about how the existing constitution was being messed with, not about the rights of people who didn't have any rights. People were brainwashed to see things in a certain way, even those who weren't Nat supporters. My parents did not go on demonstrations, did not get up early in the morning during the bus boycott to drive people walking the nine miles from Alexandra into town. When the bus company finally gave way, 'Azikwelwa' – we will not ride – was replaced by a new slogan, 'Asinamali' – we have no money – and a new campaign, for a £1-a-day minimum wage. My parents did not speak of these things.

If any discussion about politics came into our childhood home, it was so contentious that you needed armour plating to survive the battles. Even though they both did nothing, my parents were at different ends of a continuum. And the arguments were not about the politics outside for long. It only took a moment for them to deteriorate into personal slanging matches.

When the authorities were bulldozing Sophiatown, people collected in the hall belonging to the Church of Christ the King. Trevor Huddleston was still there, and he and his curate were trying to prevent the police breaking into the hall. Dad was ordered to go with the police and certify that the crowds in the church hall were a health hazard, so the police could evict them legally. He complied, following orders. He may have been ashamed, but by then he'd got himself into a position where much of his job was about obeying his superiors and not asking questions. Farm jails, inhuman prison conditions, Sophiatown … he couldn't stand back and see what was happening, in the Health

Department or in the country as a whole. It's as if he didn't have any alternative framework. Everyone he knew and respected told him that apartheid was necessary and best for everyone – black as well as white. The propaganda about the danger of people mixing across the colour bar was so powerful ...

People like my Dad really believed the end of apartheid would be the end of civilisation as they knew it. There were so few white people saying anything different, especially not among people he mixed with; and the few who did speak out were, apparently, deeply suspect, treasonable communists. I think my Dad's racism was only part of the story – like lots of people, he could be kind and compassionate at times to individuals, as long as there wasn't any inconvenience or threat to himself. But he couldn't have faced up to his own ethical compromises without admitting that he might have hitched his wagon to the wrong horse, and that would have meant a major identity crisis. He'd have had to ask what his whole life's work had been about. And he couldn't do that – not even long after, when they'd been back in England for years. Being a hero who stood up for things wasn't for him. It never had been.

For my Dad, the demeaning stereotypes and fear which denied blacks their rights and equality were all taken for granted – as unquestionable as the sun setting in the west. But my mother ... how to explain away the speedy collapse of her political sensitivity when she first went to South Africa? She was not ignorant or in-different to politics or to injustice; nor was she callous or selfish.

Mum didn't like what she saw but she wasn't prepared to stick her neck out. At the end of the fifties, when she started going on the annual marches to mark the end of integrated universities, Dad was quite furious. He didn't want her to be involved, and he was really anxious that, if it came out in the open that his wife was 'political', he would suffer in his job. She also lived in a very sexist environment. It was difficult enough to have a full-time job in the world she moved in. None of Maurice's friends had wives who worked. She probably couldn't have made a political stand without leaving him completely; indeed, she tried to leave a couple of times. And he hounded her: turned up at her office at the university, threatened to humiliate her in front of the professor, and made her come home again.

By now I was fifteen. I was reading the papers for myself. Through the Lewsens, I knew people who'd filled their cars with black people morning and night, back and forth between Alex and Johannesburg during the bus boycott. At school one day, Jud Fry told me her mother had joined the Black Sash. I got into an argument with a classmate, Sally, because she said it was right that black people should not have the vote. They weren't fit for it. I got so angry that I smacked her across the chest. (She was a lot bigger than me.) Everyone standing round was shocked. It was becoming harder and harder to understand anyone – my parents, my school friends; I didn't understand myself either. And it was harder and harder to stay silent. I remember wondering whether I was completely mad, because I didn't seem to have the same ideas as anyone else I knew. You could say things were getting at me.

The things overheard on buses ...

'I'm just so fed up with my maid Bessie/Florrie/Lizzie. She is so unreliable and I can't trust her. I leave rand notes out sometimes, just to test ...'

'I know exactly what you mean. It's impossible to get an honest maid these days. And they want to be paid ten rand. And they're cheeky too. Now I like the mission-educated Nyasa girls. They're cleverer than the others, I think, learn quicker.'

'Really? I've just had to get rid of a girl from up north. She was *hopeless*. She could hardly understand anything we said. She said she knew how to cook and use the washing machine but she was *hopeless*.'

Or at our own dinner table ... 'Bessie/Florrie/Lizzie, I've shown you how many times where to put the little knife. Here, *this* side of the big knife, and forks and spoons for puddings up *here,* facing like *this*. What's the matter with you, girl, can't you remember *anything?*'

'She'll have to go. It's hopeless.'

'No, please, Master. I'm sorry, Madam. I will remember it next time, Madam.'

'You'd better, or it's *out*. There are plenty more where you came from, don't forget.'

Buyers' market. Young girls from the reserves, desperate for the pass that would allow them to stay in the city and earn, would come to the door asking for work. Men with hats in their hands, about to be endorsed out of the city, would beg to be allowed to dig our garden. In the days before I left home, we did not keep servants for long (though after I left they had the same woman servant, Rosie, for fifteen years). Some spoke hardly any English and none of us spoke any black African language, not even the pidgin Fanagalo.

More remembered conversations … I get up to go to the loo at midnight, and find Joseph, an elderly man who doubles up as house 'boy' and garden 'boy', slumped at the kitchen table on one of the hard chairs. The neon lights glare down.

'Why don't you go to bed, Joseph? It's late. You've got to get up at quarter to six. You don't have to sit up here at the kitchen table, waiting for the folks to come back. We'll be okay.'

'No, Missie Hilary. I must stay up. The Madam and the Master don't let me go to bed till they come back. They say I can't hear from my room down the back if there is trouble here.'

True, Joseph's room is attached to the garage at the bottom of our long garden, on the other side of the fence with the granadilla vine and the yesterday-today-and-tomorrow bush, whose flowers fade over three days from the deepest blue to the palest grey. And though I and Gay and Jon are respectively fifteen and thirteen and six, the 'boy' must stay up to guard us.

And the one-way conversations held only in one's own head – pointless conversations which would just lead to more trouble if one really expected answers … *Why do they eat different jam to us – the cheap melon and ginger which we all hate? Why do they only have the white marge which tastes like mutton grease? Why boys' meat, which has to boil all morning and smells disgusting? Why chipped tin mugs and special plates kept in a separate part of the larder? Why do we pay them so little, and expect them to get to the townships and back in one day on*

Sunday when it's miles and the transport is so hopeless? Why are they only allowed to wash in the sink in the laundry room and not use our bathroom? Why ...?

I once asked one of the maids passing through for a month or two what she thought when Verwoerd was shot. I received a very circumspect reply that could not possibly incriminate. But later I was invited – reticently – into her room, a small, dark adjunct to the storeroom where we kept the suitcases and the surfboards, my bike and junk, to see pictures of her children. I had not been in there before. It had a concrete floor; her single iron bedstead was on bricks, she had stuck pictures from magazines on the walls, and the photos of her children were in cheap frames on a dressing table made from a nasty table with a broken leg which had been thrown out of our house.

Once a husband came and stayed over, illegally – his pass was not in order. My father was adamant that he must leave. He was given a day's grace and then he must be gone. Where did he go? Where could he go? Once, our maid's two little children arrived to stay, brought by a woman from the townships. The maid came and spoke quietly and humbly to my mother. They played peacefully in the yard and slept in their mother's single bed. My mother gave them some of my brother's hand-me-downs. Then, without explanation, they left again.

Little windows into a world existing alongside ours, just out of sight, secret, unknown. I started to see that through their eyes, our world was ridiculous, cruel, inexplicable, justified only by the power of hiring and firing. Though my parents would sometimes go silent when the servants came into the room, and picked up where they left off as they went out with the tray and the dirty dishes, they often talked in front of them as if they weren't there. So we were intimately known to our servants – the petty arguments at the dinner table, the irrationality of adults who required things done just so. Adults who could not contain their disappointments and indulged in childish tantrums, two-day-long silences and inexplicable reconciliations; and who still expected fresh home-made scones and buns for tea on the stoep on Sundays.

Served with white gloves.

A woman from Zimbabwe once told me that her father had beaten the black people who worked for them before her eyes, and that her mother, a nurse, had verbally abused them without giving it a thought. 'So what made you different?' I asked the question which always puzzles me. 'I'm not sure,' she said, 'but I think it was that I read so much. I read everything I could get my hands on, and it made me question the things I was hearing and seeing around me.' I read too, but I don't think this explains it.

My natural rebelliousness, which had been provoked by the mindless restrictions of boarding school, was now all channelled back into my home. I metamorphosed into a model pupil at school, but became a difficult daughter, opinionated, arrogant and self-righteous. I refused to sit at table and be waited on when my mother pushed the electric foot bell beneath the carpet to summon the servant on duty to clear the table or bring the next course. I insisted on taking out my own plate and would linger in the kitchen. I argued about my father's job and accused him of being a lackey of the government.

'Just stay out of this,' they said when they argued with each other, which was increasingly often. I took no notice. I added my tickey's worth to every argument: which day the washing was done and why my father couldn't expect to have a clean shirt if he couldn't remember such a simple thing; why the toast was burnt or the coffee too weak; why there were only two vegetables instead of three with the roast meat; who was responsible for the salt cellar being empty; the consistency of the vegetables; instructions to the garden boy; the character of one of my father's colleagues; my mother's refusal to play bridge. My mother corrected him and put him down, and my father found equally hurtful ways to vent his frustration and anger. Often I was ordered to leave the table. I would take my plate and finish my meal on my bed, while the rest of the family sat in silence, chewing and swallowing as the servants brought the next course.

The day came when I got caught up in a mammoth row between them. It didn't matter that I had said nothing inflammatory to spark it, since the drama was played out following a pre-ordained script. I was my mother's daughter, I was wicked, I was a troublemaker, everything was my fault. Working himself into a rage of terrifying irrationality, Dad rushed to the study, where he hid his pistol (only used once, to my knowledge, to frighten off a dog) and pointed it at me. I batted it away with a large French dictionary off my mother's shelf and fled into my room. I stretched myself out under Gay's low single bed, furthest from the door, pulling down the blue cover. Gay sat on my bed, facing the door, her feet at my eye level; when Dad came looking for me, she swore blind I hadn't come in there and was probably hiding in the garden. Dad stormed around the house and garden searching for me. I was trapped in our bedroom, since all the windows in our room were protected by burglar alarms and bars – keeping us prisoner as well as keeping intruders out. Eventually he shut himself in the sitting room with a bottle of brandy – a man who hardly drank.

Later, in a state of shock, my mother and I slipped out in the dark, cold winter's night and walked two miles through completely empty streets to the house of a friend, who put us up for the night. I did not see the rest of my family for a week. My mother's friend took us back by car late the following morning, after my father had gone to work and my brother and sister to school. I packed a little bag of clothes and another of my mother's friends came to fetch me and took me to her farm in the countryside, feeding me Cadbury chocolate as we drove. When she took me home at the end of the week, I was ready to be told the parents had decided on divorce. What other solution to this mess could there be? Instead, I found the whole episode was wrapped in silence. No one referred to it. Polite conversation at the dinner table: pass the butter, may I have some more potatoes please?

I learned that fights are dangerous and finally learned what Gay had known all along, that the best protection was to stay out of them; to become involved, whether unwittingly or voluntarily, would lead to getting badly hurt. The day-by-day management of this new persona required that I did not say what I thought or show what I felt. That would give the whole game away. I learned never to cry in front of anyone; to keep my face impassive whatever happened. I became distrustful, even of my mother, who I'd thought was my ally. After a while, this mask was so effective that I really didn't hear anything any more. I was completely switched off, closed in on myself. My body was there, my mind was elsewhere. The quarrels, the bitter accusations, the verbal sideswipes at the servants did not penetrate. My matric exams were almost upon me and I had a good coping strategy. I would work my way out of this mess. There was a precedent, since it had been my mother's solution too.

University. Finally associating with Jewish boys, as my father had dreamed. But something had gone wrong with the fantasy replay of his own student years, transposed to the southern hemisphere. These boys were angry and outspoken, political – writing for the student newspaper, standing for president of the Students' Union, arguing with lecturers, stirring us up about the Pass Laws, about the Congress of Democrats, about the Treason Trial. Students were going to the Trial and demonstrating outside the courts. The Act segregating the university had been passed, but there were still Indian and black students in my classes. They let me know what apartheid looked like from their side of the fence; they might be the black peril, but, by God, true symmetry: we were the white peril.

It was 21 March 1960. We were strolling up the wide path towards the main steps of the university, coffee over, lectures ready to begin again, when the news of the massacre at Sharpeville and the declaration of the State of Emergency spread as fast as fire through dry newspaper. We were incredulous, horrified. Hastily we counted heads in the group standing together on the steps: more than ten people. An illegal gathering. We dispersed, not knowing quite what to say or do. None of us was taken in by the official explanation of Sharpeville, in which unarmed blacks shot in the back were not the victims but the perpetrators of violence.

But this was the year of living like a chameleon, drawing on all the years of practice at being a Jew in a gentile world and never getting found out. Like a chameleon changing colour and blending in wherever you put it down, I could be whoever I wanted to be. I walked defiantly down the hill from the university to our house with James, a black student in my politics class, by my side (but at a carefully chosen time, when my parents wouldn't be home) – not caring that white strangers were staring in disapproval and black strangers in fear and amazement. He sat on our stoep with a cup of tea and proclaimed, 'Yes, this will be mine one day.' The gardener hoeing in the rose garden was in earshot and looked as if he'd been hit.

Nobody from my class at Roedean went to Wits. I found new friends among the girls who were also doing English and French and history. None had gone to expensive private schools, and I kept quiet about Roedean. In my first year, still only sixteen, I joined the choral society and sang in a Gilbert and Sullivan operetta, dressed in rather unbecoming peasant style with a big bow in my hair. I wore my swimming costume and a ridiculous sash across one shoulder, and rode through town on a float in Rag Week.

Sometimes I was a character in a Scott Fitzgerald story, living it up with rich, spoilt white kids, jockeying for social position. I went on picnics with the white boys who drank too much, and played chicken in their sports cars on the winding rocky roads leading to the Magaliesberg. Pass that car on the blind bend. One, two, three, nothing coming the opposite way, made it this time. One, two, three, and you were dead. At Retiefskloof or Hartbeestpoort Dam, we camped by the waterfalls, made campfires and drank from the large jars of cheap wine we'd hauled up the rocks. I started to smoke to show that I wasn't a kid anymore. We sat for hours on the lawn outside the university library, gossiping and eyeing up the boys. Some of my friends were drum majorettes, marching and twirling in tiny skirts in front of the university pool while the rest of us sat on the wooden steps in the amphitheatre. We practised rousing songs, which we'd sing, arms linked, for the big intervarsity rugby match against Tukkies. Not having a clue what the words meant, we swayed and stamped to *Gaudeamus igitur* –

> *Gaudeamus igitur*
> *Juvenes dum sumus.*
> *Post jucundum juventutem*
> *Post molestam senectutem*
> *Nos habebit humus.*
> *(Let us rejoice then*
> *While we are still young.*
> *After a pleasant youth*
> *After a troublesome old age*
> *The earth will have us.)*

– with the same crude and raucous enthusiasm as the nonsense song:

> *Oompa, wally, wally, wally oompa,*
> *Oompa kwa, oompa kwa ...*
> *Oompa oompa, stick it up your joomper*

Through one of my father's friends, I was invited to join a group of young Jewish people who listened to classical music in the semi-darkness of their wealthy parents' houses in the northern suburbs, taking turns to choose the composer of the evening. The group took themselves very seriously, and though it was good to be among people who were open about their love of music, I desperately wished there was a little more humour, more light-heartedness.

Now that I was a university student, even though I was still only sixteen, my parents' control loosened. My father sat me down one day and, with barely managed embarrassment, offered to get me contraception if and when I needed it. I didn't – yet – but I was touched and grateful at his generosity and the implicit message that sexuality was not shameful. Perhaps I had also learned to let go of them a little.

Uit die blou van onse hemel, uit die diepte van ons see,
Oor ons ewige gebergtes waar die kranse antwoord gee,
Deur ons vér verlate vlaktes met die kreun van ossewa —
Ruis die stem van ons geliefde, van ons land Suid-Afrika.

| Chapter 8 |

EWIGE GEBERGTES

My second year at Wits marked a new beginning. By then, I was becoming more discriminating about the people I wanted to be with, and I moved into a new circle of friends. We'd still sit in a circle in the sunshine on the lawns outside the library, gossiping about who we fancied and who was going out with whom, but I started to feel that my mind was being stretched, not just by what I was required to study but by my new friends themselves.

Ronnie sauntered up one day, wearing his white lab coat and shapeless, dark-brown corduroy trousers with holes in them where acid had splashed. Later I would find out that, when the dark-brown cords were taken away by a washerwoman to be scrubbed by hand in the township (and brought back neatly pressed, along with his shirts), he would wear his only other pair of trousers, a paler brown corduroy, also dotted with random acid holes. I discovered that he didn't own and never wore underpants. That he didn't own pyjamas.

It was not love at first sight, since he was Patty's boyfriend. She was a close friend, and I actually thought he was unattractive and difficult. Then that relationship broke up, and towards the end of my second year, what had been a platonic friendship between two people in the same crowd started to become deeper; he was miserable and lonely and he confided in me.

He was on the rebound and so was I, except I was trying to come to terms with losing my father's love and affection. How else can I explain my gratitude that someone appeared to value and love me, wanted me near him, lit up when I came into the room? Ronnie said I was what he needed, what made it possible for him to face the world. I was flattered that he wanted to know what I thought and read, to discuss ideas with me. This had never happened before. Boys were frightened off by any sign of brains or ideas, and any girl who knew the score understood how to pretend stupidity. Don't mention that you'd got distinctions in matric, liked reading and classical music. And now here I was, attractive to a man, not a boy, who was unconventional and unafraid, who liked Bach and Handel, who was full of adventurous plans which cost nothing and took us everywhere. I knew I had found my soul mate. And then there was sex. Since I was fourteen, I had set very precise limits on all those boys who were allowed to undo my bra or stroke me through my pants, but never insert a finger under the elastic. Child of the fifties, I believed in one true love and I was prepared to wait. True love was a girl's destiny, her reward and fulfilment.

Newcastle is a small, mainly Afrikaans-speaking town in northern Natal, built originally around coal mines and later steel. Newcastle is where Ronnie spent the first seventeen years of his life. The Boers and the British fought there in the first Transvaal War of Independence, and the town was an important provisions post in the South African War. That was in our one and only history book, the-all-purpose-for-all-classes-in-all—white-schools author-ity on what we needed to know about our country's past. We did not learn that in 1913, the year before Gandhi left South Africa for good, Newcastle was the starting point for a great march of 2 200 Indian labourers, women and men. They walked from New-castle to the Transvaal border, where Gandhi was arrested and jailed for the fourth time. Indian workers throughout Natal came out in sympathy, in the biggest general strike the country had ever seen.

Ronnie's father's family were originally from Aberdeen in Scotland. Ronnie belonged to another restless, wandering family, contributing to the vast Scottish diaspora in the colonies. The grandfather emigrated to Perth some time in the late nineteenth century, and Ronnie's father Ronald was born there round the turn of the twentieth century. But in the late 1920s he emigrated too, this time for the east coast of South Africa, finally settling in Newcastle where he opened a butcher's shop. Not long after, he married Edna Paterson, whose family had emigrated from Ireland earlier in the twentieth century. Yet another family which had said goodbye for good to tiny, economically destitute villages in damp climates and struck out for new lives in the sun. The Patersons were Catholic, and Catholicism became the religion of the family, not least because Edna's devout mother came to live with the new young family not long after they were married. She helped look after the new baby, born in 1935 and called Ronald after his father, while his parents went back to work.

Ronnie didn't care to talk much about his father, but there were a few posed family photos, taken with someone's Brownie in the late thirties and after the war. Apart from his height – they were both over six feet tall – Ronnie didn't really resemble his father. Ronald was far more muscular and burly, handsome in the fashion of contemporary film stars: a bit like Errol Flynn, with slicked-back hair and a moustache. There was also one of Ronnie himself, aged about four, a beautiful child with a soft brown fringe, huge eyes and a shy smile: a little boy-angel in a Renaissance painting of the Virgin and Child. I never saw any photos of his mother Edna, but he said he looked more like her.

Ronnie was just four when war was declared. His father was one of the first to volunteer, along with quite a large contingent of English-speaking men from Natal. After training, he was sent

to North Africa. He was one of the Desert Rats beaten back by Rommel at Tobruk; he may have been one of the 11 000 taken prisoner straight away at Tobruk, or perhaps one of the few South Africans who escaped capture, fought on and eventually drove the German troops west to Tripoli after El Alamein.

During the war, and after her husband came back but effectively abandoned the family, Edna managed on her own in the butcher's shop. After a while, she couldn't make ends meet and the shop was taken over by someone else, though she continued to work there till her health failed. In these years, Ronnie sometimes helped out – behind the counter, or hanging up the carcasses in the vast, cold storeroom at the back of the shop. Just as I, the doctor's daughter, knew about vitamins and minerals and roughage and eating healthy brown Bremmer bread, so Ronnie knew about meat. He learned the skills of cutting a carcass into joints. He knew which cuts needed long stewing but would be tender and economical. He knew that cheap ribs of lamb were delicious on a barbecue. Appraising marbling and colour, he could instantly select the best steak from a display.

At home, his grandmother was in charge. There were now two children, Ronnie and his sister, born right at the start of the war. Young Zulu nannies looked after them and both children learned some Zulu. Early on in the war, when he was six, his grandmother decided that Ronnie should go not to the local Afrikaans-speaking primary school but to the English Catholic convent. Later, his sister joined him there. Sometimes, reminiscing about our school days, Ronnie and I talked about the convents we had both attended. But while my time at Springfield with the Dominican nuns had been without rancour, Ronnie had bad memories of narrow-mindedness and cruelty. He remembered the nuns as authoritarian sadists, inflexible and self-righteous; any child who challenged their many secular rules and religious certainties was punished by beating. They didn't stand for any kind of personal opinions, which they called insubordination. Once, when she was about eight years old, Ronnie's sister was tied to a tree with a rope for several hours. They used to beat Ronnie with a short, thin stick on his bare legs and the palms of his hands. It was pointless to complain to his grandmother, because she would never take his part against the nuns. His mother did go up to the school to complain about the treatment that his sister had suffered, but it didn't do much good against their moral certainties. Ronnie learned early on, by bitter personal experience, lessons about authority and power, and how the odds are stacked in the struggle for justice.

Later, he moved from primary school at the convent to the Afrikaans boys' high school. His Afrikaans was already passable, from mucking about with kids in the neighbourhood, and now he became fully bilingual. He was in high school when the Nationalist government came to power and put in place Christian National Education for whites, the mirror image of their strategies to control the future of blacks through Bantu Education. As a nominal Catholic, he was allowed to abstain from Dutch Reformed Christianity, which permeated the school – but by then he despised religious zealotry of any sort.

Even in his second language, high school was not intellectually demanding. He was too small and too slight to be any good at rugby and wasn't in any other teams, so he had plenty of time on his hands. He started to read anything he could find, first going through everything lying about the house – his grandmother was an eclectic reader. Then, when this supply was exhausted, he formed a special relationship with the town librarian. She was gratified to keep the unexpectedly rewarding youngster supplied with books, which she'd order from Pietermaritzburg. Still, there were plenty of hours with nothing particular to do, and when he wasn't helping his mother in the shop and didn't have homework, he took to hanging around the back of the bottlestore with the Indian boys – not making a song and dance about it, which would have attracted the hostile attention of his classmates.

He found several of these boys easy-going and accepting. It was a young Indian boy who first got Ronnie smoking and drinking, squatting under the gum trees in the dusty places behind his parents' general store. The Indian boys were not concerned that Ronnie was small for his age, did not have a father on the scene and wasn't particularly good at rugby. One or two had ambitions to leave their town and go to university, perhaps into professions like law or medicine.

So, Ronnie managed to straddle two worlds. He talked and dreamed and smoked with the Indian boys behind their shops. He went to school, hiked and camped in the hills, and fished and swam in the tributary of the Tugela River near his home with the white boys from town. The river was slow-flowing and infested with bilharzia, which makes you lethargic and anaemic and attacks the kidneys; but miraculously, Ronnie stayed healthy.

His father, Ronald George Frederick – what a Germanic, regal name – came back from the war damaged and brutalised, a casualty without visible scars. A man who had been prone to violence and drunken rages in peace time, he came home even more likely to take refuge in the anaesthesia of alcohol. Before the war, he had sometimes drunk too much, and occasionally vented his rage on his little boy and his wife, under the baleful but helpless eyes of his mother-in-law. One day, a year or so before he went off to the war, when Ronnie was little more than three years old, he held the child's head under a tap till he nearly drowned. When Ronnie was only four, he beat him almost senseless with his leather belt. Ronnie never knew what he'd done – perhaps nothing. Probably it was the booze conjuring up paranoia from trivial or imaginary slights. So when he was ten and the soldiers came home, Ronnie was anxious and ambivalent, though his six-year-old sister was intrigued about her Daddy, whom she'd never seen, and excited to meet him. Ronnie's nose was put badly out of joint, because even though he was just a child, as the only male in the family he'd been treated as 'the little man', indulged by his mother, grandmother and sister, who adored him. For a while, Ronald senior re-exerted control, and the mother-in-law and wife had little option but to accept the new regime.

Ronnie's little brother was conceived then, in that brief period of reconciliation after the war ended. He was nicknamed 'Mousie'. Mousie was a sturdy, adventurous little boy, popular and happy-go-lucky. He looked like his big brother – the same widow's peak, his straight hair pushed up into a V in the middle of his forehead; the same round face, freckles and big eyes.

When he was nine and Ronnie was already at university in Maritzburg, Mousie went on a school camp at Howick. One day, he was climbing the rocks at the top of the Howick Falls. He lost his footing on one of the great ledges of rock, steep and smooth, high above the pool below. He fell but managed to cling to a stout bush growing on a ledge. There were people around – some of the other kids who'd come on the camp, some adults. They struggled for hours with ropes and climbing gear, trying to reach him, but they couldn't get near; eventually, he couldn't cling on any more …

Mousie's death replayed itself as a recurrent nightmare, so that eight years later, when I met Ronnie, he was still getting flashbacks, seeing Mousie hanging up there with aching arms, desperately waiting for someone to rescue him.

Ronnie's mother pretty much fell apart after Mousie died. She was ill anyway, with elephantiasis – a ridiculous name for a serious and terribly painful disease, a horrible affliction. Carried by mosquitoes, it causes your legs and ankles and arms to swell up to huge proportions. Edna could hardly walk and she was in great pain. She was in her late forties when she died. The illness claimed her, but really she died of a broken heart after her little Mousie fell at the Howick Falls.

After the war, Ronald senior went on longer and increasingly destructive binges. Ronnie desperately wanted to admire and respect him. At first, Ronald would disappear for just a day or two, then for weeks at a time. In the beginning, Ronnie would sit at the window in the evening, watching and waiting for him to come back. He'd refuse to move out of earshot of the phone, in case his father rang. But after a while, Ronnie became cynical and resentful. When his father stumbled back into town, he'd be dirty and ragged and often ravenous. His face became increasingly ravaged. There was so much alcohol in his system that he was permanently drunk. Sometimes he'd be maudlin and weep pathetically, asking forgiveness, and promise to reform. After this had happened a few times, Ronnie no longer believed any of it; he watched his father in the grip of the demon and knew the promises were just words.

Meanwhile, not surprisingly, his mother had acquired a new 'friend'. She was still quite young and, before the elephantiasis set in, very attractive, with huge, dark-brown eyes that her sons inherited. The high-minded Catholics at the convent school and the priests at the Catholic church, which his grandmother dutifully attended every Sunday, went to town with their judgements and disapproval. It was bad enough that the father had abandoned the family and become a drunk, but for the woman to openly consort with another man was unforgivable.

Many years later, when we were in flight from South Africa, it was a Catholic priest in Tanganyika who helped Ronnie and me when we had nothing. When I learned about liberation theology and the rebel priests confronting fascism in Latin America, I wondered about the Catholic hierarchy in Newcastle in the early 1950s, which had showed no generosity towards this wayward family. The whole family got ostracised on both counts – because of the father, and because of the mother. The sad truth was that though Ronnie didn't respect his father, he was humiliated that his mother had taken up with another man. The man who moved into his mother's bedroom and sat at their dining-room table in his father's place did his best to be kind to the children. But Ronnie cold-shouldered him, punishing both him and his mother in the resentful, judgemental way of teenagers, who have so little experience of adult emotions and sexuality and only feel their own pain.

In the brief glimpses Ronnie gave me of his father I learned about more humiliation. His father had been gone for many months when one day, the boy saw him wandering into town, a broken-down, ragged man of the road. He went to the butcher's shop, probably to beg his wife to give him some money. Shortly afterwards, he came out hurriedly, stumbling and swearing, and wove drunkenly back the way he'd come.

Ronnie decided to follow him, staying a short distance behind, ready to slip away quickly if Ronald stopped and looked back. But he didn't stop and he didn't turn round. He kept going out of Newcastle itself, past the mine dumps towards the black township. Ronnie watched him go into a shack. He came out again with a black woman who was holding his arm and smiling up at him. There were a couple of coffee-coloured toddlers hanging on to both their legs. Ronnie never discovered anything more about these half-brothers or -sisters. They were younger than Mousie and are probably alive somewhere, perhaps also knowing and wondering about their white half-sister and -brother, who had lived not far along the road in a house much more spacious and well appointed than their own.

The last time Ronnie saw his father was when he was already at university in Maritzburg, studying for a B.Sc. The Goldfields Corporation had awarded him a scholarship, which took care of all fees and boarding expenses. The science degree hadn't been his preference. Though he had done well at school in pretty much everything, what he really wanted was to be a writer and study English literature, and possibly politics and philosophy. But living on the breadline as the family did, the real imperative was a training that would lead to reliable job prospects, and anything allied to the mining industry guaranteed this. When he was in his matric year, Edna studied the ads in the papers to see what was on offer. To her credit, she did not insist or even hint he should go straight into paid employment and start bringing in some money. Instead, when she spotted the ad for the scholarship, she enthusiastically sent for the papers, got Ronnie to fill them in, and made

sure he went for the interview. I was at boarding school at Girls'
Collegiate in Pietermaritzburg at the same time as Ronnie was an
undergraduate at Scottsville – we may have passed each other in
town as I trooped to church in a crocodile with the other senior
boarders, in our white dresses, white socks and pale panama hats.

One day, when he was still in first year, living in prefab huts
that made up the university residence, he saw a ragged, unshaven,
weather-beaten man sitting on a bench just outside. In a brown
paper bag he held a bottle of 'white lightning', the cheap and
deadly alcoholic brew made from fermented sugar cane. Ronnie
was desperate for him to move on before anyone from the residence saw this old-before-his time, broken-down tramp and put
two and two together. But the man waved at Ronnie and, taking
pity, he approached and asked if he was alright. Ronald wasn't
very coherent and it was obvious that he was very drunk. It was
pitiful and painful. Slurring his words, he kept repeating that he
was so proud of his boy, that he loved him despite everything. He
knew he'd been a rotten father, but he begged Ronnie to forgive
and help, and not turn against him. So Ronnie went into his dormitory and got whatever small change he had. Then he said he
had to go to his lectures. He squeezed the rough, grubby hand his
father held out and, in a sudden gesture, leaned down and hugged
him. Truly, Ronnie hoped he'd be gone when he came back, and
indeed, later that afternoon, there was no one on the bench. The
paper bag lay crumpled behind it, along with the empty bottle.
Ronnie never saw his father alive again. One night not long after
that, he was found by the roadside near Maritzburg, having drunk
himself to death.

Mousie fell to his death not long after. Then old Mrs Paterson
died, and a few months later there was yet another funeral, this
time for Edna, Ronnie's mother. Ronnie was just twenty-one and
his sister not yet seventeen, the two of them the only survivors.
Ronnie was his sister's guardian, but his scholarship certainly didn't
run to looking after her, and he was in a state of shock at the suc-
cession of tragedies and deaths that had hit the family. Thankfully,
neighbours who'd been friends with Edna took his sister into their

home and saw her through the final years of schooling, before she also left Newcastle for good to train as a nurse. The house on the wrong side of the railway tracks, along with its meagre contents, was sold. The proceeds went mainly to help his sister's adoptive family, and then to set her up in her nursing training. It was a bleak time.

Ronnie had to do National Service while he was still at the University of Natal. Students were not pulled out of university for two years in those days, but had to make up the compulsory time piecemeal during their holidays. This meant he couldn't get a job, which would have helped keep him solvent. He'd chosen the navy rather than the army, imagining that it might be less macho and because he'd always liked water – he was a good swimmer and a champion diver. But the navy training was not really very different from the army. Even in the navy, there were hours of mindless square-bashing and painting coal white in preparation for some dignitary's visit. The all-white navy was as racist as Ronnie had predicted, but growing up in Newcastle and among his peers at university, he'd had plenty of practice at keeping his mouth shut about his increasingly unpatriotic views.

Ronnie had shot up and was over six feet tall, and though skinny, he was strong. Unlike my cousin Mirrie's son, a delicate, sensitive Jewish boy who did National Service much later, no one pushed him around or bullied him; he did his training with university students like himself. But though his peer group was not the problem, someone as anti-authoritarian as Ronnie could not submit for long to commands to attack the kaffirs, or to the seemingly pointless regime, designed to humiliate the squaddies and break their spirit. Before his dishonourable discharge for insubordination, he'd acquired a new passion and a new skill. In the navy he learned to be a first-class marksman. He once tried to teach me to shoot on a rifle range near Johannesburg, but the rebound of the gun against my shoulder so bruised me, and my inability to shut my left eye and take aim through my right so humiliated me, that I gave up straight away. Why or who would I want to shoot anyway?

In London, where he kept an airgun, he once shot at crows from the top-floor window of our flat, because their cawing early in the mornings was driving him crazy. He set up a target on the apple tree in our small garden and practised, to the terror of our elderly neighbour. When he died, after we'd lived apart for many years, I found the airgun and a much bigger rifle among his things as my daughter and I tried to sort a life's accumulated possessions. I wrapped the guns in a blanket and took them back to my basement in London. For several years they sat there. I had no idea what to do with them. I knew that he (and I) should have had a licence to possess them, but didn't know how to get one, without admitting that I was already breaking the law. Then the police declared an amnesty – anyone could hand in their firearms at their local police station, no questions asked. So with relief, I bundled the guns up in their blanket, which somehow couldn't possibly hide their shape and identity, and drove to the police station. The larger one was almost as big as me. I walked into the station holding them awkwardly under my arm, barrels pointing towards the floor, and plonked them down on the police counter. The attending officer unwrapped the long parcel carefully. He blinked, and some sad people slumped on the bench in the entrance area, waiting to report a crime, looked stunned or giggled. A small, middle-aged, well-spoken white woman wasn't anyone's idea of a person who would need to take advantage of a gun amnesty.

After he got his science degree, there was no home for Ronnie to return to and no reason to go back to Newcastle. Anyway, he was committed to working for Goldfields, to pay back the scholarship. Now he moved up to Johannesburg to work in their research labs. Looking in the small ads in the newspaper, he found a room to sublet in a shabby house in Yeoville. The main tenant was a gentle giant of a man called Stefaan. Stefaan was a good bit older than Ronnie, in his mid-thirties, and in a way was like the father – or perhaps older brother – that Ronnie might have wanted. Though Ronnie was technically his lodger, the landlord–lodger relationship relaxed totally and they became good friends. Stefaan was a man of few words, kind, softly spoken, tolerant and dependable. 'Ja, nee,' he would say philosophically from time to time, economically summing up his even-handed view of most things. He was Afrikaans, but in his job at the Jo'burg Technical College, where he taught courses in pottery and textile design, he spoke slow, accurate, sing-song English, heavily inflected with the accents and rhythms of Afrikaans. He was incredibly strong and could lift a medium-sized motorbike singlehanded. He was a man who could do magic with anything mechanical, even though he had little aptitude for making a living. He was unworldly and un-materialistic, and you felt he belonged in another century, when things were simpler and less frenetic.

Other people had a carpet and a lounge suite in their sitting room, but Stefaan kept the engines of two cars and a motorbike in there, laid on sheets of newspaper to catch the oil, along with boxes of parts and all his tools. He'd removed a door to get the motorbike inside and not bothered to replace it. In the yard, two cars stood on blocks, stripped of their engines, which had been taken inside. The stoep was an Aladdin's cave of discarded junk. It was closed in with metal-framed windows and wire meshing to keep bugs out. On the concrete floor, there were piles of house-hold objects – a kettle with a dead element and its plug removed; a useless toaster with broken springs, its side arms hanging loose; a gas water-heater which had once served a kitchen sink. Stefaan believed he shouldn't throw anything away that might come in useful. He couldn't care less about fashion or short-back-and-sides – there was always grease ingrained in his skin and dirt under his nails. Ronnie worked alongside Stefaan in the workshop in the sitting room, learning how to fix engines. When he bought his own second-hand motorbike, small, red 'James', it came into the sitting room too, to be stripped and thoroughly serviced under Stefaan's supervision.

It was during this period that I met Ronnie. He'd already set out, step by difficult step, to reinvent himself, creating a new identity that had nothing to do with the boy who'd grown up in shameful circumstances in Newcastle. He seemed determined to come inside from the margins of society, and in South Africa in

the fifties, brains, race and colour were on his side. Even at university, he'd started on this personal journey. He understood there
was a world of difference between the training which leads to a
job and the reading and thinking which makes you an educated
person. He kept himself open to new ideas – composers he might
listen to, authors he might enjoy. By the time I knew him, he had
a vast collection of Archiv recordings by Deutsche Grammophon:
Bach's Goldberg Variations and the unaccompanied cello suites,
all the Handel Concerti Grossi, Beethoven quartets, Palestrina,
Vivaldi and Monteverdi. The records were kept in several wooden
orange boxes, sorted alphabetically. Though the sound quality of
his record player was tinny and thin, he listened to music for hours
lying on his mattress on the floor, often in the semi-darkness, with
the curtains drawn.

It was not easy to run from his past, which clung to him like a
shadow in the sun. Depression and sometimes rage triggered by
small events frightened his friends. His moodiness was notorious. Drinking was often the way out – nothing special among the
white boys, the chemists, dentists and engineers with whom he
mixed. A prickly, difficult person, more intense, more sensitive to
the nuances of mood than anyone I knew. Ronnie's moods were
like some sort of powerful poison in his system, paralysing him and
preventing him from getting up or leaving his room. He'd drench
himself in Baroque music, hoping to wash away the sadness that
often seemed to overwhelm him. Lying there, he'd chain-smoke
till the big clam shell which was his ashtray nearly overflowed and
his room stank of cigarette stompies.

But luckily, it wasn't like that all the time, or he would not
have survived and nor would our relationship. Mostly, he was
full of energy and enthusiasm for new ideas and new places to
go, always wanting to talk about what he was reading or music
he'd just heard. We talked politics, what we thought of what was
happening in the country and how wrong it all was. We talked
about how hard it was to live in my parents' house, and how they
covered up the cracks in public. He suggested that I read poetry,
and overcome the dislike which my English teacher at Roedean

had managed to instil. He gave me Yeats and Robert Frost, Eliot and Dylan Thomas. Ronnie read and passed on to me James Joyce and Faulkner, Carson McCullers, Kerouac, Hemingway and Philip Roth. We talked about Brendan Behan and the simultaneous energy and destructiveness of alcoholism; what we thought about the explicit descriptions of sexuality and sex in D.H. Lawrence and Henry Miller. Together we read, in English, Sartre's *Nausea* and Camus' *The Outsider*. Neither of us really understood what these books were about, and it never occurred to us to discuss them with my mother, who'd read them in the original French and would have given us a short lecture, if we'd only asked. We talked about existentialism as if meant something, but what was happening to us was more subtle – a world of ideas and experiences opening up and showing us the insularity and narrowness of the world we lived in.

Ronnie bought *Classic* magazine, with its articles and stories by black writers I'd never heard of before like Nat Nakasa and Lewis Nkosi, and *Encounter*. We had no idea that *Encounter* was funded by the CIA and was part of a master plan to indoctrinate people against communism. We met Lewis Nkosi at the mixed parties we started to go to, though we never met Nat Nakasa – who went to New York on a scholarship and became so depressed and lonely that he committed suicide. Another tragic story of exile from those years.

By now, the research team in the Goldfields laboratory had organised for Ronnie to do a PhD at Wits University. It wouldn't be convenient to continue living with Stefaan, since he needed to be near the lab to watch the experiments at night. He took a room in Phineas Court, above a Greek café: a bleak, ugly concrete building with metal windows. Stefaan helped him get his mattress, the boxes of records and books, the plank and bricks which were his bookcases, up the two flights of concrete stairs and along a dark corridor, with time-switches controlling harsh lighting from fluorescent tubes. The room was sunless, looking over an internal yard. It had rather nasty patterned curtains, and Ronnie bought squares of cheap grass matting to cover some of the bare floorboards. A black man, employed by the owner of the block, knocked softly in the mornings and waited with his brooms and bucket and mop till he was invited in to come and clean, or till he judged the room was empty and he could use the keys he'd been provided with. People warned Ronnie about theft, but nothing was ever stolen. The showers and the toilets were along the corridor and you queued for your turn. I never saw any women living in Phin's. People would stare at me when I sometimes stayed over, standing with a towel wrapped round me as I waited for my turn in the shower, feeling conspicuous and embarrassed.

Phin's was literally just across the road from the main gates of Wits, right next to the statue of a Springbok. Now he was a full-time student again, he got to know a new set of people – some who came to have greasy-spoon breakfasts or suppers in the café downstairs, some whiling the time away between lectures, or, instead of lectures, playing pinball. Ronnie first met Mike Schneider hunched over the pinball machines, banging and tilting in a manic attempt to get the machine to disgorge its tokens. He introduced Ronnie to some of his friends, most of them Jewish, several still at university. Unlike Mike, who worked for his uncle, they were doing their training in architecture, dentistry, medicine. Mike's friends were different from the people Ronnie had known before: self-deprecating, more cynical perhaps, liable to be openly critical of the government rather than indifferent. Once again, Ronnie started living a double life, with two sets of friends who had little in common and who didn't really know of each other's existence.

The food at Phin's café was cheap but monotonous. Ronnie found a German restaurant in Hillbrow, owned by Heinz and Margrete Schmidt. They had come to Johannesburg soon after the war. We were never sure what they'd been doing in Germany before and during the war, and we never asked. Both of us knew Germans who found the political climate of South Africa a congenial alternative after the war. Steering away from political discussions, not mentioning that I was Jewish, and eating huge portions of homemade sauerkraut, sausage and roast pork at the restaurant, where they kept a table for Ronnie, was just another of many compromises that were part of life.

He had a key to the university laboratory, so he could go in and work till the small hours of morning, alone, without any distractions. I sometimes came and sat in the lab, bringing a book – there was no room for conversation as Ronnie concentrated on his measurements and calibrations. The experiments needed checking every few hours; the results were written down by hand and the mathematical calculations done laboriously without computers. I gave him a slide rule for his birthday the first year we were going out together.

Ronnie moved easily and cheaply round Jo'burg on his motorbike, James. Thanks to Stefaan, he could fix it himself when it spluttered to a halt. He took himself off into the veld on voyages of discovery, past the yellow mine-dumps of the southern suburbs, along the wide roads leading to the dusty towns of the goldfields, each with their huge, ugly, threatening Dutch Reformed church, their dry-cleaners and low shops and houses with corrugated roofs and shady stoeps, their whites-only hotels and men-only bars. In these places, carts drawn by ancient horses would drag into town with families of black people: old men, women, children. Black women and men sat on the concrete stoeps in the shade, their feet grey from the dust, watching and waiting for change. These little dorps were very like Newcastle; Ronnie would quickly establish if anyone spoke Zulu, and start a conversation.

Or he would go north out of Johannesburg, towards the Magaliesberg mountains, on winding roads overhung with rocks where the aloes clung, where the dung beetles toiled patiently up and down and the ant hills were four feet high. You could smell the heat rising off the red earth, and the pink feathery grasses refracted the light as the sun went down.

In the year I started going out with Ronnie, I discovered a South Africa that I'd only glimpsed from the back seat of my parents' car, speeding on the highways to our annual holidays in the Cape. Now, I rode pillion on James, both of us without helmets or jackets. We turned off the main roads on to stony side roads, and then bumped over dry hummocks of grass towards trees which we guessed hid a river. We found huge pools in the shadows of shiny, smooth rocks, and stripped and dived into water so cold and pure that your skin burst into goose pimples with the shock. Then we'd lie naked on a rock till we were quite dry from the sun. Once, we saw a python sunning itself nearby; paralysed with fear, I tried to remember that snakes were more frightened of people than I was of them. But the stories from my childhood, about mambas so fast they could catch up with a car and crawl in through the engine, were hard to eradicate through an effort of will. Sometimes we'd turn towards one another and lazily make love on the rocks, and I'd squint into the setting sun with the spare towel under my head. Sometimes we forgot to watch the time and had to dress in a hurry, so that Ronnie could get me home before night fell. There was no twilight: from one moment to the next, the sky would be completely streaked with gold, pink and red, lit up as the sun sank through the dust of the mine dumps, and then filled with the myriad stars of the southern hemisphere.

Together we explored the wide landscapes of the Transvaal – the huge skies, the rivers, the kranse and the vlaktes honoured in the National Anthem, which we sang along with 'God Save the Queen' at all official events. Even though it belonged to people I'd started to think of as the enemy, the rhythms of the hymn to the land I loved, in any language, moved me more than any phoney salute to a monarch 6 000 miles away. When I was younger, re-peating the Lord's Prayer in Afrikaans at the Van Jaarsvelds' farm, I'd played with the music of 'en die heerlikheid tot in ewigheid'. Now I sang to myself loudly on the back of the bike, the wind carrying my voice away, playing with the alliterations and repeti-tive suffixes and prefixes of 'Die Stem': 'Ons ewige gebergtes … ons vér verlate vlaktes … die stem van ons geliefde …'

It's not hard to understand why we ended up together, two needy outsiders, desperate to find warmth, security and acceptance. I was nearly eighteen, and finally, it seemed, I was with someone with whom I could stop pretending. I could peel away the mask that covered so much: the embarrassing, tactless and unaccept-able characteristics my father so hated; the things I had to hide from other boys I knew – my taste for classical music and love of reading; my rage and frustration at the divided world we were living in; my longing for something to help me break out of the uptight, destructive suburban world that trapped my parents. Now, with someone who understood from his own bitter experience, I could talk about the mess and hypocrisy in my home, the outsider feelings, the dreams of doing something with my life, the determination not to repeat the destructive relationship that my parents had fallen into. I'd never known anyone like Ronnie before, and I'd never known people like his friends, or experienced the adventures that now seemed to open up every day we were together.

At Wits in the late fifties, before the universities were segregated, it was still possible for whites to sit in the canteen and have a cold drink or coffee with blacks and Indians – the last cohort of non-white students. Shortly thereafter, they were shunted off to the tribal universities in the middle of nowhere, with their fancy architecture and their empty libraries. There were black and Indian students in my politics class, but I was too intimidated and insecure to talk to anyone in that group, white or black, feeling always that I was there on sufferance. Through Ronnie, however, I started to meet and become friends with black people for the first time.

In the lab at Wits, Ronnie introduced me to some of the black assistants – men with no surnames, invisible to most of the laboratory staff and students. Ronnie's lab assistant, Andrew Mabaso, once told him wryly that a white man had poked his head round the door and, looking straight through Andrew, had said, 'Oh, so there's no one here then.' In his easy, unselfconscious way, Ronnie gained the trust and the friendship of some of the assistants, like Andrew and Elias Sobuza. He remembered not just their surnames but the names of their wives and children, and was invited over weekends to their homes in the townships. He bumped along on his motorbike, searching the endless identical roads, where house numbers ran into the thousands. The wives and children treated him with shy, polite deference, this strange white friend who laughed easily, sitting sprawled at their rickety tables with his long skinny legs in flapping brown corduroys. He'd bring some Castle beers, smoke his pipe, share his cigarettes, and go at dusk with the men to a shebeen. They carefully avoided talking politics as such, but conspiratorially joked about the craziness of apartheid, in which not they but the white man was in danger of being arrested for entering their shabby, unglamorous, forbidden world.

Ronnie had a love affair with jazz, but it was not exclusive, and when he introduced me, I fell in love too. We discovered the jazz bars downtown, and the Indian cafés where the colour bar blurred and blacks, whites, Indians and coloureds sat in semi-darkness together round the unstable formica-topped tables, the air hazy and sweet with the smoke of dagga and cigarettes. In the bars we listened to music made by men who would later be world famous, when South Africa's jazz musicians fled their country for Europe: Kippie Moeketsi, Hugh Masekela, Dudu Pukwana, Dollar Brand – melding the rhythms, the energy and the melodies of township music and kwela with the mind-blowing, heartbreaking improvisations of America. They turned both of us on to South African jazz. Already Ronnie's record collection included Dave Brubeck, Miles Davis, Charlie Parker, Dizzy Gillespie and Thelonious Monk in a separate orange box, so you didn't need to search for John Coltrane, Coleman Hawkins and Cannonball Adderley among Bach and Haydn. He always had his mouth organ stuck in his trouser pocket and would often accompany the musicians; although he had no formal musical training, he could pick up tunes and improvise pretty much anything.

Once we borrowed a friend's scooter, for James did not have the strength for the journey, and took off for a weekend of camping without knowing quite where we were going. We ended up in Mbabane, across the border in Swaziland. Night was falling, and we crept through a wire fence and unrolled our sleeping bags under a tree. Next morning we woke to thwacking sounds – *thwack, plop, thwack*. We were right in the middle of a golf course. We scrambled away hurriedly before anyone could accost us. Later, we took a road which went high above the town and sat on the edge of an escarpment, looking down onto the valleys below. We greeted a passing Swazi man, who invited us to join him and his family at his cottage nearby. We leaned against the wall in the sunshine, sharing a calabash of beer.

We slept there, and the next day found our way to the house of a student Ronnie had known at Maritzburg University. It was a large, beautiful, open-plan farm house, with polished wooden floors, great windows open to the light, African artefacts tastefully displayed and Alsatian dogs barking and wagging their tails. The friend was not there, but his parents welcomed us graciously and invited us to stay, though we'd never met them before and had arrived unannounced. We didn't tell them where we'd spent the previous two nights. It was all part of seeing how far we could live in two worlds.

Back in Johannesburg, we went down to Fordsburg and ate in the Indian cafés, found the jazz clubs, went to parties and danced with people who never entered the social world of country clubs, tennis parties or braais. I was finding a new identity for myself, defying convention. I felt like a rebellious moth, breaking free from the restrictions of a cocoon. More than anything, innocently enough, I responded to being loved and wanted for who I really was. I thought I could escape the repressive conventions of the fifties, which decreed that girls should long only for marriage, babies, and cooking in a lovely kitchen. I was seduced by the raw excitement and freedom of spur-of-the-moment exploration of the countryside and the city. A world from which I had been excluded, had hardly known existed, opened up for me. A world where one could sit on a mine dump, watching the setting sun as the last rays lit up the whole sky in chocolate-box streaks of pink and gold through the ever-present dust that hovered over the Rand. I was in love with Africa, as well as the man who was sharing its glory with me.

I was spending less and less time at home, but the necessity to leave permanently had not disappeared. My father made it clear that, till I was out of the house, relationships within the family would be dangerously volatile and sour. My mother started to make enquiries about my going to university in England, and on the basis of a postcard with all the College crests which I had bought in 1952 on a visit to Oxford, I chose St Hugh's. The application papers arrived, the reading lists, the exemplar questions for history. In December, the telegram came offering me a place and an exhibition. St Hugh's did not require that I come for an interview; I was accepted, sight unseen. That I did not really want to leave South Africa, that I really wanted to be an architect, that I didn't know why I was going to Oxford, except that it was the only way to get out of home ... these things were not discussed.

In September 1960, I left my parents' house for good on my way to Oxford. I would soon be nineteen, the same age that my father had been when he went to study in England. Ronnie came with me on the train to Lourenço Marques in Mozambique – where six months before, on Inhaca island, one night on the sand with a snake in the tree above us, I had lost my virginity. For two nights, I smuggled Ronnie into my room in the Polana Hotel in LM, all part of the package deal.

Twenty years later, I saw a documentary about Maputo (as Lourenço Marques has become). The palm-shaded courtyards, the spacious rooms of the Polana Hotel, were sheltering refugees from the Mozambique war. There was no running water, no servants with fezzes and red sashes taking the orders for cold drinks and Castle beers, no discreet white-suited orchestra providing a backdrop of contemporary tunes for dinners of crayfish and piri-piri prawns.

I took the coach with the other passengers to Lourenço Marques airport, for the first lap of the journey to England. Within a few minutes, a bearded, middle-aged man asked to sit in the empty seat next to me. He was Arthur Goldreich, and he said he'd been watching me in LM. He'd noted that my boyfriend had gone home without me. My companion was married, an architect. So, what was the problem? Did I really imagine that my boyfriend would be faithful when I was gone? Come on, don't be so naïve! I had beautiful breasts, he said appreciatively; my tight, pale-green sweater was the perfect colour to set off my olive complexion. Simultaneously anxious, flattered and intrigued at this attention – could I handle it, could I set boundaries and make sure they were respected, should I be concerned about his wife when he plainly was not? – I was entertained all the way to London with anecdotes, information and insights about how to study a sculpture, what made this building remarkable and that one mediocre.

Some years later, he and his wife would make headlines in the Johannesburg papers. Along with Anne Marie Wolpe, Arthur's wife Hazel was arrested when Arthur and Harold Wolpe bribed a warder and made a dazzling escape from Marshall Square police station. Arthur, I discovered later, was a crucial cog in setting up Liliesleaf farm in Rivonia, where Mandela hid till finally all the leaders of the ANC were captured there in 1964. Arthur's journey to London at the same time as me was not an innocent business trip, but part of intricate diplomatic dealings to obtain funds for the ANC underground. As for Harold and Ann Marie Wolpe, they were still in my future.

In those days, Africa was a broken jigsaw of places where South African planes were forbidden air space and could not land. The tiny charter planes carrying South Africans to Europe stopped where they could to refuel, often for days at a time. First we headed north, over the huge sprawl of the Rift Valley, flying low enough to see herds of animals racing across the open land to the west. We landed at Entebbe in Uganda at night, in heat which shimmered around us. Then westwards across the bulge of central Africa, to Kano in Nigeria. Another hop to Lisbon, where the fascist police in their grey uniforms were everywhere. The plane refuelled, and on we went to England.

St Hugh's, Oxford ... my South African identity continued to haunt me. A black student told one of my friends that he wanted to put a bomb under my door, as all whites were complicit in apartheid. I rushed every morning to the pigeonholes, hoping there'd be a letter from Ronnie, who seemed to have forgotten me. The letters came sporadically and only fuelled my homesickness. I worked hard at my weekly essays, but my heart was not in it. I was just waiting for the summer holidays, to go home again.

We really thought we had a purpose
We were so anxious to achieve
We had hope the world had promise
For a slave to liberty
Freely I slaved away for something better
And I was bought and sold
And all I ever wanted
Was to come in from the cold

- Joni Mitchell -

| Chapter 9 |

COMING IN FROM THE COLD

In late September 1961, my parents saw me onto a chartered plane at Jan Smuts Airport, with my arm in a sling but able to manage my suitcase in my right hand. Ronnie was not there to see me off; he lay in a semi-coma in a large ward in Johannesburg General Hospital. I flew into Brussels and struggled with my suitcase and broken arm onto the train which took me to the Hoek of Holland. Then to Felixstowe, then London and finally back to St Hugh's College in Oxford.

I felt a mixture of numb despair and disbelief. How had this happened, what was I doing here? 'Don't worry about a thing,' my parents had said as they booked my flight. 'As soon as Ronnie is recovered, we'll make sure he joins you in England. He can finish his PhD there. But you must go back. You can't leave Oxford now.

You have a long life ahead of you. Don't throw away this opportunity.'

Flashbacks of the past month in South Africa tormented me as I cycled aimlessly round Oxford, often in tears. The white Volkswagen Kombi van – driven, it turned out, by a drunk – had picked us up as we were hitchhiking out of Newcastle, where we'd gone for Ronnie's sister's birthday. 'Please slow down,' one of us had said anxiously, sitting on the back seat behind the driver and his equally drunken friend as he slewed and skidded round the bends of the mountain pass leading out of Natal towards the Transvaal – a fall of thousands of feet on one side, a cliff on the other.

'Moenie worry nie, safe as houses,' he slurred, opening another bottle of beer.

'This is dangerous, I want to get out of here,' I whispered to Ronnie.

'We can't, just hold on,' he whispered back. 'We'll ask to be let out at Volksrust – that's the next town.'

We hit the cliff at speed, without warning. The driver had wrenched the wheel round as the van skidded in the drizzle on its smooth tyres, just avoiding hurtling to a certain death down the mountain side, unprotected by any containing fence or wall. The back of the van flew open and Ronnie was propelled like a cannonball onto the tarred road. I found myself in a large basket in the back of the van. Serendipity: saved by vegetables.

On the road, Ronnie lay screaming in agony. I found I could not move; I tried calling to him from my vegetable-packed nest, but no sounds seemed to come. Aeons later, an ambulance arrived. Ronnie screamed without ceasing as they lifted him onto the stretcher. I was lifted out of the basket and put on the other stretcher.

Volksrust Hospital did not boast an X-ray machine in 1961. The surgeon operated on the mangled leg and encased it in plaster of Paris. I sat by Ronnie's bed, mostly without talking. He was barely conscious, overwhelmed by agonising pain. His sister arrived from Newcastle, and went again. Time passed in a blur. On the third day, I spoke to my father on the phone: 'He seems delirious, he's not making any sense.'

Within hours, my father had organised an ambulance, and we were taken three hundred miles through the starry Transvaal night to Johannesburg. I went home with my arm in a sling and Ronnie was admitted to Jo'burg General. They operated on him the next day, but he was in such a dangerous condition that they could do nothing about his leg. Fat from the marrow of his shattered bones threatened to invade his brain, causing an embolism. A few weeks later, the surgeons tried again, this time taking a piece of bone from his hip to insert into the leg, and grafting an enormous flap of skin and flesh from the calf of his unhurt leg onto the shin of the damaged one. He lay in agony, unable to move, one leg growing onto the other one. I do not know how good the pain medication was in those days, and I do not know how he survived.

When I got on that plane, I didn't even know if he realised that I'd gone. I was doing everything in a fog, on automatic pilot, unable to find the energy to dispute the decisions being made on my behalf.

At St Hugh's, I struggled to focus on the weekly essays and the one-to-one tutorials. Classical economics seemed a million miles from the realities of people's struggles to survive in the townships in South Africa, and from my developing ideas about a fairer economy. Geoffrey Warnock, who tutored me in a shady study in Christ Church Quad, made no attempt to hide his contempt for my feeble efforts to master Boolean logic. His wife, Mary Warnock, my personal tutor at St Hugh's, was kinder about my insights into existentialism, which at least seemed to have something to say to my depression and feelings of worthlessness in a world where God was dead and I seemed to have lost my way. Conscientiously, I attended the big second-year Politics, Philosophy and Economics lectures by famous names in vast tiered halls; but almost immediately afterwards, I'd forgotten what I had been listening to. Riding my bike, muffled in scarves and with the hood of my duffel coat over my head, I felt as if I might drown in the grey drizzle.

I now lived with five other second-years in a house in St Margaret's Road in North Oxford. My friends, generously recognising how I suffered from claustrophobia and the cramped physical horizons in England, had offered me the biggest front room, looking out over the garden. On the wall, I hung a huge piece of driftwood shaped like a heron in flight. I'd found it one day near a river in the Magaliesberg, and carted it back − first to Johannesburg on the motorbike, and then in my luggage to England. A woven cloth from Kano in Nigeria, in rich ochre colours, was stretched across the single bed, scratching any exposed bare skin when I lay on it. I'd bought it on one of those strange meandering journeys between South Africa and Britain, avoiding countries where South Africans could not pass, for all to know that I came from Africa. I turned on the tiny electric heater and played my *King Kong* and Miriam Makeba records over and over on the rackety gramophone I'd bought.

> *King Kong, brave as a li-on*
> *King Kong, king of them all*
> *King Kong, nothing can stop him*
> *That's me King Kong King Kong.*

My friends sang this to try and cheer me up, but my smile was weak and insincere. I sang 'Laku tshoni 'ilanga' along with Miriam on the record player and alone on my bike. I rode around aimlessly in the rain on Sundays, not wanting to be with people, hoping that if I rode far enough, I'd find something that would spark my interest and cheer me up.

And finally, it seemed I couldn't fight the tide any more. I couldn't stop crying. I couldn't work, though I tried. My mind was in another country, another time. My tutors wanted to know why the standard of my essays had gone on a ghastly slide. I knew I was wasting my own and everyone else's time, and my parents' money. It would be better, surely, to admit defeat and go home. Mary Warnock was solicitous and kind. Married herself, with a large number of children, she seemed to understand that I was incapable of concentrating, guilty and traumatised. 'It's alright,' she told me, 'there is a provision for people to do their degree in four years if necessary. Go home and come back within the year, so that you can complete in the allotted time.'

Could I have done otherwise? For us girls, the B-side of 'Peggy Sue', 'Heartbreak Hotel' and 'Just walkin' in the rain' was a sense of responsibility and mission: our power to fulfil the dreams of the boys whose lives would be ruined by our perfidy, our selfish desire to get educations or have lives of our own.

So in this endgame with my future, pop songs and my peer group delivered the checkmate. Certain that my destiny was to be someone's own true love, I betrayed myself and my parents' convictions: that education was as important for a girl as for a boy, that I must be equipped not just to make a living, but to have a profession. Forty years on, I can only try and understand, not judge too harshly that idealistic woman-child, indoctrinated by the conventions and values of the fifties. The choice was impossible, from anyone's perspective. I remember telling myself that even if Ronnie was brain-damaged or physically disabled for life, it was my duty to care for him, and that it would be callous and cruel to walk away. 'Stand by your Man' was written, I believed, for me.

Anyway, it would all turn out fine because, so I told myself, in six or nine months both of us would be on a plane back to England to continue our respective academic careers. In the basement of St Hugh's, my boxes of records, my books, a tea chest full of things I could not take back on the plane, the driftwood, my bike and the beautiful mirror I'd bought in a shop off St Giles waited for me. I thought I would be back for them. Soon.

It was a decision which would determine the trajectory of my life for the next twenty years.

Somewhere towards the end of January 1962, I arrived home. I was on my own when I landed at Jan Smuts Airport, since my parents were holidaying in Europe and Ronnie was still in hospital. I found a flat in Hillbrow, within walking distance of Jo'burg General, and set out to find a job.

As the months went by, with operation after operation delaying the date of Ronnie's discharge from hospital, I told myself I didn't care if I couldn't go back to St Hugh's – after all, I had a degree, I didn't need another one; getting married and living happily ever after was my ambition. My friends wrote to me from England. This one was going out with that one, second year was a doddle, no exams, they missed me, the Beat poets had come to do readings in Oxford, it was great; someone had been to see *West Side Story* in London and thought of me because they knew how much I loved music; they hoped I was okay and that things were turning out well for me. With love from.

After Sharpeville, the South African economy was in crisis. How could I support myself with my degree in politics and history and my Saturday and holiday experience working in shops? The answer was a job as editorial assistant for *Optima* magazine, run from the Anglo American headquarters in town. Editorial assistant – well no, typist and dogsbody more like it. Unable to type, I was despised and intimidated by the outgoing secretary, who was pregnant and who saw through my pretensions instantly. I enrolled in an evening touch-typing course at the same technical college where Stefaan had taught. My well-trained pianist's hands served me well as I learned to type to music with my eyes closed, using all ten fingers. Soon, at Anglo, I no longer needed stocks of Tippex to mask the mess I made, trying to produce decent copy from the material which Sam, the editor, plonked on my desk every few hours.

At editorial meetings, I had to be reminded that my role was to take the minutes and record decisions made by the men, not to have opinions. Finally, one day I was called into the Managing Director's office. Sam stood meekly to one side as I was told that I should find myself a niche where I fitted better, and that I could work out my notice till the end of the month. Was it that I couldn't type well enough? Had someone reported my friendship with Isaac, one of the black messengers, with whom I chatted in the corridor, and for whom I'd tried to organise a collection when his spectacles got broken?

More likely, my impassioned objections at the most recent editorial meeting to a proposed article confirmed beyond doubt that

I was a dangerous and opinionated radical who didn't know her intellectual limits. The article was by an eminent scientist known to the Anglo board; it revived the nineteenth-century Galtonian argument that Africans had measurably smaller brains than Europeans. It was the first and only time I have ever been fired from a job, and I was neither ashamed nor upset — not then and not now.

It did not take me long to find another job — this time at the university, working for Professor Black, a friend of the family. He overlooked or, more likely, didn't care about the defects which had marked me down as a failure in the corporate world of Anglo American. I was made a technical assistant in the mining department, responsible for invoices, looking up articles, occasionally rewriting the prose of the research workers and, most time-consumingly, soldering millions and millions of wires together for some endless experiment at the rock face. I stayed there for two years, back on the campus where I'd been an undergraduate, where my mother and Ronnie, when he finally came out of hospital, also worked.

In July 1962 we got married, in a brief window between operations. I was twenty and had to get written permission from my parents before the wedding could take place. Ronnie's leg was still encased in plaster and he was on crutches for the secular ceremony on the stoep of my parents' house — which turned into a drunken party, thanks to the punch doctored by pure alcohol from the laboratory. Gossips observed my stomach with interest, but I was not pregnant. The pressure to get married was more insidious, more mundane. In the first flat I rented, the landlady came snooping round and checked the cupboards to see if there were any men's clothes hanging there. When Ronnie came out of hospital for a few weeks and came to stay with me, she told me she could not have immoral women living in her block. I told myself I hated the flat anyway and found another place in Hillbrow, run by a couple who were less openly judgemental, but the pressure was on from all sides. Why had I come home if I didn't intend to get married? I wasn't going to disgrace myself and my parents by living in sin, surely? What if I got pregnant? Did Ronnie love me or did he not? If he did, he would surely want to marry me, now that I had given up university for him.

Getting married, wearing an engagement and gold wedding ring, being happy ever after – these were all part of my fantasy. During all those desperate adolescent years, unwilling witnesses to our parents' disintegrating marriage, Gay and I had consoled ourselves that we would do things differently. We would learn from their mistakes, would try and build something positive from the mess we were growing through; we would know what to avoid, how to behave with love and dignity. Marriage for me was not just a fifties dream of feminine fulfilment, but the way I would prove my character. Or so I thought, then.

I planned the wedding with my mother, enthusiastically. My parents were far from happy about my decision to leave Oxford and marry Ronnie, but had realised that their very objections were making me more stubborn. Now I can see that Ronnie himself felt trapped and pressurised, unable to find a way out of the dilemma. He was not indifferent to what I'd given up, or unaware of what my family had done to help him through the agony of the post-accident months; we all knew that my father had probably saved his life by his prompt action in getting him from Volksrust to Johannesburg as he sank into a coma. But was all this a reason to get married?

We lived for a while together in the one-roomed flat in Hillbrow, while Ronnie was still in hospital. It was a dank, murky, depressing place. We ate sitting on the mattress in the room where we slept. There was a kitchenette and tiny bathroom, where the electric light was kept permanently on because the window was so small. Someone's idea of interior decoration had been squares of black and yellow lino, laid in a diagonal pattern over the entire floor. When I woke in the morning and stared at this giant draughts board, my eyes jumped; I felt nauseous. I bought grass matting to try and cover it, but nothing really worked. It felt like being trapped among a thousand wasps.

Despite the holiday cooking course at the tech which I'd taken when I was still at school, I struggled to produce edible meals.

Once, Ronnie chucked the under-cooked beans on the floor in disgust and stormed off to eat at the Schmidts' café nearby. He didn't want the scones and fruit tea-cake that I'd learned to make. I needed to economise and chose cheap cuts of meat, served with plenty of vegetables. We'd been given a pressure cooker for a wedding present, but the slabs of boiled brisket with potatoes and carrots which they'd taught me to cook went bad before we could finish them. And I used to hover anxiously, expecting the whole thing to blow up, hurling the meat and vegetables at the flyblown ceiling – as it had done when I'd tried to cook oxtail.

Coming home in the evenings after work, I had to steel myself to face the bland, beige front door, the hated yellow and black tiles, the streaked walls and the gloom. The pop songs had promised that married life with my beloved would be bliss, but all that I seemed to have gained was anxiety: about Ronnie's sudden outbursts, about his and my depression. Finally, focusing on the yellow and black tiles as the source of my misery, I insisted that we could not live there any more.

We were lucky. 'White Norman', who lived in a squat in an enormous, crumbling mansion in old Parktown, not far from my parents' home, said there was space there for us too. So one day we moved our few belongings into two rooms upstairs in the front part of the house. Number Four, Trematon Place was the oldest double-storey house in Johannesburg. It had been built in the 1890s by a mining magnate who got rich in the gold rush. Unfortunately, his architect forgot about stairs. You reached the upstairs rooms from the magnificent dining room and ballroom, both with stuccoed, painted Italian ceilings and murals on the walls, by a staircase so steep it was more like a ladder. It was a makeshift solution, installed after the whole house was finished, when the owners realised that there was no way to get to the bedrooms from the ground floor. This staircase was too narrow and winding to take furniture up, so our things – the double mattress, the second-hand single bed that made do for a sofa, the table and chairs which my mother's friend Isobel had given us – were hauled up outside the house and pulled in through the huge French windows that opened onto the verandah.

It was Isobel who'd owned the shop where I had bought the pink angora top years before. She'd been my mother substitute as I struggled through adolescence in my parents' home. Now she lived with her family in one of the wealthiest parts of Johannesburg, on the Westcliff ridge – with a swimming pool in the huge sloping garden, and many, many rooms for all her children. It had not always been like this. Her story was a fairy tale. Isobel and her husband and children had lived in a very modest little house with a tin roof, up the road from my parents. She'd befriended an old, destitute man with no family – making sure he was fed, inviting him to meals at her house from time to time, getting him to hospital when he needed to be admitted and visiting him there; no single other visitor ever came. When he died, she was the only person at the funeral – which she arranged. Then they found a will. He was no pauper. He was rich. Very, very rich. Everything was left to Isobel. With the money she bought the grand house in Westcliff. So we had a cleaned-up table and chairs from Isobel's shed, which I'd painted white. The single bed doubling as a sofa was covered with the same Nigerian bedspread that I'd had at St Hugh's.

The ground floor of the house in Trematon Place was crumbling and unsafe for human habitation. Ronnie brought two motorbikes, which he intended to fix, into one of the back kitchens, and laid out the dismantled engines on the metal and enamelled counters built around the huge, useless stove and vast, catering-sized kitchen sink. The electricity dated from the beginning of the century. We stripped the plugs off the lamps and poked the wires directly into the sockets. Sometimes the whole house was plunged into darkness when the aged electricity system failed, but we always had candles and camping lamps ready.

'White Norman' was a medical student who was more interested in art and sculpture, with which he filled his huge, light studio. In the middle of the studio, there was always some enormous clay figure on a stand, covered with damp cloths, that he was working on. He painted the wooden floors white and hung unbleached calico over the windows.

We were surrounded by artists. For a while, Nikki, who was Greek, had the middle rooms. She brought back bags of olives, haloumi cheese and pastries from her father's shop for us all to share. We went with her to the Greek cafés where people got drunker and drunker on retsina and sang in Greek and danced in circles in the middle of the floor, holding their hands up high. Nikki turned one of the bathrooms into a blacked-out darkroom with red lamps. In the other, bigger bathroom across the corridor, which we all used, her black-and-white photos floated in the enormous freestanding bathtub, which stood on curved legs on the marble floor. She simply left the water running, hour after hour. The photos were hung up to dry with wooden pegs on string across the bathroom, and strips of negatives fluttered against your face like moths. She brought Penny to live there with her.

Beautiful Penny, a rosebud child from Rhodesia, with wrists like twigs and long delicate hands, had been abused by her stepfather, and run away to Johannesburg. After Nikki and Penny moved, we dropped in on them in their one-room bedsitter. Like us, they had lengths of material from the Indian shop draped over the windows, a mattress directly on the floor and painted wooden orange-boxes holding all their possessions: kitchen utensils, food, clothes, records. The bed was crumpled; Ronnie, always uncomfortable with the couple's relationship, later remarked that the aftermath smell of sex was unmistakable.

In the colourful chaos of the Indian shops downtown in Diagonal Street, whose interiors and clientele reminded me of my aunt and uncle's and grandparents' shops in Cape Town, I bought hessian to glue over the crumbling plaster in our rooms. In these same downtown shops, seldom frequented by white people, we bought lengths of cheap cotton cloth imported from Mozambique and Swaziland, printed with enormous red fish, elephants, guinea fowl and stylised flowers with slogans in Portuguese, which we pinned over the windows. We had no fridge or oven, just an electric hot plate, plugged into the ancient, unsafe wiring system. On this I cooked for whoever came – dropouts and beatniks, and black people needing a safe place to stay rather than make the long journey on overcrowded trains or unreliable buses back to their township homes.

People would turn up at night, and call up from the overgrown semicircular driveway, where seventy years before the horse-drawn cabs and first motor cars of Johannesburg's smart and wealthy set had pulled in. Silent, dark-haired, meditative 'Black Norman' (so called to distinguish him from blond White Norman, the sculptor) loved jazz and rolled joints from dagga which he grew in pots on his windowsill; Basil the draftsman sang Billie Holiday songs mournfully, accompanying himself on his guitar.

> *Sunday is gloomy, my hours are slumber-less*
> *Darling the shadows I live with are numberless*
> *Little white flowers will never awaken you*
> *Not where the black coach of sorrow has taken you*
> *Angels have no thought of ever returning you*
> *Would they be angry if I thought of joining you?*
> *Gloomy Sunday ...*

After we had gone, Basil moved from dope to harder drugs, and finally OD'd. Black Norman? Perhaps he died too. Did they play 'Gloomy Sunday' when they buried them? The statistics for un-natural deaths – white and black – were mounting in those days just after Sharpeville.

One winter night, long after we'd gone to bed, Lennie, Ronnie's old friend from Newcastle, arrived unannounced and threw pebbles at our sash window till we pushed it up to see who was there. He'd hitched all the way from Basutoland with a lump of shiny stone in his rucksack. He was certain he'd found gold, and insisted that his friend Ronnie-the-scientist inspect and give technical advice, straight away. For a while he moved into our living room with his skinny girlfriend. They took over the single bed-sofa and sat around all day, smoking joints and giggling and eating whatever I served up at night. Then he took off much as he had come, suddenly, without planning, this time to the Cape. He left the skinny girl behind, in tears and pregnant. She stayed for a while longer, then must have gone home to her parents. Five years later, in England, we bumped into Lennie again. He was as handsome as ever, a con man with soft curls, wide bright eyes, white teeth and a convincing smile. He was now a born-again Christian, the preacher for a fundamentalist sect in South London; the skinny girl and his child not referred to, left behind somewhere in South Africa.

For a few days, a strange young man with extraordinary, vivid orange hair slipped watchfully in and out of White Norman's part of the house. Then he vanished. After he'd gone, Norman told us it was Ronnie Kasrils, who'd been at school with him, his thick, curly black hair dyed in preparation for his flight out of the country.

Barney Simon put on *The Maids* in the larger of our downstairs 'ballrooms'. Years before it became fashionable, the play was performed without curtains, scene changes taking place as we watched. The audience brought their own cushions and we warned people not to applaud too enthusiastically because of the fragile ceilings, which might collapse on our heads. We were breaking a much more serious law than the building regulations, since there were white and black people sitting together.

When we had parties, we used Norman's huge studio upstairs rather than the ballrooms, beautiful though they were. Cheap booze, home-grown dagga in our joints, live music played by black jazz musicians, black people without permits to be there who would need to stay the night, blacks and whites dancing and going off into the garden together – all this meant we needed to keep a watchful eye out for the police. Even sharing alcohol with a black person was illegal in those days. Most of us were practised at vanishing into the dark as silently and speedily as ice melting in the sun if the alarm call came that the police were on their way.

Sometimes Prince's huge black Daimler would pull into the drive. Who knows how Prince made his money – drugs, prostitutes, illegal booze; we didn't ask. He dressed better than any of us and always had large amounts of cash on him. 'Too late, too far to go back to the townships tonight,' he'd say with a big smile.

'It's okay, Prince, come on in – have you eaten?' we would say, and fetch the spare sheets for the single bed out of the tin trunk that had brought my belongings back from Oxford, now covered with cushions and a bright cloth from the Indian shop. In return, the next day, Prince would chauffeur us to wherever we wanted to go, sitting in the back of the Daimler like true Madam and Master.

More often, it was Willie, called 'Ntinyan', or Eddie who stayed over. Like me, they were both just twenty-one, workers at one of the big cigarette factories in Johannesburg. When they stayed, we'd

sit tight and refuse to open our door to the other people in the house. We knew them through the Work Camps Association – a multiracial organisation in which young people got together to do voluntary work outside the borders of South Africa on various community projects. We couldn't do anything inside the country because it was illegal for blacks and whites to mix in this way. I was now the secretary of the Association, keeping all the information in my desk in the Mining Department. We'd had some good holidays with the Work Camps people, over the borders in Swaziland and Bechuanaland (now Botswana), travelling together – blacks and whites – in hired minibuses, camping at the work site, digging ditches and building foundations for schools.

I learned new songs there, harmonising to guitars and mouth organs round campfires when the sun went down, drinking beer and trying to keep the mosquitoes away with smelly citronella smeared all over us. I learned to sing in harmony: songs about Mandela coming to power ('Mandela uyezo, uyezo, sina amandla') and all the words of 'Nkosi Sikelele', which was illegal when we crossed back over the border into South Africa. Willie taught me a beautiful lullaby about a bird dressed in white. Ten years later in England, I sang it to my children.

Nda vi lizwi kwe lontsholo
Nda kha nge landa sondela
La li si tsholi si thiti li ti li ti li
Ntjilo ntjilo I mmandi lontsholo ...

When I was a little girl, my mother taught me French through songs ('Il était un petit navire, qui n'avait ja–ja–jamais navigue'; 'Quand trois poules vont aux champs, la première va devant'). Now, how I wished I had been able to learn Xhosa or Zulu the same way.

After Sharpeville, as the regime became more repressive and paranoid, the Work Camps became the only opportunities left to mix legally across the colour bar; the only chance to get to know people without worrying about police appearing to break up the party and drag everyone off to the cells of Marshall Street police station. The huge Johannesburg prison – The Fort – loured over us from the top of the hill next to the university. We walked in the shadow of its walls nearly every day. Somehow you forgot about it.

Willie and Eddie both hoped to go to university, but their qualifications, acquired through Bantu Education, were not good enough to apply. By then, university for them would have meant not Wits but Turfloop, one of the new African universities built hastily in the middle of the bundu, with pathetic libraries of empty shelves and handpicked staff loyal to the regime. We gave them private lessons at our one and only table, Ronnie teaching science and maths, me English and history. We hoped to enter them for the Cambridge A-level exams, the papers for which we'd obtained through the Wits University night school, where I had also started working. Here, cleaners, factory workers, domestic servants and messengers came to be taught by people who were mostly younger than they were, students in these same rooms themselves during the day. Already, the night school was being harassed by the police – it did not follow the prescribed syllabus for Bantu Education. Exhausted, hungry, with so far to get home, our students struggled to concentrate and we struggled to teach, faced with the disaster created by fifteen years of Bantu Education.

One evening, before the date for the A-level exams, Willie and Eddie arrived together for their lesson. But there were to be no lessons any more. They had come to say goodbye. Willie had a bag full of records – Blue Notes, Cannonball Adderley, Thelonious Monk, John Coltrane. 'You keep them, they're for you. Remember us by them,' he said. 'We're going. We can't stand it any more. We can't tell you anything, but wish us luck.' I still have the records. I found out what happened years later, though I never learned the details.

Perhaps like the 'nurses' driven out of the country about the same time by Mike Schneider, who was dressed as a priest, they disguised themselves – maybe as women – to slip over the border and make their way to an ANC camp in one of the friendly African territories. Here they were either trained as soldiers, or sent on to get an education in one of the countries that supported the ANC in the long years of its struggle – Eastern Europe, Scandinavia, Russia, Algeria. Eddie became the ANC representative in Sydney; Willie went to Howard University in America on a scholarship, married an African-American, became an engineer, and eventually got a teaching job at a university. Two able, talented, ambitious young men who were able to make something of their lives, among the millions whose lives were blighted.

One terrible winter night at Trematon Place, we were woken by the spinning lights of a fire engine and the screaming of sirens outside our bedroom window. We rushed out in our dressing gowns, and moved Ronnie and White Norman's motorbikes well away from the shed that was ablaze in the grounds of the house next door. The house was used as a ballet school – before she went to the Royal Ballet School in England, Gay had trained there under Faith de Villiers. The firefighters connected their hoses and after a while the flames died down. In the lights of the fire engine, we watched in horror as they went in with spiked sticks and used them to pull out a completely blackened, burnt corpse. We could hardly breathe with the smell of burnt flesh.

An elderly black man, who had been screaming in near hysteria and struggling with the fireman holding him firmly, lurched forward. 'It's my wife, it's my wife!' he cried.

'She's dead, old man,' the fireman said; the blaze safely quenched, they went away.

We took the old man inside, all of us in a state of shock. 'Oh baas, oh madam, what am I going to do? What am I going to do? How will I manage without her?' he sobbed. He and his equally elderly wife had been living in the shed and, because it was so cold, had made a fire inside. They had fallen asleep and the fire had gone out of control. He'd got out before he was asphyxiated, but had not been able to rouse his wife.

Ronnie gave him a brandy and we put him to bed in the single divan bed. The next day, we put a mattress in the shed at the bottom of our garden for him. Ronnie gave him a pair of corduroys, a shirt and his duffel coat, for he had nothing left from the blaze, and got hold of tranquillisers from somewhere. He explained to the old man how many he should take at a time. So, while we squatted in the house, for a time we saw the old man, a squatter at the bottom of the garden: sometimes alone, sometimes with other black people who also inhabited the sheds and outhouses of the white people's mansions, huddled in coats round open fires, trying to keep warm in the freezing Jo'burg winter. Then he disappeared.

We were still living at Trematon Place when Andrew Mabaso, the assistant in Ronnie's lab, invited us both to his home for lunch one Saturday. We found our way easily on the broad straight road leading out of Johannesburg towards the newly built township of Soweto — a road which fifteen years later would carry the tanks and Saracens filled with armed soldiers and police, attempting to crush the unstoppable uprising of children and young people. We cruised slowly along identical roads, distinguishable to our eyes only by numbers, scrutinising the identical breeze-block houses, their anonymity softened and personalised by small tokens — a little flower garden of marigolds, white and blue ageratum and red salvia, its borders marked out with stones; a brightly painted window frame, lace curtains carefully draped. Children stared at us curiously. There were no other white people to be seen anywhere. At Andrew's suggestion, we parked the bike round the back, out of sight, and went indoors. Mrs Mabaso had prepared a tasty meat and vegetable stew, but she laid the table for only three, not sitting down with us to eat. She hovered anxiously nearby, urging seconds before our plates were empty. The children peeped round the doorway of the only other room, bedroom to them all. There was no electricity, and a lantern hung on a hook on the wall.

We had brought some beer, even though it was illegal for whites to give booze to blacks, and when the bottles were empty, Andrew suggested that we go to the nearby shebeen. It was still light outside when the sound of a siren stopped the laughter and singing in the shebeen and the police crashed in. Andrew and two of his friends were put into the Black Maria by black policemen. Ronnie and I were put in the back of a police car driven by a huge white policeman, his flattened head spiky with a recent crew-cut.

At the police station, he ordered us to stand in front of him and sat himself down behind his wide wooden desk. 'Man, this is no joke. Ek jok nie,' he said. If we had missed the meaning, his tone and body language left no doubt about his anger.

He bombarded us with questions, giving us no chance to answer any of them. 'You've made me miss my rugby game. I was called here right in the middle of the game. What the hell is going on? Who are you? What are you doing here? Do you have a permit? Where is your permit? Nobody, but *nobody* comes into *my* township without a permit, and without me hearing about it. Who are you visiting? What is your connection? You're politicos, aren't you? Communists?'

We had not thought in advance how to play the situation if we got arrested, and now we had no opportunity to work out a story; nor did we know what Andrew would say when his turn for interrogation came. Through the window, we could see him being led into a cell at the side of the station.

I pulled from my repertoire my poshest, most English accent, hoping that I could play the innocent and that the ruse would not backfire. You couldn't be sure — some Afrikaner policemen would go out of their way to show their contempt for the English. I smiled as winningly as I could and tried, despite my anxiety, to force my face into a sexy come-hither smile.

'Oh sir,' I said, 'I am a student from England, on a visit to your wonderful country. We were invited to lunch by someone who works in Ronnie's laboratory. I'd never been to a township, I had no idea I needed a permit, it's all completely innocent, I promise you. We're really not interested in politics at all. We are not at all political, never have been.'

I crossed my fingers, praying that, if things deteriorated, he would not trace me further than my British passport and realise that this 'foreign student' was an impostor, one of the opportunists who had renounced South African citizenship at the time of the Republic. I'd claimed my birthright as a British-born citizen and acquired my navy-blue passport with a lion and unicorn on the front. This entitled me, it announced in small print on the inside of the back cover, to the protection of the United Kingdom authorities — but not, it warned, if I broke the law of any country I was in.

The policeman made notes and looked us up and down. It was impossible to know if he was convinced by our story. Perhaps the truth, that we really were innocent, carried us through.

'Right,' he said eventually, when he'd finished recording the incident in his ledger. 'I'm taking you back home myself. I want you out of here. I don't want to see you here again. Is that understood? You want to come into my township, you get a permit like everyone else. And don't bloody ruin my rugby game ever again.'

'Yes sir. We are very sorry, sir.'

The policeman hitched a trailer on to his car, and a black man ran James up the ramp and secured the bike. We sat in the back, silent ourselves, as he drove silently. By the time we were back in Johannesburg, it was dark, the night obliterating the veld and revealing only the long straight road, lit by occasional car lights coming towards us.

We turned into the driveway of Trematon Place and unloaded the bike, and now our chauffeur finally introduced himself. 'Swanepoel', he said, by way of farewell. Soon to be Major Swanepoel, the notorious Special Branch interrogator and torturer, whose responsibility for deaths in custody would only be fully exposed years later, through the Truth and Reconciliation Commission. The same Swanepoel who later interrogated my mother when we fled.

The following week, Andrew told us he'd been kept overnight in a cell and questioned relentlessly. But he had nothing to tell, nothing to hide, and finally they let him go, warning him too not to flout the law.

And now it was September; my year out was up, I was due back at St Hugh's to complete my degree. Believing that I could have my cake and eat it, I booked my plane ticket back to England, to take up my place at Oxford before my time ran out.

The truth was, I didn't know what to do. My parents wanted me to go back, of that I was sure. I wouldn't be long apart from Ronnie this time. The endless operations were over. We would start again together in England. But only one year from our wedding, the marriage wasn't going well and I wasn't sure that it would survive another separation. Ronnie seemed to find pleasure in putting me down; there was even an occasion when, in a replay of a fight with my father, I threw a dictionary at him. He was drinking too much, taunting me, it seemed, by disappearing overnight without saying where he'd been. A week before I was due to fly, I visited Isobel, whose judgement I trusted.

'There is no question,' Isobel said with all the certainty of a happily married woman twice my age. 'Your place is by your husband's side. You should be making nourishing home-made pea soups for him to come home to, not rushing off like this.'

The next day, I went into town to cancel my plane ticket. The chartered company running the flights had gone bust; it seemed like an omen. I lost my money but didn't care. I was surely able to draw the right conclusions from the available evidence: Isobel was happy and my mother, the one with an academic career, was not. To be happily married to my man was all I craved. As Joni Mitchell sang, all I ever wanted was to come in from the cold.

Some things that happened for the first time,
Seem to be happening again,
And so it seems that we have met before,
And laughed before,
And loved before,
But who knows where or when?

– Rodgers and Hart –

| Chapter 10 |

BUT WHO KNOWS WHERE OR WHEN?

Ronnie knew Mike Schneider long before he and I met and got married. Ronnie and Mike used to play pinball in the Greek café at Phineas Court, outside the main gates of Wits University. For a while, Mike arrived at our house in smart clothes to take out my sister Gay. Hooray – a Jewish boy! My father was delighted. Then Mike started going out with one of my friends from university, and Ronnie and I fell into coupledom with Mike and Fleur.

Mike recruited Ronnie into the organisation when he came out of hospital, sometime after our wedding in 1962. It was then still called the National Committee for Liberation, a heterogeneous conglomeration of people who in retrospect seemed united only in their hatred and defiance of apartheid – ex-communists, liberals, members of the ANC Youth League, Trotskyites. The founders had met in prison, after the Sharpeville Massacre had galvanised opponents of the government, strengthening their determination to hasten the day of revolution. These were the days when the ANC, led by Mandela, determined to move from their previous position of non-violence, and Umkhonto weSizwe (MK) and ANC guerrilla warfare were born. For a while, MK and the NCL were in alliance.

The actions of the NCL read like an adventure story now – part farce, part heart-stopping derring-do. By the time Ronnie was recuited, Mike had already been part of a number of daring escapades, including donning the disguise of a priest and driving twenty nurses over the border into Bechuanaland. Denis Higgs, a mathematics lecturer at Wits, was another central person in the original NCL whom we knew well. He and a couple of others tried to destroy the records at the Bantu Administration Tax Office, using glass cutters. But they'd used golden syrup to deaden the sound of breaking glass, which blunted their cutters. Another time, they tried to bring down the electricity supply into Johannesburg. After hours of sawing and huge blisters on their hands, the pylon finally came down, plunging the eastern suburbs into darkness.

The NCL operated for quite a while and was responsible for some of the sabotage attributed to the ANC. Then, in July 1963, a raid on Liliesleaf farm in Rivonia, on the leafy outskirts of Johannesburg, netted virtually the whole of the leadership of the ANC, except for those who had already fled the country. By the end of the year, the so-called Rivonia Trial had put the black leaders of the ANC onto Robben Island and the whites into Pretoria Central Prison. Only Rusty Bernstein was acquitted; he fled the country before the Special Branch could pounce again. Even though Harold Wolpe, Arthur Goldreich, Mosie Moolla and Abdullay Jassat made their dramatic, headline-grabbing escape from the notorious Marshall Street Police Station, and Joe Slovo and his wife Ruth First had already fled, the government was openly jubilant, claiming they had destroyed the last vestiges of opposition. The mood among those people who wanted and waited for change was low. But the sabotage continued, to the dismay of the Special Branch. It was not MK. It was us.

When Ronnie told me about his conversation with Mike, I insisted that I wanted to be involved too. 'Impossible, this is not girls' work. It's dangerous, it's too difficult. You don't have the skills.'

I persisted. Ronnie said he would talk to Mike and others in the cell. Finally, reluctantly, I was admitted. There were a few other women involved; despite deeply entrenched attitudes among the men that women were not psychologically or physically equipped to handle the stress, there were things we could do, and women were less conspicuous in some situations. Ronnie and I had not been publicly involved in demonstrations and belonged to no political grouping. I'd been out of the country in England for most of the previous two years, and the first months after coming back to South Africa had been spent trudging up and down between work, the flat and the hospital. Ronnie himself had spent most of the previous year in a hospital ward. But for the one incident with Swanepoel, when he'd been called away from his rugby game to deal with us in the townships, we were fairly sure we had no police record. Our anonymity could only be beneficial.

When I chose my pseudonym, I thought of feisty Kate in *The Taming of the Shrew*. A fundamental principle of the African Resistance Movement (ARM) – as we called ourselves after the original name, National Committee for Liberation (NCL), was abandoned – was that people would not get hurt. Our aim was to keep hope alive, make people realise there was still an active opposition, through sabotage of installations on which the smooth running of the economy depended. We hoped to undermine international investor confidence in the economy and create alarm and despondency in government and business circles. We would do this by destroying pylons which took electricity in great footsteps across the countryside, railway bridges which carried workers and goods alike into town, and radio transmitters. But no people.

We had no power base among the huge black majority. We knew there were too few of us to do more than contribute to destabilising the economy and so, we thought, speed the inevitable, eventual downfall of the regime. We believed, too, in psychological warfare: our power to shake complacency, create anxiety and uncertainty. Sabotage has been called the weapon of the weak. It is likely that we achieved nothing at all, at great cost to members of the organisation who were caught and imprisoned, and to those whose characters and lives were largely destroyed when they became state witnesses. Living as we do now, in a world threatened by terrorism, which does not respect human life, I am glad that I was never involved in wounding or killing anyone. But in 1962, childless and just twenty-one years old, I was thinking about the day when I would be a mother or a grandmother, and my children and grandchildren would say, 'Okay, so where were you? What did *you* do?' I wanted to be able to hold my head up when these questions came. I knew there were three choices for us white South Africans sickened by apartheid: leave (as many decided to do), collude and try to placate our consciences with the excuse that there was no other path open to us; or join the revolutionary cause. I was certain that in my lifetime things would, could change. I would be alive to see it. I might even be able to say I had contributed.

In my new role as a member of ARM, I met one or two people with new names and familiar faces: Hugh Lewin, whom I'd known since we were both at school, to be called Mark from now on; and Mike, who was now Luke. It took a while to remember this. A man whom I'd seen around on the campus many times but never spoken to was also part of our small cell. Denis Higgs had an accent from having lived most of his life in England. Denis, with his slight stutter, his unimposing, forgettable face, his capacity to be invisible in a group, his cool and his courage, had been in the organisation from the days of the NCL and was central to the ARM in Johannesburg, He was one of the few English expatriates who did not get seduced by the enticing fictions of white South Africa into justifying their economic and political supremacy. At his unostentatious, single-storey brick house, the lace curtain at the front window would twitch as you pulled up on the gravel driveway. Ring the bell, and his 'maid' Holly, in pink dress with white cap and apron, would shyly open, standing aside demurely as you greeted her: 'Hi Holly, Denis here?' Then, because it was only us, nobody official, nobody in a uniform, nobody for whom the pretence must be maintained, she'd come and sit on the sofa with us. She didn't join in much as Ronnie and Denis discussed 'business', but her body language belied any suggestion that she was really 'only' the 'maid'.

In May 1964, Denis and Holly disappeared. We went to their house and it was all closed up, curtains drawn. We feared that they had been arrested, but reckoned we would have heard somehow. Immorality Act cases were big news, and it would have hit the papers: 'White university lecturer disgraced: caught in bed with his maid' – some titillating, prurient headline that would not need to mention the Immorality Act; after all, who had anything but a black maid? There would have been an old photo, perhaps showing him at some function at Wits, surrounded by other white academics, or one that was fifteen years old, when he was barely out of school and only recognisable to his friends. The depiction of Denis and Holly's affair would bear no resemblance to the relationship they had as established lovers and partners. But the judgement of the liberal English press – the *Rand Daily Mail, The Star* – would also be much milder than the judgement that would come from the courts, in due course. Holly, as the black lawbreaker, would automatically receive a harsh jail sentence. Denis would perhaps also go to jail and, ultimately, would be shamed and forced to leave the country. Everybody knew – this had happened before.

Some time later, a letter came from Denis, postmarked Lusaka in Northern Rhodesia (now Zambia). It did not explain why they had decided to go, or how they had got out, whether separately or together, in disguise or legitimately. Denis had a British passport but Holly only had her pass book. If Denis drove them out in his old, battered car, did Holly sit in the back seat like a meek black maid, in her pink uniform? Or did she, in a rehearsal for what would happen to Denis himself some months later, lie claustrophobic and terrified, bundled into the boot as he went through the border? Perhaps they were just sick to death of the games they had to play; perhaps they'd had a warning phone-call, saying the police were on to them. Perhaps Holly had said she couldn't go on living like this, she was sick of this madness and she was going back to her folks in the Northern Transvaal. Perhaps Denis had said, Why don't we both go, together, we'll get out, we'll go someplace where I can get a job and we can live openly together. His letter gave nothing away. Anyway, they were okay. Goodbye and good luck.

In the months in which we were active, I met very few other members. Still, Ronnie and the others did talk, with the radio on to drown their voices. I knew we in ARM were not all white, despite what at least one history book has to say; we were not all students; and we were not all men. If you'd asked us then about our political ideology, it would have seemed naïve, without clarity or a programme to achieve our goals. We wanted universal suffrage, now; we were thoroughly disillusioned with the gradualism and reformism of the Liberal Party, which also aimed for black suffrage – eventually, sometime in the future, time not specified. Several of the group had been or were still members of the Liberal Party, which was not banned, even if it was harassed. By then we knew that Soviet tanks had crushed Czechoslovakia's 'Prague Spring' and that the student leader, Jan Palach, had set himself on fire in protest at the death of their independence movement. So most of us were alienated from and hostile to the Communist Party. Yet, we hoped for an egalitarian society in which the huge disparities of wealth, power and status of apartheid South Africa had vanished. We understood that racism was at the very heart of inequality, the poison in the well, and that everything that upheld it also upheld inequality and injustice. But we did not really know how to demolish racism and its effects.

Some people in ARM were members of or had close contact with the ANC, but Ronnie and I were not among them. Some were still members of the Liberal Party, where I suppose they had cut their teeth, politically, but that was not us either. Some, on the whole older than us by ten to fifteen years, had great experience of political action and had steeped themselves in theory and policy discussions. We were younger, not part of that experience; by the time we joined, vigilance and security was so tight that we would never have discussed policy with them, even when we did meet. Baruch Hirson, who was one of the older generation of theoreticians and activists in ARM, once gave me a lift to the university when he saw me trudging up the hill. I was alone in his car, I knew who he was and he knew who I was. Neither of us acknowledged this, and idly discussed the heat.

One or two members had been prominent student leaders, which made them much more vulnerable to surveillance. Indeed, the Special Branch broke the ARM eventually by going through the lists of student leaders and hitting on the right one.

The discussion within the ANC about the necessity to abandon peaceful protest was happening simultaneously within the leadership of the NCL/ARM, and had filtered through to us much lower down the ranks, even though Mandela's speech in the dock at the Rivonia Trial justifying the turn to violence was still eighteen months ahead. Mandela's riveting words would echo round the world: 'I have cherished the ideal of a democratic and free society in which all persons live together in harmony and with equal opportunities ... an ideal which I hope to live for and to achieve – but if need be ... an ideal for which I am prepared to die.' We hoped not to die, but we did know that if we were caught we might face a very long sentence in prison.

Separately, long before the Rivonia Trial, we in ARM had also come to the only possible conclusion about resistance – that speaking out, standing in line with banners, working through reasonable, legal processes to further the cause of equality and justice were all totally futile in the face of a police state which believed absolutely in its own cruel and repressive systems and had no respect for law or human life. We'd done with useless peaceful protests, waiting for rotten tomatoes to be thrown in our faces by supporters of apartheid. We knew that banning, house arrest, solitary confinement for ninety days without trial or charges, or torture and death in detention were the punishments the Special

Branch had in store for 'traitors' like us. But unlike Mandela and the leaders of the Communist Party, which worked so closely with the ANC leadership, though each of us no doubt had our own vision of the society we hoped for, there was no coherent political philosophy or programme for what would come next.

It was only years later that I started to become aware of the nature and the wider history of the organisation that we joined. In the early sixties, the police crackdown on dissidents was terrifying, merciless. Our lives were at stake, and security in ARM was very tight and very effective. Until the trials started, people like me didn't know the names of ARM members in Cape Town, Port Elizabeth, East London or Durban, though I did know these cities had ARM cells and we tried to coordinate our actions for maximum effect. All I knew was that we were a group of young people united in our anger, disgust and opposition to the barbarities of apartheid, determined not to collude, but to do something to force forward the moment when the system would finally implode.

There was certainly theory about what sort of society would come after the revolution, but for most of us it was couched in broad statements – democracy, freedom of speech, shared resources. We didn't actually talk about this, and few of us had any notion of how these momentous changes would happen once the tyranny had been overthrown.

Ronnie said that the catalytic moment for him was seeing a newspaper photograph of a young coloured boy whose head had been blown off by a Sten gun. Ronnie often emphasised the moral issues as opposed to the political ones. In his speech at my brother's bar mitzvah in 1963 (we arrived on our motorbike, to the disapproval of the more conventional guests), he advised Jon to beware of the most fatal epidemic in South Africa – moral sclerosis. All the medical men and women there knew what he meant, even if they were embarrassed at the social gaffe of introducing politics into the proceedings. Nadine Gordimer, who lived up the road from us and was a friend of my mother's, was at the ceremony, and Ronnie's impassioned speech appeared soon afterwards in one of her novels.

As for me, looking back with incredulity at my own political naivety at twenty-one, I now understand how a police state grooms and tranquillises young people into becoming unquestioning supporters of its ideology. It also prevents dissidents from knowing quite what to do instead. It was not just what they told us about ourselves as the master race, or how they set up the foe – the *swart gevaar* – as childish, primitive and dangerous, people we should never get to know personally. It's what they *prevented* us knowing. They left us floundering without personal friendships with black people which would have challenged the stereotypes, without historical or contemporary analogies and models of better societies, without any sense of what else might be, without real opportunities for the critical dissection of society which is essential to open minds. We didn't even learn about the rise of Nazism and the Holocaust – presumably, this might have opened up some nasty, slimy cans of worms.

At home, there had never been the kind of conversations that might have educated me. When I was at Wits, one or two of our lecturers tried, god knows, but anything that smacked of liberalism, socialist analysis or Marxism was forbidden in our curriculum. We didn't even talk about what democracy meant. So, in a three-year politics degree, we never studied the theoreticians of the Russian Revolution, or the precepts of the League of Nations or the United Nations. We learned nothing about how the British had tried to establish a welfare state after the war. We had no television – another manipulative exercise by our government to keep us ignorant. We didn't know that The Platters, crooning 'Smoke gets in your eyes', or Billie Holiday were black. We didn't know what was happening in the southern states of America, had never heard of Alabama or Little Rock or the legal battles for civil rights. This news was censored out of existence long before our newspapers got to us – sometimes with the whole front page missing.

The books we might have studied to help us understand theoretically what was happening, draw conclusions about our own society and consider a new order, were all banned. It is true that we read Aristotle and Plato, went through the precepts of the American Constitution, heard about Fichte, McCarthyism and the intellectual roots of Nazism at the beginning of the twentieth century. But I had no idea how the socialism I claimed to believe in worked in practice. I am ashamed now that in my undergraduate years I didn't try and find out more, didn't think outside the box on my own. My teachers didn't dare do so openly themselves, and didn't encourage debate. They lectured at us. If any of them ever discussed the Freedom Charter, or the Women's Charter, or what a democratic, socialist state meant in practice, it was not with us.

There was something else. I was one of only two girls in the final-year politics class. The other one was Portuguese, from Mozambique – Teresa Simoes-Ferreira. I recognised her face years later on television, when she made unconventional speeches on behalf of her husband, John Kerry, the Democratic candidate for the American Presidency. In those days, long before the Women's Movement, we were definitely girls, not young women. (Perhaps this was right for me: I went to university when I was just sixteen, and was still eighteen in my final year.) What's more, in that generation, 'girls didn't do politics'; they studied psychology, English, sociology, history of art – safe subjects that seemed suitable for future wives and mothers, just as white, middle-class women in earlier generations had prepared to be ornaments through learning housecraft and a little music.

Several of my male peers in the politics class at Wits would later become professors of this and that in English and American universities, or members of the South African government when apartheid was finally dismantled. They were smart and articulate and the lecturers found them interesting. We girls who broke the conventions by choosing to study this male subject sat quietly at the back. We were never invited to speak; our presence was tolerated with puzzled patronisation that we never queried. We were used to it, and didn't really expect the lecturers and professors to remember our names. And they didn't. After many years, I met one of the 'boys' who'd been in that class. We recognised one another, and reminisced about what we'd done with our lives, discussed our failed marriages, our children. Then he said, 'You and Teresa – I remember you both well. We lusted after you, you know! You were so beautiful, so remote ... we didn't dare talk to you.' And I told him that what I remembered was not being beautiful or remote, but being too scared to put a foot wrong in that room full of confident, opinionated males, all so sure of themselves. I would never have volunteered anything uninvited, broken into the self-referencing male domain, challenged the invisible barriers that kept us out. Easier by far to withdraw into silence – and save what I thought I knew and understood for essays and written exams.

It was no different in ARM. On the whole, assumptions about girls and women meant that political conversation dried up when we joined a group. The men went quiet. It was assumed that we could neither contribute nor would be interested. Even worse, when Ronnie went off to meet Mike or Hugh or Raymond – the men in ARM – I was not invited to join them; I was left at home.

But blaming others does not really explain why I didn't know how to go beyond a sense of moral outrage. Was it the legacy of my schooling – unquestioning, copying off boards? In first-year sociology, the only subject where I tried to be critical and argue against some of the ideas we were being fed, I just scraped through in the end-of-year exams. It was not difficult to realise that, just as at school, successful students reproduced the official line.

My brother, who went to a private boys' school, says it was different for him; his teachers encouraged them to debate and question. Later he went to school in England and to university in London. But in my curriculum, anything that might have helped me dissect our political and economic system, not just in order to criticise but to develop a realistic alternative vision, had been airbrushed out of existence. Sadly, I wasn't at Oxford long enough; I should have learned the nitty-gritty of the kind of democracy that might replace the corrupt system I had grown up in. It's not an excuse, but an attempt to understand why I knew so clearly what we wanted to destroy – a passion that came from emotional outrage at injustice – but had so little sense of what it would mean in practical terms to replace the mess our predecessors had created.

And then, just at the age when young people join political groups, engage in those earnest, idealistic, formative discussions late at night that open your eyes and your mind, the crackdown came. State of Emergency. Detention without trial. Dissidence = Treachery.

Through the last months of 1962, the whole of 1963 and till we fled South Africa in the middle of 1964, we lived life in the half-light. At weekends, we went out on James to recce jobs, driving all over the Rand searching for pylons that were standing alone and could be taken out without hurting people, or railway bridges that would disable a whole line. I was deputed to go and buy Westclox alarm clocks. I went from one jeweller to another, buying only one in each shop, and brought them home for Ronnie and the other men to turn into timers in the big room that was also my studio and our study. I organised a PO box in Hillbrow under an assumed name, and collected mail which came to us from the ARM people in the Cape.

For 'jobs', as we called them, we could not use a car belonging to anybody in the cell. We only had James, our unreliable motorbike, but it was not too difficult, from time to time, to fabricate pretexts for borrowing my parents' Peugeot. This was one of those moral decisions that define you as an outlaw: not only was I knowingly breaking laws, which could lead to imprisonment or possibly even death, but I was breaking a personal code by involving my parents without their knowledge or choice.

When we left, the Peugeot was impounded, and my mother was questioned by Lieutenant Swanepoel of the Special Branch. He did not say whether he remembered meeting us at his police station in Soweto and kindly giving us a lift all the way home to Parktown.

My role as driver was to bring us near the pre-ordained spot, decided on during one of our recces, then turn off the car lights, slip into neutral and cruise in the dark to the place where the men would slip through the fences and plant a charge at the foot of a pylon. I drove for Hugh, whom I had to remember to call Mark, and another man in the group – sometimes Ronnie, though it was understood that, in general, we should not go on jobs together. I would wait in the dark under some trees, with the engine barely idling, careful not to allow my nervous foot to press the accelerator and rev inadvertently. When the men slipped back through the wire fence, I had to pull off, still without lights, and change into gear, judging the acceleration so perfectly that the sound of the car could not be detected. In those far-off days, you did something called 'double declutching', which I never understood and never mastered. So I waited in the dark, my eyes on the luminous face of my watch, watching the lights of a lone vehicle approaching. Please God, don't let it be the police, on their way to a roadblock, who might decide to check on a car parked without lights in the middle of nowhere (the Immorality Act). It approached, lighting up the road all round me. Please God, don't let it stop, don't let it illuminate the veld where the men crouched in the long grass. For a moment, the headlights bounced all over the Peugeot, reflecting in the mirror and blinding me; then it was gone again.

The men returned and slid quickly into the back seat – but, paralysed with fear, neither my body nor my mind could remember how to put the car into gear. 'Put your foot on the clutch, get into first, *go* for God's sake,' Hugh-called-Mark hissed.

It was hard to admit my fear in front of the men – there was always the possibility that this would only prove to them that girls were not fit for this work, and play into their own mythology that men do not get afraid. This was not true. They would be shaking and, once back home, would throw back hard alcohol, brandy usually. I'd go to bed and go through each moment of the night again and again, reliving the fear that we were being followed, that I could not start the car. When I fell asleep, I would dream that I had forgotten how to drive, and sit paralysed at the wheel as Special Branch surrounded us in slow motion, shone torches into our terrified eyes, broke open the car windows with their truncheons, pulled us out at gunpoint.

The next morning, we would listen to the radio and buy the papers to find out what we had done. We read in the papers that we were a group of communists, highly trained in Russia. We laughed in nervous recognition of the much more banal reality, but under the laughter was the knowledge of what happened to people caught and convicted for treason against the State.

Ronnie was out a lot, and it was understood that I would not ask questions. He went to Cape Town to see ARM people, Mike and Adrian and Tony, leaving me to move from Trematon Place to our new flat – a converted stable in nearby St Andrew's Road – on my own. My mother was angry and appalled. There was nothing I could say to explain. Another time, I went to Cape Town with him, also to see ARM people. People would advertise in the newspaper for someone to share the driving on the thousand-mile journey through the Karoo. Though Ronnie had driven a motor-bike for years, he'd never had a car, and never got his licence. But I had, taught by my father when I was eighteen. In his 'GG' government car, a huge Chevy, we drove round and round the rugby ground near our home; I'd learned to reverse through the rugby poles. So it was that I found myself at the wheel of a Daimler as powerful as a jaguar, sitting on a cushion so that I could see over the steering wheel, both Ronnie and the owner of the car sound asleep. In the silent South African night, I struggled to prevent my foot from taking us over a hundred miles an hour as we purred along the endless straight road in the Karoo night, under the infinite stars. In Cape Town, we stayed briefly with Mike in his flat near the sea; Fleur was away, and he gave us his double bed.

Ronnie went to visit Adrian Leftwich one evening while I stayed in Mike's flat, alone. The rules about security were stead-fastly maintained: Ronnie did not tell me then what they had discussed. What I did not know, I could not reveal to the Special Branch if I was caught and interrogated. I think now that this must have been when Ronnie got together with Adrian to produce a new manifesto for ARM, which tried to hold a wavering position between sabotage without deliberate loss of life and terrorism: 'ARM will avoid taking life for as long as possible. ARM would prefer to avoid bloodshed and terrorism. But let it be known that if we are forced to respond to personal violence – and we cannot forget decades of violence, torture, starvation and brutality against us – we shall do so ... For the present, ARM will inconvenience and confuse ... disrupt and destroy ... strike where it hurts most.'

It was a time of discussion and disagreements about policy and strategies. Some felt that sabotage was pointless and should stop, and that ARM should take another role. Others felt that the strict embargo on hurting people was preventing any real impact and progress. Revolution was not possible without loss of life, they said. Others again – me among them – were adamant that to move from sabotage to terrorism was to slide into murder.

We left Cape Town again in a different huge car, using false names. I shared the driving with the car owner, making up stories about our little holiday at the Cape to keep him happy.

Back in Johannesburg, Ronnie would return home late at night, either from his laboratory or from ARM meetings. He was always exhausted, and though he'd usually had a few beers on his way home, he would continue drinking, brandy mostly. We were both strung out, close to breaking point. We didn't talk much – about anything. The days of discussing what novel we were both reading, what we thought of a new jazz record from East Coast America, planning a weekend away with friends in the Magaliesberg, or pushing a few odds and ends and some food into a bag small enough to carry on the motorbike and getting out of town for the day – they were over. Everything now revolved round hiding our lives and staying one step ahead of Special Branch. We mocked them, made jokes about South African policemen having no brains, just pumpkin seeds rattling around in thick skulls; but it was all bravado.

Once, Hugh/Mark was at our house when an old friend dropped by. I pushed Hugh into the cupboard under the stairs and he stayed there for over an hour, till I could get rid of her. It was not safe for anyone to know that we knew each other. Once or twice, we visited Holly and Denis and sat around drinking with the curtains drawn. But otherwise, it was not so much that we kept our social and political lives completely separate, but that we totally closed down the social life we'd developed when we were still squatting at Trematon Place. The false smiles and camaraderie were quite beyond us both by then, but more centrally, we no longer wanted to take the risk of being caught in some raid on a mixed party where booze and dagga were being shared with black people. A mistimed encounter with one of Swanepoel's henchmen was out of the question now that there really was something to hide and other people's lives, not just our own, were at stake.

We never 'went underground' in the sense of changing names, hiding ourselves and vanishing from jobs and family, though we stopped seeing many people. We became more withdrawn, refused invitations, didn't go to public places where trouble might just happen. Daily we both went to work, me to the mining department at Wits, Ronnie to the lab in the chemistry block. I had my own office, which I'd inherited from the person I'd replaced – a man in his sixties, who had made a lifetime's job of filing papers, ordering stock and keeping records of every little experiment and its research paper. Hour after hour I soldered wires together. I developed a reasonable filing system, clearing the back of a drawer for the Work Camp records. Some of the mining engineers flirted with me, unaware that I didn't find them interesting or attractive, but mostly I was invisible to them – someone to fill in orders, find or file papers in a filing cabinet. The two secretaries in the next room – one a middle-aged woman with bleached yellowy hair with grey roots, the other a young Indian woman that Prof had hired, breaking the taboos – the engineers casually patronised without being openly rude. Farida sat on her own at her desk; no other Indians ever came into the department, and the only other black people who came there were messengers and cleaners. She and I sat on the lawn at lunch time, away from the engineers and among the arts undergrads, and chatted about husbands and recipes and whether we wanted babies. Normal stuff. Ronnie and I went to her house in Fordsburg for supper after she left to have a baby, and she explained about being Ismaili, and the picture of the Aga Khan on their wall. She gave me the recipe for the delicious curry she'd made for us.

Meanwhile, I borrowed books from the Wits library about

the Algerian resistance and the heroes of the Special Operations Executive secret agents in the Second World War. I read about women who had resisted capture and torture – Odette, Violet Szabo … trying to bodybuild my own courage, looking for hints about how I might survive in solitary confinement or under interrogation. I was already preparing myself for what I knew would be the most difficult challenge – solitary. I memorised the words and tunes of a thousand songs so that I'd be able to keep myself going if I was arrested. We had agreed that if anyone was arrested, we'd hold out for forty-eight hours, whatever happened, to allow anyone who was still at liberty to get away. I believed I could do this. I did not know then what I do now about torture.

Then I couldn't even face going to Wits anymore. Farida had gone. I'd had enough of the mining engineers and their crude sexist jokes and their thick skins and their racism. I'd had enough of the strain of pretence; it was easier to be on my own at home, even if I would miss the regular pay. So I decided to set up a little business making batik cushions and wall hangings and leather ties and bags. I went downtown and bought leather skins direct from a wholesaler, which I stretched and pinned out on our one table to cut. The patterns I made from ties and bags that I'd unstitched to see how it was done. Bolts of unbleached calico were propped against the wall in the studio. The smell of melted wax and dyes pervaded our kitchen. The batiks dripped in the sun from the washing line. Looking back, I am bewildered at my confidence and belief that I could just do all this, without training. The batik hangings and cushions, the ties and the leather bags were not well made and I only sold a few.

After a few months, I started to get bored and lonely and read the ads in *The Star* to see what I might do. A job was advertised at King David School to teach English. Ronnie had been taught by the Head years before and he still remembered the lessons on Shakespeare, which he said were inspired – involving the boys acting most of the parts, and thinking about the language and the issues in terms of their contemporary lives. Ronnie coached me in a mock interview, in which I said what he believed the Head would want to hear. He took me to the interview on the back of the motorbike. Inelegantly, my best red dress with spots and white collar and cuffs was pushed up to my panties so that I could sit astride the passenger seat. Clinging to Ronnie's waist, I tried to cover the bare patch where stockings met suspender belt with my duffel coat as we drove out to the school.

His memory and coaching worked well – I would be teaching Standard 6 when the new term started after the winter holidays. 'One thing, though,' the Head said before I left. 'I do hope you're not political? No? Oh good. The last woman who had this job left without even telling us goodbye. She was political, and she fled over the border. Left us completely in the lurch. Children sitting in class waiting and no one turns up, and no notice to me or the secretary that we needed cover. Completely irresponsible. I really don't want another politico. You won't do that, will you? No? Good. That's settled then.' I went home with the syllabuses for the classes I would teach and started planning lessons. Imaginatively, I thought, I would somehow use the punning name of the latest pop group to hit the charts, pushing Little Richard and rock 'n roll into the shadows: The Beatles.

We knew in our hearts that our days were numbered. What we were doing could only end in one of three ways – being arrested and sent to jail for a very long time, fleeing the country, or leaving voluntarily before they caught us. In preparation, we had sold much-loved but weak and unreliable James and bought a powerful second-hand 650 AJS. We started to collect information about going up through Africa on a motorbike: buying maps, ascertaining when the monsoon rains would make roads impassable, where civil war or hostility to South Africans would make our journey impossible. I wrote letters trying to obtain visas for the countries we'd need to pass through on our projected journey from Johannesburg to Cairo.

In our place in St Andrew's Road, there were entrances in the front and the back. At the front was a stable door leading into the kitchen. An outside staircase led up the side of the old stables to a huge room which had been a barn, where Ronnie prepared explosives and I laid out the cloth for the batiks and the leather for the handbags and ties.

Mike Schneider arrived at the stable door one night in early July, one step ahead of Special Branch. I was on my own there. The game was up, he told me. We all had to get out as fast as we could. We'd been waiting for this moment for months and were at least mentally prepared. With an extraordinary combination of courage and chutzpah, Mike had walked straight past the police watching for him at Cape Town airport, even going back to the waiting room for his warm winter coat. He'd bought the coat specially for this journey, dicing with his luck by slipping into a store in Cape Town even when the Special Branch were out looking for him, and using his uncle's credit card. By some inexplicable coincidence, he'd seen his cousin at the barriers at Cape Town airport. By then, the cousin knew he was on the run, and though their eyes met, both kept up the pretence of staring at a stranger. The most minute alteration in timing could have led to such different outcomes for him – and for us. As we struggled to keep control of our fate, it was hard to believe in anything other than chance and contingency in our lives.

In Cape Town, Adrian Leftwich, former student leader and central member of ARM, had been arrested and his notebook taken, in which, fatally and unforgivably, he had written the names of people involved in the movement. We did not know yet that Adrian had started talking almost immediately, a failure of courage and solidarity which was to haunt and ruin his life for ever more. Worse, Mike's girlfriend Fleur, who had gone ahead of him into the flat when they'd realised that Special Branch were waiting for them there, had also been arrested and had probably talked. She was not part of the movement, deeply hostile to Mike's involvement and knew all our real names, since she'd known us long before we adopted pseudonyms.

I drew all the curtains in the stable-flat in St Andrew's Road and left Mike hiding upstairs with something to eat. He was exhausted from the ordeal of his escape from Cape Town, surviving on adrenalin and cigarettes, and perhaps he slept. I put a notebook and a pencil in my pocket, locked all the doors, back and front and at the top of the stairs into the barn, and set out on foot to try and find Ronnie and Hugh, who I thought was with him. I had a number of ideas where they might be, and hurried along the familiar roads where I'd ridden my bike throughout my adolescence. I climbed through the fence and down and then up the sides of the empty ditch round the fields at the bottom of the university, up through the empty grounds and into Hillbrow. There was frost on the ground in the icy winter night of the Highveld. My footsteps left dark patches on dry grass where I walked close to the hedges and walls, avoiding, where I could, the paved areas lit by bright streetlamps. I skirted the dark high walls of the prison – the Fort. The streets were deserted, just as they'd been all those evenings when I'd walked to the hospital and back – to the horror of friends and family, who did not hesitate to tell me that my recklessness was openly inviting rape and murder.

Finally, I found our motorbike parked outside a bar. Women

were not allowed in bars in those days, but I stood at the door and peeped in. There was no sign of Ronnie. I quickly scribbled a note and fixed it to the seat of his motorbike: 'Butch sick – needs a vet. Come back immediately with a car.' Our dog Butch, given to us for safekeeping by Basil, the Billie Holiday lover, had disappeared many months before, but I hoped that the reference to needing a car would be read as a signal to come back with Hugh, in his car. Then I hurried back as fast as I could, the way I'd come: avoiding the main roads, creeping in the ditch and along the hedges in the university grounds, slipping out briefly onto the pavements where I could not avoid the roads, and sliding in through the back entrance of the flat.

Now I started to put a few things together in a small rucksack, reckoning that as soon as Ronnie returned, we would need to leave. The little canvas rucksack did not hold much. Warm clothes, socks, a spare jersey (it was the depths of winter); both our degree certificates so that we could get work when/if we were in a safe country; our passports (mine British, his South African); a map of South Africa; the two or three pieces of semi-precious jewellery that I owned, which I imagined I could sell if I needed to: a malachite pendant given to me by my parents as a reward for my good matric results and my purple amethyst engagement ring, which I seldom wore. My post office savings book. My duffel coat, a stripy scarf I'd knitted for myself and my woollen gloves. Going without gloves was unthinkable. My fingers would be blue and stiff from the Raynaud's disease, incapable of holding anything, and I would be crying silently from the pain. One day, they said, like frostbite, you might find that your fingers just drop off. It was particularly bad in the icy Highveld winter. Sandwiches – my doctor Daddy had taught me what I needed to know years ago: without food I was liable to collapse uselessly from chronic hypoglycaemia.

I was too late for Hugh, though in the end it didn't matter. He and Ronnie had been together, visiting John Harris, another member of the cell. After they left John, Hugh had dropped Ronnie off outside the bar, where Ronnie had left his bike, and gone back to his girlfriend's flat. Ronnie first went into the bar for a drink and then went back to the bike. He found my note tucked under the leather strap that crossed the seat. Guessing what it must mean, he returned immediately. He did not bring the bike into the yard, but parked it up the road, silently, and like me, crept in through the back entrance. He noted a white Volkswagen, the car that the Special Branch always used, parked with its lights off just along the road; two men sitting in the front seat, watching our driveway.

Mike came downstairs, but there was no time and no need for him to explain to Ronnie what had happened. Without turning on the lights in the downstairs room, we felt around on the table for the things I'd packed and left ready, and locked up. Carrying the little rucksack, our only luggage for a journey that would take us thousands of miles, all three of us wearing our warm winter coats, we slipped out into the dark and one by one made our way to a little field nearby, hunching down and staying close to the hedges. Giggling nervously at the idea of travelling three up on the motorbike, we decided that Ronnie would have to go and get help for Mike. He crept back to his motorbike and pushed it away down the road before he started the engine and drove to a phone box. In the winter night, Mike and I sat shivering in a dark spot away from the streetlamps on the frosty grass, waiting for him to return. That night, the temperature dropped below freezing, and in the early morning it would snow. Finally, Hugh arrived in his car, following Ronnie who had waited by the phone box, and they both parked out of sight of the flat. Ronnie and I crept to the bike and drove through the quiet night to Rosemary Wentzel's house, on the outskirts of Johannesburg. We did not think we were being followed. Mike and Hugh arrived by car later.

We sat around all night, whispering, taking care not to wake Rosemary's small children. We tried to contact whom we could, to warn them. Difficult with the black members of the group – they had no phones. Someone had gone to Durban and could not be reached. Nobody slept. Rosemary made us coffee. I wrote a long letter to my parents, explaining what had happened, asking their forgiveness for the dreadful, inexplicable way I'd been behaving, hoping they would understand. I enclosed the key to our flat. Go in when you can, I asked my mother. You will have to pack it up. Please pay next month's rent in lieu of notice. My library books which needed to go back were on the table. I hoped they would not be interrogated, but I had little hope they would be immune. I sealed the letter and left it with Rosemary, asking her to post it in three days' time, when we should be safely out of the country. I do not know where and when Rosemary posted that letter, for she too left that night. But when she eventually got the letter, and went to the flat, Dorothy found the sandwiches I'd made for the journey still lying on the table with the library books.

During the long night, I sat on a bed with Hugh, listening while he justified his decision to stay. I remember the sadness that overwhelmed me as I realised there was nothing I could say to change his mind; his Christian conscience made him believe that he must stay and take the consequences of his actions, even if it meant prison. He gave us what money he had. He too did not sleep, but went straight into work as normal the next day. The Special Branch came quite early to his office to arrest him. They interrogated him, acting as always in tandem: good cop, bad cop. They tortured him, tried him and sent him to Pretoria Central. No remission for good conduct. We would see him again seven years later, 6 000 miles and a lifetime away.

Mike and Rosemary packed up her car in the dark hours before dawn, put the sleeping children in the back and set off towards Swaziland. An unbelievable and inexplicable decision, since this small country was totally surrounded by South Africa and an equally hostile Mozambique, still governed in those days by fascist Portuguese who colluded with the South African government. Mike – Rosemary perhaps – did not feel confident that they'd be able to find their way out of the Transvaal into the safe territory of Bechuanaland. This was even more incredible, since only a couple of years before, masquerading as a priest, he had driven the van full of 'nurses' over that border.

Light was just starting to break up a heavy sky when Ronnie and I left Rosemary's house. The snow that had fallen during the night was crusty and crisp in the dawn, and now we shivered and clutched our duffel coats round us in the cold that comes after snow. We knew where we were going – via Mafeking (now Mafikeng) into Bechuanaland. Not north over Beit Bridge, the route we'd taken to the work camp at Serowe, but west, the shortest route to the border, which was only a few miles from the small town of Lobatsi on the other side. We'd waited for the breaking dawn because Ronnie thought we would be less suspicious. Without helmet, visor or proper scarf, Ronnie was soon almost too cold to hold the bike on the road. I gave him my scarf and my gloves and we stuffed the degree certificates into his leather gloves, attempting to give him one more layer of protection against the biting air. I realised with horror that I could not drive the bike if anything happened to him. Theoretically, I knew how to, but it was a very heavy bike and I'd never actually tried. It was not the moment to learn.

As the sun rose on our last morning in South Africa, melting the snow, we passed through the small towns of the Transvaal. We stopped once, just long enough to buy some oranges from a man by the side of the road, but we did not want to waste any time. We did not know how far ahead of the Special Branch we were, or whether they'd be waiting for us. Sometime in the late morning, we drew up at the border. There was a heavy metal pole blocking the road. The official came out and took both our passports, mine a reassuring navy with its lion and unicorn, Ronnie's the green South African document, decorated with a springbok.

'Ons is studente, Tukkies – Universiteit van Pretoria,' Ronnie said, judging that he would make a more favourable impression on the border guard if he spoke Afrikaans. 'Op vakansie. Ons neem 'n klein vakansie in Bech. Net twee of drie dae. Ons het gehoor praat van die fantasiese mooi voëls anderkant die grens.'

'You didn't have to go overboard,' I said to Ronnie when the official disappeared into his hut, taking our passports with him. 'For God's sake, bird-watching! Supposing he'd known anything about birds and asked you?'

Ronnie pulled the bike right up to the barrier. 'Listen,' he said, 'if there's any hint of trouble I'm going to make a break for it. I'm going to just ride the bike at the barrier and ride luck fuck. You hold on tight, that's all. Keep your head down. The barrier isn't fixed, it should just swing back with the weight of the bike.' We waited with the engine running in neutral, trying to appear non-chalant, in reality more terrified than we had ever been.

The man returned and handed us the passports. 'Okay, man,' he said. 'On your way. Enjoy your holiday. Enjoy the birds.' He pushed the barrier aside and we rode slowly through to safety. Half a mile down the road, where we could no longer be seen, Ronnie stopped the bike. We got off and looked back towards South Africa. Both of us were crying openly. 'Goodbye, my country,' I whispered to myself, 'I will see you again. But who knows where or when?' Inappropriately, inexplicably, the Rodgers and Hart song slipped into my consciousness and I sang it to myself, soundlessly.

> *And so it seems that we have met before,*
> *And laughed before,*
> *And loved before,*
> *But who knows where or when?*

For evermore, when I hear that music, the memory of standing looking back towards the border, shivering in the icy morning air all those years ago, comes back to me. Saying goodbye to my beloved South Africa. We'll be back, we said. And then we started to laugh with hysteria, relief and exhaustion.

An hour or so later, the border official picked up the phone. It was a message from the Special Branch. 'Watch out for the Mutches coming through on a motorbike,' he was warned. 'Dangerous communists, saboteurs. Don't let them through. Hold them and call us.'

Ma kube njalo — Let it be so
Ma kube njalo — Let it be so
Kude, kube ngunaphakade — Forever and ever
Afrika! Mayibuye! — Come back Africa.

| Chapter 11 |

MAYIBUYE AFRIKA!

By lunch time we were cruising slowly in the dusty main street of Lobatsi. 'Do you know Fish Keitsing?' I asked a man sitting by the side of the road. 'We're looking for Fish Keitsing. Can you help us?' Showing no surprise, the man directed us round a corner to a group of small houses, packed together on a slope.

Fish was 'away' but his wife made us welcome, also apparently without surprise at our unannounced arrival. It turned out that, a while before, Rica Hodgson and her husband Jack had come through Lobatsi. They were members of the CP and also on the run from the Special Branch. Propped against a wall stood a large painting donated to the Keitsings by Rica. How on earth did this happen, I wondered. Did Rica paint this in idle moments while they waited to move on? Nobody explained.

To our embarrassment, we were treated like esteemed VIPs and given the only bed in the little house. Standing on bricks behind a curtain, it clearly belonged to Mrs Keitsing and Fish. The rest of the family slept communally on mats on the floor, and in the days we were there, Mrs Keitsing joined them. There was no running water, no electricity and no kitchen. We helped Mrs Keitsing fetch water in large plastic containers from a standpipe a little way down the hill, which was then transferred into different-coloured plastic basins to be used for rinsing the plates, washing the children and washing clothes. Mrs Keitsing made a fire between stones in the mornings, allowing it to smoulder through the cold days. Each morning, she made porridge in a big iron pot on the fire. We ate from tin plates, sitting on flat stones and wearing our coats against the winter cold. In the late afternoon, she cut up vegetables and small bits of meat – probably goat – which went into another big pot and stewed slowly till sundown. Again we sat with the family on the flat stones and, using our fingers, ate small quantities of the reheated leftover porridge with a dollop of the stew and lots of gravy. The tin plates had been rinsed since breakfast. It was clear that the Keitsings had very little money, and that two more adult mouths to feed was putting a strain on the household. Without discussing it, we gave Mrs Keitsing what we could from our wallets, keeping a little bit back so that we could have an excuse to sit in the bar with a beer.

After we'd found Fish's house and put down the canvas bag which held all our belongings, we asked directions to the police station, to claim political asylum. We were fingerprinted, the officer pressing each finger of each hand one by one into the pad of black ink, and then onto the document recording our arrival. I was too tired to think much about this first official recognition of my criminal status. We made our statements to a noncommittal British official. 'Take care,' he said as we were leaving, 'this place is crawling with South Africans. You're not necessarily safe just because you're over the border. I'd advise you to get out of here as soon as you can. I've already had word that they're looking for you. They are furious that you got through the border.' He smirked. 'That guy probably had all hell to pay for letting you through.'

Early the following morning, a black South African came to the Keitsings' house, asking for us. News had travelled fast. We were invited to lunch with Moulvi Cachalia, his daughter and our visitor, Robert. All were ANC people who had fled South Africa and were temporarily living in a safe house nearby. Moulvi Cachalia's daughter gave me the recipe for the curry which we ate for lunch, and we all went for a walk up the nearby koppie. At the top, Moulvi stood looking back towards South Africa, almost visible in the clear afternoon air. 'They try to deprive us of our country and our human rights, but not forever,' he murmured. We did not see him again.

In Lobatsi's only hotel, Ronnie and I sat at a corner table, making a beer last as long as we could. Burly white South Africans in short-sleeved shirts spread their thighs on the bar stools, displaying bulging genitals beneath their very short, tight shorts. Their muscular, hairy legs and arms claimed the space along the bar as they guffawed in Afrikaans about their victories with girls, at rugby, shooting game.

A young Englishman came into the bar, glanced around, then came and stood by our table with his back to the fellows at the bar. He spoke softly, in English. 'Hi. New to this town, I guess? Not seen you around before. I'm Alex.' He held out his hand and we both shook it, one after the other. 'I run a school up-country, in Francistown. Just down here for a visit.'

'Sit down. Have a beer,' Ronnie said. We told him our names and talked about casual things: the unexpected snowfall in the Transvaal, the birds in Bechuanaland. By some extraordinary co-incidence, it turned out that Alex had once gone out with the sister of one of my closest friends in Johannesburg, where he had lived for a while. We made small talk about occasions when we might actually have met. Discreetly, he did not quiz us about our reasons for being in Bechuanaland. He didn't ask questions we would have fumbled to answer, like what we thought of our room at the hotel, or the food. He did not ask how long we were planning to be in the Protectorate. It was easy to pretend we were just up there for a quick break. In fact, Alex knew already why we were there. He also knew that we weren't staying at the hotel, or even camping, as might have been assumed, but with black people up the hill nearby. He had come to the hotel to find us and he was there for a purpose. The English official who'd taken our finger-prints and registered us as refugees a couple of days before had let him know we were in town.

'See you tomorrow? Same time, same place?' he said when he left after half a pint. We stayed on. There was not much to do, and we were very conscious of taking up space in Fish's small house where we could not offer Mrs Keitsing much help, after we'd fetched water and helped clear away the plates from breakfast.

We met Alex again at the hotel the following day. He was as discreet as ever, avoiding any hint of secrecy or conspiracy in front of the same meaty South Africans drinking at the bar. We drank a beer together and then went for a walk up the dusty road towards the gentle hill where Moulvi and his friends were staying.

'What do you intend to do next?' he asked as we walked. 'You obviously can't stay in Lobatsi forever.'

We didn't know. When we had left, a few mornings before, our only plan was to get safely out of the country. The dream we'd had, in a time when it was still possible to plan – to ride up Africa on the bike, Johannesburg to Alexandria, and then a boat to Marseille, and across France – needed money and very different luggage from our single canvas bag. Now that we'd fled with only my post-office book containing a few rands and two pieces of not very valuable jewellery, it was not at all clear what we intended to do for money. We had no spares for the bike if it broke down, and no tools other than the basic ones we carried all the time in a small compartment beneath the seat; no water containers, no cooking utensils, no maps. We didn't need Alex to tell us that even the first leg of our dream journey would be foolhardy and irre-sponsibly dangerous.

'I've just come down in a big four-wheel-drive Jeep and it was a struggle,' he said. 'The road is too bad for you to go much

further on your bike. You won't make it. I'm going back to Francistown tomorrow. Want a lift?'

That night, Fish Keitsing returned from wherever he'd been.
As with his wife, there was no suspicion and no interrogation. It
seemed enough that we'd known to ask for him, and had volunteered the names of the people who'd instructed us that his was
the safe house we must find in Lobatsi. We explained that we were
going to move on the following day, to Francistown. With almost
no money left to give him, Ronnie offered the 650cc AJS. Fish
accepted politely, but without embarrassing effusiveness, never
abandoning his reserve. He knew how to ride a motorbike, and
Ronnie explained as much as he could in a short time about the
workings of the AJS. We never found out if he was able to use it,
or if he sold it. Nobody in their right mind would want to make
long journeys on a motorbike over the Protectorate's sandy, rutted,
dangerous roads, where you would ride for miles seeing only
beautiful birds by the roadside – and wait for hours for someone
to pass by if you broke down. As for spares ... maybe the AJS rotted
away in a back yard, a white elephant which no one could use.

We left before the sun was high in the sky, while it was still very
cold, and drove all day across dry, thorny countryside. Alex had
brought sandwiches and cold drink, and his tank held sufficient
petrol for the journey, so we stopped only to stretch our legs and
pee. We didn't try to talk much, not with the rattling and banging
of the Jeep, but just dozed or stared out of the window. This
time, I did not offer to drive. Finally, we arrived at the school in
Francistown. We were offered a choice of beds in the dormitories,
built of breeze-block and very like the school we'd helped build
near Serowe when we were part of the Work Camps Association.
They were cool and spartan and empty, all the children having
gone home for the winter holidays. We could have bathed in a
different bath every morning if we'd so pleased.

Now I was glad I'd pushed my post-office book into the
rucksack when I'd hastily packed on that last night in South
Africa. I'd worried that the South African government would have
blocked my account, but they hadn't caught up with this detail yet,

and the Francistown post office was able to give me my meagre savings. Alex didn't want any money from us, either for petrol or for food. I bought some cheap cotton material, a length of denim and two zips in a local shop, borrowed a treadle Singer sewing machine from Alex's wife and made myself a dress and a pair of jeans. It was warmer in the day in Francistown than it had been in Jo'burg, and besides, I hadn't brought enough clothes in the canvas bag to wash anything and get it dry, and still have something to wear. Thank you, Dorothy, I said to myself as I pinned a newspaper pattern to the material. Who would have thought I'd be so glad of that winter holiday course at the technical college when I was fifteen? Along with learning how to plan a full meal, cook bobotie, melktert, banana-and-date loaf and salt beef with carrots, I'd learned to make patterns from scratch for dresses, trousers or shirts, how to insert a zip and attach a collar.

We registered with the Resident Commissioner and confirmed that we had political asylum. Every day we went and signed in, the only whites waiting in the sun in a long queue of many, many refugees, all staying at the ANC camp called the White House just outside Francistown. At the school, we passed the time reading Alex's books and playing with his small children. We walked for miles in the late afternoon and evening, when the sun was no longer at his height. When Alex came too, he pointed out rock formations and named the strange colourful birds. He loved the solitude in this country made for contemplation and meditation. July 9th, when we'd fled, seemed an age ago. We waited patiently, living each day as it came, with no real idea about what we would do next. It was enough that we were safe. And so the days passed.

We heard the news of the Johannesburg bomb on the radio. John Harris, the man Hugh and Ronnie had gone to see the night Mike came to warn us, had been arrested. The police had ignored John's warning phone call. An elderly woman had been killed, many people injured, and John was in custody for murder. Oh God, people were never supposed to get hurt. What had gone wrong? With horror and fear, we read the first report in the *Rand Daily Mail,* arriving from South Africa a day late.

The following morning there was a phone call for us from Johannesburg. Listening for a moment in silence, Ronnie passed the phone to me. It was a journalist. The news of our escape from South Africa was in the press, on the front page. The Special Branch had made available the photo of me which came from my old, abandoned South African passport – of course, they must have found it when they raided the stable; there were allegations that we were associated with the bomb. How did the journalist know where to find us? Who had given us away? Perhaps one of the meaty men in the bar at Lobatsi had noticed us with Alex and that when he left, we had gone too. Who knows what money had changed hands, who in Lobatsi had been tempted by the promise of a few easy rands?

Ronnie put his finger over his lips in a warning signal to me to say nothing. Though the journalist threatened to make up a story which would be worse for us than if I gave him some information, I rang off. By now, both Alex and his wife knew who we were and why we were there. They accepted the situation without comment, never asking us to explain ourselves or inviting confidences, but treating us like any ordinary visitors come to stay for a few days. We asked them to block any further attempts to speak to us.

The journalist who'd tried to get his interview was as good as his word. Shortly thereafter, a story about me appeared on the front page, riddled with inaccuracies, along with my passport photo.

That evening, we were getting ready to go and eat with Alex's family when the whole school building shook with an enormous explosion. In Johannesburg, we were used to rumblings and little earthquakes when old, disused tunnels in the mines below us caved in. This was different: a roar that could only have been caused by a bomb. Alex's children started to cry. The littlest arched her body in her high chair, legs straight out in front, and howled with fear. The older one jumped off his seat and ran to his mother and hid his face in her lap, shaking and crying. We went outside, but we could see nothing across the veld, no smoke or flames to mark what might have happened.

The next day, we discovered that South African vigilantes had blown up part of the White House. The Resident Commissioner called us in to speak to us personally when we went to register. We were told that the blast had been meant for us. An eye for an eye. Fortunately, no one was hurt this time, but the Commissioner was adamant: we must get out of his town, out of the Protectorate. The British could not take responsibility for us. He would arrange our passage out. We must be ready to go the following morning. Did my British passport help? I never thought to ask.

We must both have been in a state of shock as we packed our meagre belongings into the rucksack, saying goodbye and thank you – doing what we had to do without any sense of control over our lives. We'd been in Bechuanaland for less than a week and now we were moving on again, like hunted animals, with barely time to get our bearings. We reported at the police station as we'd been instructed, and were taken by an official to the small airstrip, where a tiny Piper plane was waiting. We were stuffed into the cramped space behind the flying doctor, who was being taken to Maun, in the northern part of the Protectorate. Our South African pilot offered his opinion of the terrorists responsible for blowing up Johannesburg Station and what he would like to do with them, personally. We smiled as if in acknowledgement, but did not compound the duplicity by actually agreeing with him. We did not know what he'd been told about our identity and did not dare to ask.

At Maun, standing at the bar, we noticed that our names and photos were on the front page of the newspaper that a white man was reading. Taking his beer with him, Ronnie went and stood outside, where no one could glance up at his face and back at the photo and make the connection. One glance at the newspaper and I found I needed to go to the toilet immediately, also out of view.

Now the pilot was ready to leave again. The doctor had stayed behind at Maun, so we were the only passengers to the northern border. Swooping and diving low over the Okavango swampland, so low that we thought we must touch the tops of the flat dry trees or crash into the koppies, our pilot explained with a hearty laugh that he wanted to give us the opportunity to see close up the huge herds of buck, zebra and wildebeest, fleeing ahead of the shadow and roar of the plane. He must have known then who his passengers were, but since he couldn't openly disobey the Resident Commissioner's directive or find a way to hurt us without hurting himself and his plane, he must have decided that his best revenge was to scare the living daylights out of us.

Bumping hard on the narrow airstrip, the plane came down at Kasane, on the eastern tip of the Caprivi strip, where Bechuanaland, Southern Rhodesia and Northern Rhodesia met in a narrow swampy triangle of elephants and fever trees. Sick with tension from the terrifying flight, one of us gripping the little rucksack that still held all our possessions, we made a wobbly journey on foot across the airstrip to the office of the District Commissioner. We were within sight of the Zambezi River, which was the border between the Protectorate to the south and the Rhodesias to the north and east.

Like all the officials running the Protectorate, the District Commissioner here was English. He was very tanned, with thinning fair hair and a straggly moustache. He looked as if he'd forgotten to eat for months – his khaki shorts and shirt hung off his scrawny body – but his veined nose and blotchy complexion gave the game away about how he nourished himself. He did not invite us to sit down and, throughout our interview, played with a pistol on the blotting paper before him. It was clear within a few minutes that he was completely bush happy – very drunk and as likely to shoot us as give us the permit to cross the river that we'd come for. Our explanations about being flown to the border courtesy of the Resident Commissioner in Francistown were of no interest to him. 'Dogs!' he cried suddenly, grabbing the pistol and pointing it across the desk, terrifyingly close to our heads, towards the open door. 'I shoot dogs on sight.'

'Yes, sir.'

'Rabid, fucking dogs – killed my wife. Punish them all for the sins of their kind. Did you see that dog? Shoot the bugger, don't let one of them live.'

'Yes, sir.'

'Permit? No fucking way. Sort yourselves out. Get across the river any damned way you choose, don't bother me.'

We backed out of the office, watching the pistol with care. It was blazing hot. We went and sat under a tree, where some small children sat scratching patterns in the sand with sticks. The words of a song came back through the mists of memory:

Little black Sam across the sea
Goes to school like you and me
Makes his letters in the sand
With pieces of stick and little black hands.

Some elephants strolled nearby, their ears flapping gently, their feet, which seemed almost boneless, scuffing the dust. Then we noticed a lorry waiting by the river's edge, its open back piled high with vegetables and bundles wrapped in cloth, a few men and women standing alongside. 'Where's the driver?' Ronnie enquired, and someone pointed towards a man knocking back a beer. After a short discussion, Ronnie returned. 'Get up into the lorry,' he told me. 'Huddle down under some of those bundles. He'll take us over.' The pontoon reappeared, the driver climbed into the driving seat, a great many people climbed into the back along with us, squashing into all the available space, the engine started and we swayed precariously across the wide, slowly flowing river. I imagined that the elephants waved us goodbye with their huge ears as we crossed into Northern Rhodesia.

Kazangula, on the opposite bank, was a tiny place with hardly a building, nothing to eat and no railway station. We needed to keep moving, on to Livingstone and then to Lusaka, more than two hundred miles away to the north-east, where we would look for Denis. If we could just keep going till then, Denis would give us a welcome and a place to stay. Finding Denis became our goal.

We hitched a ride on another lorry going east to Livingstone and arrived in the late afternoon. Night would soon settle over this little African town. We didn't know a soul, and we had very little money left. Ronnie went to try and find us something to eat. Hungry, frightened and exhausted, for the first time in this saga of escape my courage left me, and I sat down on a flat stone at the edge of the road with my feet in the prickly, dry grass and cried. No one approached me. No one asked me what was the matter. After a while I stopped crying. Ronnie came back with a pie and a Fanta and we tried to think what to do next.

Hitching to Lusaka seemed to be the only option, and we walked out of the town on the only road. For a long time, as the sun went down, we waited by the side of the road. Nothing came.

Nearby we heard the whistle of a train, and watched as it slowed down at what seemed to be a siding. We clambered over the rough veld to the edge of the railway line and I went up to a white man who seemed to be some sort of official. I invented a story about stolen wallet, no money left at all, need to get to Lusaka, no other way we could think of. Yes, a goods train would be coming through on its way to Lusaka shortly. Yes, it would be possible for us to ride in the guard's van; wait there, he'd talk to the guard when the train stopped.

And so we found ourselves sharing one tiny seat in the last carriage of a long goods train. When that became too uncomfortable, one of us sat on the ridged wooden floor, with the bumpety–bump, bumpety-bump of the wheels on the track reverberating through our spines. The guard was chatty, wanting to know our names and what we were doing hitching a ride on a train – normal enough questions. 'Helen McKenzie,' I said quickly (the first name that came into my head; Helen had been in the same dormitory as me at Girls' Collegiate), and repeated with a few embellishments the story I'd invented for the official at the siding outside Livingstone. He seemed satisfied. The train puffed its way through the clear night, stopping at every small siding and village; sometimes there was a platform and a name, as often as not there was just the open veld. Even in the early hours of the morning, someone would appear to hand up a sack of letters, a box making its way to Lusaka. The guard would climb down and greet colleagues and we'd be invited to share coffee and a sandwich. Our fabricated story about the stolen wallet was savoured, prompting sympathetic nods and reminiscences about other occasions when people had fallen foul of the untrustworthy natives. So we passed a long night, sharing the railwaymen's little world of camaraderie and rituals.

As the train chuffed on, we tried to doze but could not, even though we were both exhausted. It was too uncomfortable, the seat too hard and narrow, the wheels beneath us too jerky, and there was still too much adrenalin pumping through both our grimy bodies. At six in the morning, the train puffed into Lusaka station, the air cold, misty and smoky. We had been on the go without sleep, without washing, without changing our clothes, for twenty-four hours. I washed my face in the toilets at the station and looked at myself in the scratched mirror above the grubby basin. My hair, scraped back into a ponytail with a rubber band, was filthy and had started to frizz out round my face. There were huge hollows under my eyes.

We badly needed food and rest, but our first move had to be to find Denis. We stood in the queue in the post office, with the notion of asking how one could trace someone in Lusaka who'd recently arrived and was not listed in the phone book. 'Denis Higgs, English, with a British passport ... but he came from South Africa some months ago. A friend,' we explained.

The reaction was totally unexpected. The man looked at us, and then spoke behind his hand into the phone. A moment or two later, two men appeared on our side of the counter, one on either side of us. 'Will you both please come with us,' they said.

We sat in the office of yet another official, a white man this time. 'So which is it,' he enquired without a smile, 'Hilary Mutch or Helen McKenzie?' When I looked surprised, he continued: 'Subconsciously, people almost always choose pseudonyms with their own initials ... right, so I believe you were asking for Denis Higgs? I am going to ask you to stay in this office till I can get further instructions about you. You are not under arrest, but I wouldn't try and leave here. I want to warn you that you are not safe. Oh, and would you like a cup of tea?'

The door closed quietly behind us and we were left on our own – a long wait, several hours. Once I went to the door and into the corridor, intending to find a lavatory. There was a man sitting opposite, his door open. He glanced up and then followed me, waited outside the toilet, and returned to his room when I went back to my place in the office. Unable to get any further information about either Denis or why we were being detained, Ronnie and I slumped in the hard, armless chairs and drifted in and out of sleep, with little to say to one another. They say that the easiest way to break anyone is sleep deprivation. One loses a sense of reality and of time. We were too tired to be frightened or apprehensive.

When the white official finally returned, he came with an

elderly black man, who stood at the back of the office, listening but saying nothing.

'Right, first things first. I am sorry to tell you that Denis Higgs has disappeared from Lusaka. We believe he has been kidnapped by South African vigilantes, but we are not yet certain about what has happened. Second, we do not believe that you are safe here. I have instructions from Prime Minister Kaunda to look after you and help you leave the country safely. This man – Mr Chitimukulu – will take you to a place of safety and give you further instructions.' He held out his hand. 'Goodbye. Good luck,' he said.

Mr Chitimukulu introduced himself more formally in the large black Daimler which was waiting outside. Daimlers seemed to have claimed a special place in my life and I noted that this one was particularly shiny and grand. Indeed, it was one of the official UNIP (United National Independence Party) cars used to transport members of the interim government, waiting in the wings to take control with independence later that same year.

'Chief Fresh Chitimukulu,' he told us. 'I work for Prime Minister Kenneth Kaunda. The Prime Minister is concerned for the safety of opponents to apartheid in South Africa. We are concerned that we were not able to protect your friend Denis Higgs. I will take you to a hotel outside Lusaka for the moment; you must be ready at six a.m. tomorrow morning for the onward journey. You should not talk to anyone in the hotel. They will have been instructed to arrange a room for you, and you may eat in the restaurant. The bills will be paid.'

Now began a farcical interlude. The hotel, which was several miles outside Lusaka, was frequented by wealthy holiday-makers, honeymoon couples or people on dirty weekends who didn't want to be recognised by anyone who might know them. Both of us were filthy and smelly. Ronnie was unshaven, my hair was dirty and I was feeling sick and headachy from constipation, which has plagued me in all situations of stress since I was a small child. I was wearing the jeans I'd made in Francistown and had nothing clean to change into, for after being given notice to leave, I had not had time to wash clothes in preparation for the journey. Regretfully, we looked at the swimming pool – neither of us had swimming costumes. We comforted ourselves with the thought that the water was probably cold anyway. Instead, we took turns to soak in the deep bath, liberally applying the free lotions and powders and washing our hair using the little sachets of shampoo, courtesy of the management. I washed my underclothes and hung them over a chair, knowing that I'd have to put them on again, still wet, but disgusted at the idea of putting them on dirty. Finally, drawing the curtains against the daylight, we pulled back the padded quilts and slept on the twin beds. When we awoke it was dark. We must have slept the whole day away. A full-bellied orchestra of cicadas filled the night. Rather hopelessly, I did some exercises to try and get my stubborn stomach to work. Oh, what I would have done for some of the castor oil I'd avoided with such determination at boarding school!

We made our way to the dining room and chose a corner table, trying to look the part of ordinary visitors despite our grubby, casual clothes. Carefully avoiding eye contact and curious stares, we allowed the waiter to lay starched napkins on our laps. Expensively dressed, smart whites and a few well-heeled black people occupied the linen-covered tables, leaning forward amongst the silverware into the lights of candles propped in empty wine bottles. Feeling as if we'd stumbled inexplicably into a theatrical production where we were the only amateurs in a cast of professional actors, we perused the wine list and the menu. Who knows when we would eat like this again! Thank you, Kenneth Kaunda.

Chief Fresh Chitimukulu knocked discreetly on the window just before six in the morning. It was still dark, and it was cold. He did not tell us where we would be going, but merely said that due to trouble in the east, we could not take the good, direct route, but would have to make a very long detour; our journey would be more than three hundred miles and we needed to do it in one day. The roads were not tarred; some were still strip roads, which required the driver to keep the car carefully positioned, but most were rutted gravel, dusty and hardly used by motorised vehicles.

At around eight, he pulled up in front of a store in a small village, and invited us to stretch our legs and get something to eat. The choice was minimal. We bought a stale meat pie and a canned Coke, which was rather warm. Chief Fresh paid. Seeing myself in the broken piece of mirror in the toilet I broke into open laughter: I was unrecognisable. In the back seat with the window open, my face, neck, arms — everything exposed — had been covered with a thin film of red dust which had lifted off the untarred roads as we sped north-east. Only the skin round my eyes, protected by my sunglasses, showed my original skin colour. I looked like an ochre owl. I tried to wash off the dust, but it was hopeless in the cold water without soap. I went back to the car without being able to dry myself off, resigned to turning back into a red ghost as soon as we'd been on the road again for half an hour. It was far too hot and airless to keep the windows closed, and air-conditioning — even for Daimlers — was not yet invented.

Fresh drove fast and by midday we were, he said, in his own land, where he was a chief and knew many people. Indeed, when we stopped for more food in Kasama, to us just another small village like all the others, people greeted him enthusiastically, brought chairs out and placed them under a tree and tried to detain him in conversation. But he would not stop for long. We were headed for the strip of land between Lake Tanganyika and Lake Nyasa, where Northern Rhodesia met Tanganyika.

It was dusk and the central African night was falling fast. Chief Fresh stopped by the side of the road, and then led us a little way up a steep, rock-strewn hill. 'I needed to get you here before it got too dark,' he said. 'You must be careful how you go, you could fall and that would be very bad. Nobody would know you were lying here, hurt.' Already feeling bereft, we both hugged Fresh. Ronnie was carrying his new duffel coat, bought to replace the one he'd given to the victim of the fire. He gave it to Fresh, who took it with both hands in the polite African fashion and nodded his head in thanks. 'Go well. God go with you,' he said.

'Stay well, Chief,' we answered. 'Thank you.'

Now we were on our own. We clambered further up the hill and through the wire that marked the border, then down again towards the thin points of light of the little town we could see below us.

It is easy to write adventure stories; your fingers on the keyboard short-circuit the thought processes, the clichés appear unbidden on the screen before you, the conventions determine the form and the characters. The real story, more mundane, less glamorous, slips quietly away — outfaced — as the tempting excitements of fantasy narrative take over, as our heroes make their way in the darkening evening downhill towards the small town below, following a rocky path worn by children herding goats. They stumble and grab at bushes. Careful, don't fall now. Nearly there. Soon the path meets a wider, smoother road, its surface cleared of the biggest stones. It leads to brick buildings, some with electric lights. A man points the way to the police station. It is not far. No South African vigilantes here. Safe at last.

This town is Mbeya, the nearest small town to the border between Northern Rhodesia and Tanganyika (soon to become Tanzania), where Chief Fresh had brought us in a virtually non-stop journey over unmade roads, travelling for much of the way at nearly seventy miles per hour. The policeman behind the desk called a superior, who listened to our story, confiscated both our passports — mine and Ronnie's useless South African document. He would never see it again. So he became stateless, the *de facto* life of the past few weeks converted into *de jure*.

Immediately, without discussion, without any of the formalities and polite cups of tea which we'd experienced under semi-house arrest in Lusaka, we were locked into a cell at the back of the police station. Fortunately, neither of us was hungry, for there was no food. We would share one narrow camp bed, with one grey, scratchy blanket and no pillow or sheets.

The last time we slept in a police station was in the Eastern Transvaal, in South Africa. We'd found ourselves stranded at nightfall in a small town when our motorbike broke down. There was no hotel and we had very little money. It looked like rain and we had no tent, so the police station seemed a good idea. Ronnie explained our situation in his perfect Afrikaans, and immediately the policeman on duty had offered us a section of the stoep. We laid our sleeping bags on the hard cement. A bit Spartan perhaps, but it wasn't cold. During the night we heard the shouts of policemen, and the grunts and cries of someone brought in under arrest. We drew our own conclusions – one more incident of brutality to add to the enormous store that we held in our heads; but there was nothing we could have done to help the arrested man or boy. When we left the next morning, we decided not to test the limits of our hospitality by asking untoward questions.

Here, locked into the cell in the police station in Mbeya, we listened to the sighing and soft snoring of our fellow prisoners in the cells on either side of us. We fell asleep head to toe on the narrow, low bed, both of us fully dressed, though I loosened my bra and undid the button of my homemade jeans. All my clothes were looser than they'd been a few days before. In the night, I rolled off the bed onto the floor, wrapped myself in my duffel coat and put the canvas bag under my head for a pillow. Ronnie's coat now belonged to Chief Fresh and he seemed entitled to the grey blanket. I slept better without Ronnie's smelly socks in my face, and with space to turn restlessly, trying to get comfortable. I hitched up my knees, crossed my arms and tucked my fists together under my chin, the way I always do when I go to sleep.

In the morning, we heard a guard going along the line of cells, unlocking each door one by one. Our door was opened, and in the light we saw that the cells opened onto a covered concrete stoep. The toilet facilities were an open space in the corner between the cells and a dead-end wall. The downpipe from a stained basin opened directly into a sluice, which ran along the edge of the wall. The other prisoners, raggedy in torn shorts and shirts, were also coming out of their cells, and there was the loud sound of men peeing into the sluice. At the end of the wall, there was a single toilet. Below the wooden toilet door, which stopped eighteen inches above the concrete floor, I could see feet pointing outwards, wearing the sandals made from car tyres that are ubiquitous in Africa. Not for the first time I rued the poor design of the female body, which meant I had to squat or sit to pee, and not stand at the sluice as the men could.

I appeared to be the only female prisoner, in fact the only female anywhere around. The single wash-basin, which had two taps but only one in working order and only for cold water, was visible to anyone who cared to stare. I waited my turn, then faced the wall and stripped to my bra and panties, putting my clothes neatly on the concrete floor. Then as best I could without flannel or soap, I splashed my face and filthy neck, dabbed under my arms, and stuck my dusty feet into the basin. We didn't have a towel, so we did without. The deodorant was running out, but it seemed a trivial detail when no one around us had any either. I tried to brush my hair without a mirror. My hair is very thick and curly. Matted with red dust, it stood out round my head, with a curious bump from the rubber band that had held it in a ponytail all night. My scalp hurt from the rubber band and itched from the dust, but there was no possibility of washing it. I tried with little success to rinse the red dust of Northern Rhodesia off my hairbrush, re-membering somewhere about 'dry shampoos' and hoping I could brush my scalp clean, but this didn't work either. The rubber band broke and I didn't have another one, so I left my hair in a heavy, itchy Afro, years before this became fashionable. Toothbrushes were among the first things I'd pushed into the canvas bag and we still had a little toothpaste, so I cleaned my teeth without swallowing any of the water — but then succumbed and drank a little cupped in my hand, hoping I wouldn't get a stomach bug. I was not a doctor's daughter for nothing. The hazards of unboiled water in Africa had been drummed into me since I was a toddler.

No one, rightly, seemed worried that we might run away, and after we had washed we hung around uncertainly. For a long while, we sat in the sun on a low wall at the side of the police station, waiting for something, anything, to happen, someone to come and tell us what to do next. We people-watched, and people walking by stared back, loads on their heads, babies strapped on their backs with lengths of bright green, black and gold cloth celebrating TANU (Tanzania African National Union), independence, Nyerere. We were startled, for these were also the colours of the banned ANC in South Africa.

A few weeks later there was another, more emotional piece of evidence that we'd left South Africa behind. In a cinema in Dar, not 'God Save the Queen', not 'Die Stem', but the chords heralding 'Nkosi Sikelel' iAfrika' sounded out: the anthem of Tanzania-to-be, the hymn of the ANC that in 1992 would also become the national anthem of the new South Africa. Everyone stood up. The South Africans sitting all together in the little cinema auditorium sung in full-throated, interweaving, four-part harmonies – bass and tenor, contralto and soprano. In our own country, the anthem had been banned for years, and if you sang it, you expected the police to crash in, ready to arrest, smash and destroy.

Nkosi Sikelele Afrika – God bless Africa
(we sing quite softly in the cinema)
Maluphakanyisw' uphondo lwayo – Make her glorious
Yiva imathandazo yethu – Hear our prayers
(our voices and our bodies sway with the lilting harmonies)
Nkosi Sikelela – Lord bless us
(now the power of the music takes over)
Thina lusapho lwayo – Us your children

Wosa moja, (wosa, wosa) – Come, o spirit, come
(go the men, and the women's voices echo: 'wosa, wosa …')
Wosa moja, oyingcwele – Come Holy Spirit

Morena boloka sechaba sa heso – *Lord protect our nation*
(faster, more urgent)
O fedise dintwa le matshewenyeho – *End all conflicts*

O se boloke – Protect us
(the women's contralto and soprano voices soar with the sound of 'boloke')
O se boloke
(the men too, a deeper plea)

O se boloke sechaba
O se boloke
(again, an answering echo from tenors and bass)
Sechaba sa, heso – Protect our nation
Sechaba sa, Afrika.

Ma kube njalo – Let it be so
Ma kube njalo – Let it be so
(we chant in unison)
Kude, kube ngunaphakade – Forever and ever
Afrika! Mayibuye! Come back Africa.

I did not glance at Ronnie standing next to me, but felt sure that he was also holding his breath, choking on tears. Before the lights went up, I wiped my wet face with the back of my hand, ready to smile and discuss the film.

Sometime in the middle of that first morning in Mbeya, when the sun was already high in the sky, as we sat waiting on the wall, a man came up. He asked us to follow him down the road. He was in plain clothes, laughed hugely, wanted to practise his English. He took us to a small restaurant and sat with us while we ate an enormous breakfast, which he paid for. He told us that this must double up as lunch and that there would be nothing more till supper time. He pointed out the Roman Catholic mission, and waved when a young white man came by – American, Peace Corps. We were not incarcerated, but neither were we free to go.

After our meal, we went and sat on the wall as the sun moved across the sky. In the evening, our official provider of meals arrived and accompanied us to the same little cafe. No one offered any explanation about why we were being held or what was happening. For the next three nights, we slept in the cell, though we were no longer locked in. Where could we run to, even if we had the energy or will? All day we sat, moving along the wall with the sun. For even though this was central Africa, near the equator, it was winter, and we were very high above the sea. We could see Mount Kilimanjaro's snow-covered cap in the distance.

For three days, the routine was unchanged. We washed at the single basin, we ate at the restaurant, sitting on the stoep for our daytime meal. In the evenings, we went inside into a dark room and ate at a metal table covered with a plastic tablecloth printed with crazy-paving patterns and red cherries. The menu each evening was stew, possibly chicken, though this was not certain. It was tasty enough, with lots of tomatoes, carrots and onions, served with hunks of white bread. There were no cattle here, and what little milk or butter there was came down from Kenya and was expensive and not on offer to people living in the local jail. I learned to drink my tea without milk, musing that, if I'd known what the future would bring, I would've given up milk as well as sugar for Lent when I was a boarder at Collegiate.

On the fourth day, we were called into the police station for an interview with the chief boss-man. He sat formally behind his desk and invited us to draw up two armless wooden chairs on the opposite side. He explained that all South Africans coming through were automatically treated as security risks. South Africa and the United Republic of Tanganyika and Zanzibar did not have any diplomatic relations. We had been subject to the normal, routine checks through the ANC and he had just received word from Dar that our status as refugees had been confirmed. We would be granted political asylum. He stood to shake our hands across the desk and said with due formality, 'Good day. You may go now.'

When we stood, looking bewildered, he realised we knew no one and had no idea where we should go. He called one of his men to take us to a house up a steep road on the outskirts of Mbeya, giving him quick instructions in Ki-Swahili, which we couldn't understand. The dreamlike feeling, of being caught up in a current over which we had lost all control, continued. All we could do was bend like a reed in the wind or, like twigs, let the flowing river take us.

We found ourselves in a safe house full of UNIP refugees and criminals who had fled over the border, waiting for independence, when they could safely return home to the country that was still

Northern Rhodesia but would soon be Zambia. Lexicographer, older than the others, with thin, watchful eyes and a roll-up cigarette stuck to his lower lip, received us. It did not seem appropriate to shorten his name. He appeared to be in charge, and had several men move out of a room with one bunk bed in it to join those who were sleeping on the floor in the 'dining room', the 'sitting room' and the only other 'bedroom'. We had the uncomfortable sense of being treated deferentially and differently because we were white, but when we protested, we were told it was because we were a married couple that we should have a room to ourselves. Probably, our privileged privacy was more to do with me being a woman in a house full of men.

Other than the bunk bed, which had metal springs but no mattresses, there was no other furniture in the room and no curtains on the window. I worked out a temporary system to cover the glass with the dress I'd made in Francistown, wedged between the metal frame and the window, but this only worked if the window was closed, and then it was stuffy and airless. Lexicographer found me a piece of material to put over the window when I wanted to wear the dress. Bathing was in a real bath, but it was not connected to any plumbing and stood in the yard under a tree. When you pulled out the plug, the water flowed out onto the rich soil and downhill towards the road, a little rivulet that soaked away during the heat of the day, leaving only a dark mark. All water had to be fetched in buckets and empty paraffin cans from a standpipe a little way down the hill, and several people used the same water once it was heated and poured into the bath. Washing was an elaborate ritual. Since I was the only female, Ronnie had to hold a towel in deference to modesty when I stripped down, but it was a very small towel and served as nothing more than a nod to convention. The men carefully turned away when it was my turn in the bath, and I went inside when they were washing.

The cooking was shared – a huge pot simmered away for half the day on a big stove fed with logs of wood. We ate communally, standing round a big wooden table, or squatting on our haunches out in the yard. I took my part cutting up vegetables for the pot, but was neither expected nor allowed to do anything more. There were not enough chairs to go round, but mostly I did get to sit down, for there was a bit of competition to treat 'the woman' nicely and get her attention.

The men sang songs in Shona – sad songs, love songs, freedom songs. I never learned the words, but it was enough to join in the tunes, humming, harmonising. Some of the tunes were familiar from South Africa. They already knew 'Shosholoza', the miners' work song about coming down in the train across the mountains from South Africa, and we sung it as a round.

> *Shosholoza*
> *Kulezo ntaba*
> *Stimela zase South Africa*
> *Shosholoza*
> *Stimela zase South Africa*

We taught them a freedom song we'd sung at the work camp in Serowe, 'Mandela uyezo, uyezo, sina mandla!' I sang 'Molly Malone', 'Diana' and 'Freight train'. Ronnie didn't have his mouth organ, or perhaps he would have improvised along with my singing. Something about our exile triggered in my memory a satirical song I'd learned at Oxford about Richard II. It came unbidden into my brain:

> *In thirteen hundred and ninety-eight*
> *There was trouble at Westminster Hall*
> *Bolingbroke and Mowbray they had a mighty brawl*
> *King Richard decided to arbitrate*
> *But found that he had left it too late*
> *So he gave Bolingbroke a ten year stroke*
> *And he banished Mowbray for life!*

My audience was baffled, and no one attempted to learn the words or the catchy tune.

We played cards and drank skokiaan, the beer that the men brewed themselves, passed round in a calabash. It was thick and creamy-white, the texture of slightly granular soup, and lethal.

Whoever had tobacco and dagga rolled cigarettes and joints and passed them around.

One night, when we'd been sitting outside listening to the cicadas after the sun had gone down, voices were raised in anger. Ronnie and I hustled quickly indoors and did not come out till morning. Everyone in the house was still asleep, wherever they had collapsed the previous night. We knew that more than one of the men has murdered someone back in Northern Rhodesia, some with guns, others with pangas. Only one of the men, Blessed – beautiful, with a perfect body and startling, almond-shaped green eyes – spoke English comfortably enough to have a conversation with us, and he told us without embarrassment about the man he had shot: a familiar enough story, involving a woman, treachery, revenge. He'd worked in a dry-cleaners in Northern Rhodesia, and when I washed my and Ronnie's clothes in the bath water, he insisted on ironing them for us, which he did beautifully. I was nervous around him when he was stoned on dagga or drunk on the bottled liquor which sometimes appeared at the house, and his eyes became hooded and bloodshot; then, his body language transmitted aggression, though we couldn't understand what he was actually saying. At times like these, the tension of men living without women, in exile, with nothing to do but wait, filled the air with the threat of violence. But no one ever transgressed any of the unspoken rules about hospitality. In a house of murderers, we were safer than we'd been for months.

Leon, the American from the Peace Corps who was teaching at the local school, turned up and invited us to come and have supper with him. He and two other volunteers from nearby villages would also be there. He was from New York, very urbane, very politicised. All the Americans were eager to know what we thought about South Africa, and what might happen there now that the leaders of the ANC were in jail. We told them very little about ourselves, not knowing what they might repeat to the wrong people. They told us about their perceptions of Tanganyika and their mundane daily lives, which often fell short of the romantic ideals they'd had when they signed up – but which would, no doubt, be glamorised and remembered with nostalgia, turned into fascinating stories for their families and friends when they went home. They were hungry for new people who spoke English, and we too were glad to talk to people other than each other. A year later, we read an article in *Time* by Leon about his experiences in Tanganyika. After his 'gap year', he'd returned home and become a journalist, launching his career with quite an insightful account of the realities of being in the Peace Corps.

No one from the Anglican Church came near us, but the young Roman Catholic priest, who was in charge of the little mission school and the Catholic church, sought us out. He seemed unconcerned that Ronnie was not just a lapsed Catholic, but defiantly atheistic, and that I was not even a Christian. He too invited us to come and eat with him, and tactfully, gently drew me out about why and how I had become involved in violent protest against the State. I sensed that he really did want to understand, though what we'd done perhaps went against all his morality. To my embarrassment when I recollected in solitude, I realised that I'd delivered an impassioned speech from behind his sofa – about justice and equality, responsibility, agency. The priest was silent, bowed his head a little, smiled. Jesus, on his cross on the wall, also averted his eyes. I imagined that the priest was thinking, in Yeats's words: 'The best lack all conviction, while the worst / Are full of passionate intensity.'

It was not the first time that I'd felt I'd broken social conventions, and though I absolutely believed in what I had said, I felt vulnerable and rather childish, and wished I could learn not to wear my heart on my sleeve. I did not have the insight to understand how the life we'd been living had taken its toll, and so forgive myself for this emotional outburst.

Later in the evening, he asked us what we planned to do next. Taking each day literally as it came, we had not thought about how to move on, though we knew we would have to. We'd also been told at the police station that we needed to register ourselves in Dar and make contact with the ANC, who had vouched for us. We had no money left, nothing at all, and the priest offered to lend us the money for the bus fare to Dar, £5 each, saying, 'Uh, pay it back when you can.' We never did. But nor did I ever forget his kindness and practical help, and that he did not sit in judgement, lecture or preach.

A day later, early in the morning, we joined the queue of people waiting to board the bus which would take us all the way from Mbeya to Dar es Salaam. The roof rack was loaded high with bundles, boxes, fruits, live chickens in baskets. Every seat inside was taken, and people also sat on the step below the long seat which went across the back of the bus. A man had a goat on his lap, its legs tied together; it bleated in protest for the whole of his journey, till he disembarked some two hundred miles down the road. Another old man sat quietly with a panga held between his knees. The woman in the seat in front of me had a baby with diarrhoea, who cried without stopping, with a high mewling sound that penetrated the depths of my brain. The young mother mopped hopelessly at the smelly yellow shit which ran down the baby's little legs and onto the kanga cloth tied round her waist, and let the baby suck at her breast. A toddler rushed up and down the aisle, tripping on people's outstretched legs and the parcels, bundles and boxes which were crammed on the floor between every seat. She fell into passengers' laps when the bus lurched. People held her and laughed. The driver had a radio with a speaker which filled the bus with music; headache music – too loud, too insistent, too driving. There was no way to block it out. Go with it, bend like a reed, go with the flow.

The journey took all day, winding down from the mountains in the west, through countryside which became hotter, lusher and more steamy as we approached the coast. The foliage changed; now there were banana palms, huge mango trees, pawpaws growing wild. The driver stopped in villages where people got on and off. He climbed on the roof, unloading half the stuff to get at their possessions, and then chucking everything back again. The panga man and the goat man were replaced by a woman with squawking, angry chickens and an enormously fat man who smoked a smelly pipe. When the bus stopped, people came round offering bananas, pineapples, mangoes, peanuts in twists of newspaper, cans of cold drink, single cigarettes for sale.

The seats were hard and very upright, with neither armrests nor padding. It was not possible to get comfortable with your legs crammed against the seat in front of you. I'd found a place next to a shy and silent young Englishman, the only other white person on the bus. Politely he'd offered me his window seat so that I could look at the view, and passed me his *Observer* newspaper, airmail edition, three months out of date. As the bus swung precariously down the narrow winding passes of the escarpment into the lowlands, he fell asleep, slumped against my shoulder, all the way to Tabora – where he woke up suddenly and got off. Typical Englishman, I thought: we hadn't been introduced, so he couldn't talk to me. Ronnie swiftly moved into his seat, stretching his long legs out in the aisle. The old injuries from his accident, he said, were giving him hell.

It was late afternoon when we pulled into the bus station in Dar. We had the address of the ANC office; all we needed were directions.

The ANC put us into a boarding house with a few other refugee South Africans, all sponsored by the ANC. Unlike the people we were now living with, we had no role in the organisation, but like them we went to the ANC office every day to check on news. One day, soon after our arrival, we were given a message that Oliver Tambo was in town, that he wished to meet and speak with us, and that we should find him at the hotel by the beach.

Oliver ordered a chocolate mouse. Politely, I swallowed my giggles. Glancing at the menu, I realised what he was asking for. We sat with our icecreams, and Oliver with his mousse, while he tactfully probed our politics, the story of our escape and our intentions. We must have passed the test, because there were no further interrogations; indeed, we were allocated a small allowance by the ANC to survive.

The boarding house was up some steep stairs in the centre of the Indian quarter of Dar. Women were together in one room, men in another. Only Ronnie and I were a couple, but there were not enough rooms for us to stay together. Abdullay and Mosie, the two men who were already there, had left their wife and girlfriend respectively behind in South Africa when they fled, and they had no idea when they might see them again. Eleanor Anderson was the other woman, and her partner – the orange-headed mystery man who'd hidden in our squatted house a lifetime ago – was 'up-country', training.

Abdullay, a fragile and delicately built young man, weighing no more than me, had been dangled from a window by Special Branch. He had suffered permanent damage, and was liable to epileptic attacks and problems with hearing. Eleanor had been sprung from prison by the ANC and taken over the border. Eleanor was blonde. Like her partner, Ronnie Kasrils, she had dyed her hair, not orange but black, and disguised herself as an Indian woman. There were still streaks of black which had not fully grown out. She told us how her interrogators had taunted her and threatened to give her six-year-old daughter up for adoption to a good Afrikaans couple, who would bring her up as a true, honourable South African and teach her to despise her mother. That would be after they'd hung Eleanor herself for treason. She was safe now, but her young child was still in South Africa with her mother, and it was not possible to communicate with her.

The mosque was just across the road, and five times a day the mournful bird-like voice of the imam called the faithful to prayer in a minor key: 'Allahu – Akbar, Allahu – Akbar'. At the bottom of the stairs, in the narrow corridor where one entered the boarding house, Ronnie pointed out a framed picture of the Aga Khan, identical to the one we'd seen in my Indian friend Farida's sitting room in Fordsburg when we'd been invited to her home for supper.

I had lost any sense of connection to my past life. We'd only been gone a few weeks, but we were disorientated and rootless, living through each day, taking whatever came, as it came.

Izrat, the Ismaili who ran the boarding house, spoke English, and he came and talked to us most days, sitting on one of the single beds. His wife, who spoke no English, brought home-made vegetarian food the like of which I have never eaten since, not even in the best Indian restaurants in London. The August heat and humidity were almost intolerable; we took cold showers several times a day, but even as you dried off, you would be soaked again in sweat.

One day, with no explanation, when we went up to the ANC office, we were given a cheque for £50 – from London. Ask no questions ... Years later, recruited by the Defence and Aid Fund to send funds to the families of political prisoners still in South Africa and people made destitute on release from prison, I put two and two together about where that £50 had come from.

Now we could eat an occasional cheap meal in an Indian café, buy cheap swimming costumes and flip-flop rubber sandals, go to the beach. Eleanor showed me where to buy lengths of material and introduced me to a Tanganyikan dressmaker, who sat at his treadle Singer in the entrance of his shop. By the end of the day, he'd made me two loose-fitting, sleeveless dresses. I put away the jeans, the duffel coat, the socks and shoes in the rickety cupboard which I shared with Eleanor.

We were taken to meet a white South African woman called Pam, who lived in one of the spacious, shabby nineteenth-century houses in the centre of Dar, built under German rule. Enormous fans on the ceiling moved the torpid air slowly around, and there was a slight breeze through the lattices which protected the wide verandahs from the tropical sun. Later, we sat on the beach with Pam and her mixed-race child, and learned about her flight a year or two before from the Immorality laws. The news had been reported salaciously in the headlines. Joe, her lover and the child's father, was a poet and a musician, but that didn't make their relationship legal. But the relationship hadn't survived the strain, and he had gone on to America. Stranded in Dar, Pam was now living with a man who was a founder member of Frelimo, and who would be in the government of Mozambique when Frelimo finally took over from the Portuguese in 1975, after their long and bloody civil war.

We already knew that Hugh had been arrested. That news had reached us when we were still in Francistown, but we knew nothing about Mike or Rosemary. Later, we would find out how Rosemary had been tricked by the Special Branch, using her children's future as bait. She was safely in Swaziland when she received a letter, purportedly from her ex-husband, asking to meet secretly to discuss his access to their children, who were with her. She had custody, but she was in a double bind — he was a lawyer, and there was every likelihood that he would get the South African courts to reverse the decision if it went back to court. So she went to the appointed secret rendezvous near the border with South Africa — and as she drove up, her car was surrounded by police. They took her out of her own car and drove her across the border, one hundred miles inland. Then, they brought her to her own car, which another policeman had driven into South Africa, and said she could go. Disorientated and filled with anxiety, she turned the car around and immediately ran into a roadblock — and was arrested. The Special Branch denied the whole story when Rosemary's lawyer tried to protest about the trickery, which successfully delivered her into a South African jail. Caught in their trap, and with her children's future at stake, Rosemary became one of those who turned state witness. It was that or face losing her children for good.

Should she have thought about this before? Who is to judge rights and wrongs. It was a speciality of the men who acted as interrogators in the Special Branch to use emotional blackmail, and it was particularly effective on women. Rosemary was not the first or the only one to be presented with an impossible ethical dilemma, manipulated to betray themselves, the friends who had entrusted their very lives to each other, the principles they had lived by for years. Things were simpler for those of us who did not have children, but even then, we had parents and relatives who would be implicated against their will and perhaps damaged. Later, I reflected that I was glad I was no longer pregnant when we fled South Africa, despite the excruciating miscarriage I'd gone through a month or two before, which had sent me lurching along

the corridors of the Mining Department to the women's lavatories, clutching my stomach, finally to see a greyish, slimy blob in
the blood in the lavatory bowl.

Later, too, I would find out how the SB interrogators had black-
mailed and broken Lyn van der Riet, Adrian Leftwich's girlfriend.
They confronted her with each of her parents in turn. Both told
Lyn they were seriously contemplating suicide in the face of their
shame. The SB screamed at Lyn and her father that they would
make sure he lost his job. After her parents were taken away, Lyn
was beaten unconscious by 'bad cop' 'Spyker' van Wyk. Lyn was
in too much pain and too concussed to answer questions. Now
'good cop' Van Dyk appeared, and announced that they were
about to detain two married couples, friends of Lyn. One of the
women was newly pregnant. None of them was involved with
ARM. Unable to bear the possibility that they would be beaten
up as she had just been, and that her friend would probably lose
the baby, Lyn told Van Dyk where she had hidden the suitcases
containing dynamite. It turned out that the SB knew anyway,
but were playing cat and mouse with her. Now there was more
pressure from the family, with the SB colluding. Faced with impossible choices, Lyn decided to become a state witness and then
leave South Africa. The price of being granted a passport was to
remain silent in court about being assaulted. Haunted by guilt and
a sense of moral failure, Lyn believed for years that she did not
have the right to try and explain, much less ask her comrades for
forgiveness. Eventually, through becoming and being a psycho-
therapist herself, she was able to acknowledge that her guilt was
appropriate, could be voiced and let go.

The news about Denis came through one day when we were
walking along the burning road in Dar, towards the beach. He
was being held in custody in Pretoria jail. South Africans had
kidnapped him in Lusaka the day before we got there, drugged
him, put him in the boot of their car and driven him back into
South Africa. Ronnie raged and swore. All I could do was stand in
the middle of the pavement, helplessly crying for the fate of my
friend, the mild mathematician.

There was no direct communication between Tanganyika and South Africa, but now I could send letters via my sister in England, to be forwarded to my parents. Other than what had appeared in the papers, they'd heard nothing from us since the letter which Rosemary had arranged to post after we'd left, and I knew they would be worried sick, feeling angry and betrayed. I hoped that my elaborate charade of public family hostility would work to protect my mother and my father. It would be a long time before I found out what had actually happened, and how my mother had tried to deal with the psychological trauma of her interrogation by Swanepoel.

The ANC was giving us a small allowance, but we both realised we must find work. After talking for a little of moving on to Nigeria, both of use decided we wanted to stay in Tanganyika. Ronnie searched the phone book and went out walking the streets, looking for work as a research chemist and noting down the addresses of all the medical laboratories where he might apply. I got a list of the high schools in Dar at the post office, picked out the girls' schools and wrote off, offering to teach English. I thought wryly about King David, and how yet again the Head had been let down by politicos.

Before any of this came to fruition, at the beginning of September we were summoned to the Immigration Office and dealt a bombshell. A cold-eyed, unsympathetic official informed us that his government was no longer prepared to offer open house to all South African refugees who came seeking asylum. They were setting a quota on the numbers who might stay in Dar itself, and the ANC would determine who these would be; all prospective soldiers or people waiting to go into training would be sent to a camp up-country. We had a week to organise our own exit. No, there was no appeal. His was the final word.

So this was what it felt like to be 'endorsed out', surplus to requirements – the fate of thousands of black people back in South Africa. We had two cards up our sleeves and the only option was to play them both. The first was that I had a little money in a bank account in Oxford, dating from the years when I'd been there at university. I arranged through a Tanganyikan bank which was affiliated to my British bank to get access to my account. But this would not be enough to cover our air fares to London. Via London, I telegrammed a message to my mother, asking if she could help. We had very little time, and no confidence that the Tanganyikan authorities would be sympathetic while we tried to sort out the money to leave. Later, Dorothy told me that she'd gone to Jan Smuts Airport with the letter she'd written to her brother, instructing him to wire money to us in Dar. She did not dare put anything in the post in case her letters were being intercepted and never arrived. She said she searched the faces of the passengers waiting for the next flight to London, and finally approached someone who looked honest and sympathetic, asking them to put her letter in the post in England as soon as he arrived.

I wired a friend of my parents, who had befriended me when I was in England. She was a lawyer. It was a simple telegram. ARRIVING HEATHROW SEPTEMBER 9, FLIGHT XXXX FROM DAR. NEED POLITICAL ASYLUM. HELP PLEASE. She was there, waiting at the barriers with my sister. We saw her waving as we approached passport control, knowing that we would get no further. After a discreet talk with an official, out of our earshot, and once a letter with an official heading had been revealed, she was let through. With her, we were taken into a private room while our entry into the country was made legal. Hilda and Rusty Bernstein were on the same flight and also needed political asylum. They were famous – Rusty had been one of the Rivonia trialists – and the press was there to meet them. Unlike them, we slipped in anonymously and quietly, and disappeared into England.

In England, the euphoria of safety and freedom subsided, and we both struggled with depression and feelings of worthlessness. By then, the fate of our comrades who'd stayed behind in South Africa was filtering through to us, mainly through packages of newspaper clippings which Dorothy sent weekly. The guilty knowledge of their suffering, with no chance of reducing or sharing it, seemed the special price we had to pay for our escape.

We lived for a while in Paddington with Gay, joining the ballet students who boarded with Mrs Mac in Paddington, sleeping on narrow camp beds that someone found for us. One night, coming in late and not wanting to disturb us by switching on a light, one of the lodgers bumped into my bed where I lay sleeping. I was awake instantly, screaming.

Then we lived in a tiny bedsitter with a kitchen built into an alcove and the double bed taking virtually all the remaining space. We sat on the bed, we ate on the bed, I prepared our meals on a tray on the bed, and finally we cleared it and slept in it. I went off to the job I'd found in a classy shop in the West End – morning to night, six days a week, working till 7 p.m. on Thursdays and every other night till 6 p.m. I trailed to work on the bus and the Underground, returning exhausted from standing all day. But at least I was with people. I had something to do, and because it was a very prestigious shop, I sometimes met extraordinary people – African dignitaries; the niece of the Prime Minister of Ceylon, who picked up on my non-English accent and perhaps non-English demeanour, entered into conversation, and even offered an invitation to meet later.

But Ronnie's refugee status did not permit him to work. He was isolated and drifting without an anchor. Ronnie lay all day on the bed in our rented room with the curtains drawn, just as he had years ago in Phin's Court in Johannesburg, paralysed by depression, smoking – though we could hardly afford his habit, what with the price of English cigarettes. Sometimes, in the untimely heat of an Indian summer, he walked to Hampstead Heath and went swimming in the ponds. But he had nothing to do, no work; was not allowed to work, was obliged to present himself at a police station once a week as the condition of his refugee status. Finally, a letter arrived for him from the Vice-Chancellor at Wits, sent months before and forwarded by my mother. This said bluntly that he was deregistered as a PhD student due to his traitorous political activities. His despair deepened. What use had our pathetic gestures of resistance been? What was he going to do with his life now, his years of study cancelled?

By now, we'd made contact with the ANC office in London and through them, just as it seemed as if all options were shutting down, a new window opened. A doctor and his wife in Scotland with anti-apartheid sympathies had heard about the PhD deregistration. Without knowing anything more about Ronnie, they offered to take him in. The doctor was a member of faculty at Aberdeen University, and he said he could get Ronnie registered in their postgraduate Chemistry Faculty, even though his M.Sc. was not recognised in Scotland; he would have to start again from scratch. If he lived with them, his fees would be paid. Theirs was one of those gestures of generosity and selflessness that are not always recorded, but are repeated time and again by well-wishers in countries where refugees find themselves. Perhaps they thought Ronnie would be like the son they never had. With nothing else on offer, he accepted, and I saw him off on the train north to Scotland. I would stay behind in my job in the shop, moving into a single room in one of those flat-shares for strangers passing through which abound in London.

So, in one of those queer coincidences of history, Ronnie found himself in Aberdeen, where a century before, the grandfather he'd never known had been born and grown up. Aberdeen was full of Mutches, we discovered. In Scotland, like so many talented people in exile who lose their way when deprived of their country, he tried to blot out the bad dreams, the sense of hopelessness, the flashbacks, with alcohol.

When we'd been living apart for several months, I saw Robert – whom we'd met with Moulvi Cachalia in Bechuanaland, shortly after crossing the border – again in London. His mission was to contact Ronnie. The ANC High Command was interested in his skills with explosives and wanted him to consider returning to Southern Africa, to Lusaka or one of the camps in Tanganyika, to help train MK activists. Robert invited me out to supper and we went to one of the cheap Indian restaurants off the Tottenham Court Road, reminiscing about the last time we'd eaten curry together, then for beer at a nearby pub. Sitting close to me on one of the padded leather benches, Robert took my arm and suggested that we go up to his place, which was nearby. 'But I'm married,' I protested. 'I don't sleep with other men!'

He thought I was stringing him along, mocking him. Ronnie was away, why had I come to supper with him if I was going to play hard to get? It was because he was black, wasn't it? Shocked and saddened, I carefully untangled my trapped arm, stood up, said goodbye and walked out of the pub.

When I passed on the message from the ANC, Ronnie did not dismiss the proposal out of hand. I did not tell him about Robert's other proposition. I said I couldn't tell him what to do, but hoped, for our sake, he would stay in England. It was my way of trying to tell him that I loved him.

I felt myself pulled every which way, aware that precisely this sacrifice of their personal lives was being chosen and lived out by thousands of women and men – some in England, some in the African countries we'd passed through, most in South Africa itself. I am not sure why I interpreted this challenge differently from the decision, taken without hesitation only a couple of years before, that I should be involved in ARM sabotage. I'd told myself then that I was adopting a principled stand against injustice, based on a considered judgement that non-violent protest could never achieve change. Why did I feel differently now about Ronnie going back, when nothing had changed in South Africa itself? Had I started to re-evaluate sabotage as a strategy? No, of that I am sure. Was it that I wanted so badly for my marriage to work, to be the central thing in my life; that I did not want to be left behind in England; that I did not believe our marriage could survive the strain of this kind of separation? I knew what it was like being alone in England, from when I was at Oxford. At first, the pain and loneliness were unbearable. Then you started to get used to it, stopped remembering just what the other person looked like, how they talked; stopped filling your mind with the things you'd done together. You couldn't live in a cocoon or a prison cell. You made new friends, started to join in, to laugh again. Indeed, it is only the strongest marriages that survive long separations. I felt humble before those women whose husbands were in jail or 'away', and who kept the faith.

In the end, Ronnie himself decided he could not go. Only people who have had to make these kinds of choices can know how they force you to query your very identity, tear you apart.

In England, for many months I did not sing. As the weather got colder, I stood at bus stops early in the morning, and squeezed on to the Underground with people whose faces I never recognised. I allowed people to shove their elbows into my body in the crush, or poke my feet with their umbrella stalks. Perhaps physical pain was better than the emptiness I felt. When I did start to sing again, it was the songs of South Africa, the ones that might help me remember who I was, for I no longer knew.

THE SONG REMEMBERS WHEN

The ARM was very much bigger than it might appear in this book. I was a tiny, insignificant shrub, and till I read Magnus Gunther's history of the organisation, published in 2004, I honestly had no idea of the extent of the forest of which I'd been a part. Magnus spent fifteen years researching ARM and its predecessor the NCL, interviewing everyone who was still alive and would speak to him, and wrote up his analysis at the request of the South African government, which wanted to document resistance during the apartheid years.

Forty years on, some of the people in the ARM have been disgraced, some have disappeared into political obscurity and some are dead. Others have made a considerable mark in their chosen fields.

Finally, when the banning orders on political refugees were lifted, Hugh Lewin returned to South Africa, went back to his old profession as a journalist and trained journalists in Johannesburg till he retired. He wrote a book about his years in jail, *Bandiet,* and more recently published *Bandiet out of Jail.*

Eddie Daniels, a member of ARM based in Cape Town who has not appeared in this story, and was the only black person to be convicted, spent fifteen years in jail on Robben Island and became friends with Mandela. Mike still sees him.

Mike Schneider escaped from Swaziland in yet another extraordinary adventure shrouded in secrecy. Nothing is ever banal about Mike. He became the CEO for one of the largest and most important charities in the world – the Joint Distribution Committee, the 'Joint', which has its headquarters in New York. Organised around Jewish relief, the Joint has also been involved in support for Palestinians. Mike masterminded the escape of the Falasha Jews from Ethiopia, he was in Tehran when the Shah fell, he has been part of rescuing Jews from Russia and Eastern Europe. Now about to retire, he plans to devote some of the expertise gained in his current work to set up and run charities to help disadvantaged South Africans.

Denis Higgs was finally released from Pretoria jail after strenuous diplomatic action by the British High Commission. He married Holly and they went to Canada, where he resumed his academic career as a mathematician. His marriage to Holly did not last, and I have lost touch with him.

Rosemary Wentzel continued to live in South Africa and I do not know what has happened to her.

After a long exile in England, in which she created a magical garden in which many of the plants originated in South Africa, Lyn van der Riet also returned to her roots in the Cape. She had suffered a crisis of identity because of the way she'd been manipulated into betraying her comrades; she wanted to explain and ask forgiveness. Her new profession, psychotherapy, reflected her own need to come to terms with the horrible choice that had been forced on her. When I saw her shortly before she left London, I could only say that I understood what it must have been like to face the possibility of your father's suicide because of what you had done, and that whatever she'd chosen to do, she would have been racked with guilt. Lyn deserves a story in her own right, but I am not the one to tell it.

Adrian Leftwich left South Africa with political indemnity after he'd turned state witness, giving evidence which put some of his best friends and comrades in prison for a very long time. He got academic posts in universities in England, but was shunned by people who knew what he had done, and found that he could not escape his past – although, it seems, he attempted to justify himself for years. He had a number of breakdowns, and finally, after therapy, came clean in print about his immediate collapse under interrogation – but without mentioning being state witness in the trials. As Mike said to me recently, if the people who went to jail could forgive Adrian, then he could too.

Eleanor Anderson came to England and married the mystery man with orange hair – Ronnie Kasrils. He was involved in organising a variety of military actions during the period of civil war. They both returned to live openly and freely in South Africa with the return of democracy, and Ronnie is now a senior member of the South African government.

Abdullay Jassat worked in the ANC office in London in Penton Street, Islington, for many years, and returned to South Africa at the time of independence. He is still active in the ANC, though his health is poor. He never really recovered from the dreadful torture inflicted on him by the Special Branch. Mosie Moolla went to India, where he was joined eventually by his wife.

'White Norman' Seeff qualified as a doctor and worked for a while in Baragwanath Hospital in Johannesburg. He went to America, where he became a well-known photographer, doing record sleeves and photographing the rich, the beautiful and the famous.

After we'd been in England for about six years, Ronnie wrote a semi-fictionalised account of those last months in South Africa before we fled, and the nightmarish time on the run through Bechuanaland. He wrote obsessively, in his huge, scrawling, backward-facing, left-handed writing, hour after hour, every day, with a self-discipline that filled me and our small children with awe. We were not allowed to interrupt – he was the artist at work. On more than one occasion, our four-year-old daughter, whom he was supposed to collect from school, sat waiting outside the office – till finally the worried Head rang me at the school in the nearby town where I had a job, asking what had happened. This happened so many times that I gave up expecting Ronnie to remember, and organised for our daughter to go home with the policeman's wife till I could fetch her on my way home. Most evenings, Ronnie disappeared into the pub and only returned at closing time. Finally, I read what he had written – a book which glorified his role, diminished that of the black people in our cell, and depicted the woman based on me as a stereotypical, snivelling neurotic who banged pots and pans around in the kitchen, nagged and whined, and played no useful part in anything. It was a bitter lesson – and even then I did not learn it.

Haunted by the ghosts of the past, Ronnie sank further and more destructively into alcoholism. Finally, after many false starts and failed attempts at rehab, he dragged himself back into sobriety. By then, it was not possible to resuscitate our marriage. We struggled on together till we finally parted in 1981. Living in the North of England, Ronnie continued to try to expose and publicise some of the evils of apartheid, including the projects of the white South African regime to make an atom bomb. He did not complete his PhD, though he did work as a scientist for Unilever for a couple of years – putting stripes into toothpaste, as he would disparagingly say. He suffered quite a severe breakdown, though he was not hospitalised. During that time, he wrote strange and very disturbing poetry and film scripts, one of which he filmed, using his own money and amateur actors. On the strength of that, and on the tidal wave of television expansion in England in the late sixties, he got jobs first as a TV researcher and then as a director.

Ronnie died suddenly in 1992. Mandela's freedom walk from

prison, holding hands with Winnie, had been on all our television screens, and Ronnie was planning a trip back to South Africa – political amnesty was guaranteed for all those who'd been on the lists of prohibited people. But tragically, he never made it. He saw his sister and her family once before he died, when they all came to London before Mandela was freed and the regime collapsed. But he never saw his country again.

The huge gulf between Ronnie's attitudes to race and those of his family always underlined the impossibility of stereotyping white South Africans, or thinking that if you knew one person in a family, you would understand them all. When he visited us in England, his brother-in-law horrified all of us, including our children, by taking off his leather belt and whipping his young son for some minor cheekiness. I had lived away from white South Africans for about ten years by then, and could only reflect how the brutality of apartheid in fact brutalised everyone, the perpetrators worst of all. Though his sister and her husband tried to bait us, we kept the peace by avoiding any political talk.

Ten years after riding across the South African border, I had my own bike and a full motorbike licence; by then, I was determined to be a pillion passenger no longer – in my marriage or in life. The years of living with Ronnie's alcoholism coincided with the Women's Movement. I discovered that the lie I'd been living in my marriage was not unique, and that my painful experience could be explained politically, not just personally. Friends, my siblings – and Al-Anon – slowly helped restore the self-esteem I had lost, and gave me the courage to leave a bullying, co-dependent, alcoholic marriage. I was finally strong enough, and healthy enough, to rise to the challenge of a new, loving relationship. I remarried in 1987 – not to a South African, which means there is often a great deal to explain – but as they say, I am living happily ever after.

The Jewish family diaspora is fluid and no generation really seems to put down permanent roots. Of the South African cousins, four stayed in South Africa. Five packed up and left: they are in England, the USA and Canada. My brother Jon came to school in England at sixteen, getting himself a place at St Paul's School on the strength of an interview with the High Master, which he organised for himself. By 1976, after disregarding his call-up papers for the South African army, he was also an exile – largely on account of slipping back into the country to make an underground film about the Soweto Uprisings for British television. Then he was really and truly persona non grata. He wrote a prize-winning play about the Biko trial, which went to New York and was also televised. The South African authorities were not impressed with this endeavour either. Since then, Jon has won a number of awards for his documentaries, including an Oscar and a BAFTA for his film about Anne Frank, the Broadcast Award for his series entitled *Terror,* and an international award for *The War Reporters.*

After attending the Royal Ballet School, my sister Gay joined the London Festival Ballet and toured all over the world. When she returned to South Africa, she became one of the prima ballerinas in the Johannesburg Ballet Company. She married a South African journalist who worked for the *Rand Daily Mail,* but, like many honest journalists of those times, he soon fell foul of the censorship processes. They decided to leave, and ended up in Canada. Gay went on dancing professionally, and when this was no longer feasible – dancers, like athletes, are at the mercy of time and age – she became the dance director of a big arts academy in Ontario.

Despite his anxiety, my father held on for years to the belief that he was not implicated by association with his subversive daughter and son-in-law. He was a senior official in the Transvaal Department of Public Health, Acting Head of the Department; but in the year after we fled, he was demoted back to his original position and never promoted again. The man brought in was the notorious young Dr Eiselen, twenty years my father's junior. His father was Dr Eiselen, Verwoerd's Secretary for Native Affairs, author of the report which set out the principles for separate education for Bantu-speaking people. In his blindness to what was happening all around him, Dad refused to see his children's and his wife's bitter criticisms of apartheid as anything other than their conspiracy to undermine him as a husband and father.

Dad took the humiliation of demotion very personally. He was bitter that his excellent Afrikaans was not recognised, nor his years of loyal service. Anti-Semitism there might be in the official world but not, he believed, against him. His stories of how this or the other colleague – some Afrikaans, some English, none Jews – had clapped him on the back ('Hey Blair, good man'), shared their opinions and plans, were all part of his self-delusion that he was truly accepted and valued. In reality, his bosses had a master plan which gobbled up people like him and spat them out. Perhaps he imagined that his department did not know he was Jewish, duped by the phoney Scottish name, even if they couldn't avoid realising he was English speaking. So great was his insecurity and his loyalty, his deep need to believe in his life's work as 'a medical man', that he could not even start to consider that in hitching his star to this government, he would be crushed. A meek little English-speaking Jew, with an unreliable English wife, who'd kept her British passport so that she could travel safely in black Africa, a woman involved with magazines for black writers and who'd translated black authors – and a daughter and son-in-law who would have been convicted and imprisoned for treason if they had not got away … he hadn't a hope.

Dorothy and Maurice finally left South Africa after the Soweto Uprisings in 1976. For Dorothy it was 'coming home', for Maurice a very painful adjustment. He and Dorothy had visited England many times in the past, but going back to live there was not the same. He was heavily dependent on Dorothy to create a social life for them both, but his attitudes both to class and race were largely unacceptable in the circles they now mixed in. In a skewed replay of my own difficulty with white people serving me when I came to Oxford in 1960, he addressed waiters in restaurants – whatever their colour – as if they were an inferior breed, to be summoned and told off. The carefully censored memories of his student days in the thirties, bathed in the rosy haze of nostalgia for a land that had never been, were not only an anachronistic fantasy, but were contradicted by the crowded, multicultural, brash reality.

But by the time he died in 1991, after fifteen years in England, he had moved a long long way. The unthinking sexism of his generation remained – complicated by his pride in all our achievements. He would do the washing up (sometimes), but always drew the kitchen curtain so that no one saw him! He seldom embarrassed and angered us anymore with outspoken statements about white superiority, and his arrogance about working-class people had diminished. (Given his own family origins, this had been not just unforgivable but hypocritical.) After he died, I reflected that this arrogance was yet another legacy of apartheid South Africa to its white population, through that oh-so-neat conflation of race and class. Always sensitive to what would make him acceptable, maybe in England he'd learned the virtues of silence in order to keep the peace – just as I had done, in a society where my attitudes were beyond the Pale. Maybe, too, the influence of a more tolerant society, of people who offered him a different model, the opportunity to meet and talk with people of colour who were his social equals – denied him in South Africa – really did change him. I like to think so. As for his religious identity, Dad continued to struggle and search. For a while he attended Quaker meetings in Brighton. He never, to my knowledge, officially joined a shul.

After Maurice died, Dorothy lived on for another seven years, hugely enjoying her freedom and writing prolifically. She gained wide recognition of her work publicising and translating French African literature and black women's writing. She continued to travel, to climb mountains, to go camping in her eighties, with an energy that continues to inspire me. It was as if she'd been freed, not just to travel and paint the kitchen whatever colour she wanted, but to become a different kind of person. Now she came into her own, with flamboyant jewellery and a red leather jacket. When Maurice died, a new Dorothy came out of a chrysalis.

My parents lived in their house in Johannesburg for twenty-three years. This was more than twenty years longer than they'd managed anywhere else, in their thirty-three years in Southern Africa. The person who bought the house let it to

students; then it was squatted and badly neglected. My mother's carefully planned and planted garden had turned into a ruined and riotous jungle. In 1992, Jon and I found that the house had been bought by a multi-racial gay couple, who were in the middle of a major structural conversion. Little else but the intricate, embossed metal ceilings and the parquet floors of our childhood were still recognisable. In the garden, the old, old cedar trees had been cut down and were lying on the ground, ready to be sawn up and hauled away. The rare plants, organised by colour and shape, had all gone; there was no sign of the aloes, the yesterday-today-and-tomorrow, the granadilla, the great scented white camellia, the hilly lawns down which we'd rolled – all ploughed up in preparation for the landscape of someone else's dream. I went to look at the Gale Road house again when I was in Johannesburg in 2005. The old house had been demolished and a modern monstrosity erected in its place, so ghastly I couldn't bear to take a photograph to send to Gay. This hideous replacement to our former home was hard to stomach.

Although I had gone to Tanzania, to the Solomon Mahlangu Freedom College, on behalf of the London ANC Education Committee in 1981, it was only in 1992 that I finally stepped off a plane onto South African soil. I was with my brother Jon, also a banned person for so many years. Like Ronnie, our political pasts had prevented either of us entering the country when it was still under Nationalist rule, but things had changed. I was so excited and nervous as I locked up our house in London that I slammed the front door with the keys still inside. Was this some uncanny reintroduction to my once-criminal past, I thought, as I carefully worked my hand through the letterbox, reached for the keys and pulled them back – preparing for my re-entry to South Africa? Jon just smiled.

When we circled over Johannesburg and came down to land, it was almost twenty-eight years to the day since I'd left with Ronnie on the motorbike, and sixteen years since Jon had stood on South African soil. In the icy air of a winter evening, the smells, the sounds, the accents of South Africa lurched me back to the past. At passport control at Johannesburg International Airport (as we had to remember to call it) we were both ridiculously nervous – for no real reason except reflex reaction. I handed my British passport to the black official and, although I knew it was safe, I started to shake with apprehension. But the officials barely glanced up to match photographs with faces, and the new South Africa welcomed us with smiles.

Jon and I spent five weeks on a journey through the country, just ahead of the elections – virtually retracing, in reverse, the route my parents had taken nearly fifty years before, and connecting back to the beloved landscape of our childhood. This was a pilgrimage, without our non-South African partners or our children, planned for months over maps and brochures in London, to rediscover both our childhoods. So we wove around the country, on a journey to find all the places where we'd once lived or had connections.

On our way from Johannesburg to Pietermaritzburg, where I'd lived as a very young child and gone to boarding school in the early fifties, we took the long way round through Volksrust to Newcastle. The road was unrecognisable, a sleek, smooth highway through the mountain pass, with cars speeding to the coast. We could not find the winding road where the Kombi had crashed into the hillside. We ate a picnic lunch on the hill at Majuba and then went on to Newcastle. We looked for the house Ronnie had grown up in, along the shady roads, among the gum trees, but I was no longer sure I remembered where it was.

We climbed the Drakensberg and went up Table Mountain on foot, shunning the cable car. We rushed shivering and goose-pimpled into the cold sea at Qolora – winter is not a good time for swimming in the Cape. I photographed the cows browsing along the deserted coast, and the eery, rusting wrecks of huge ships which had foundered on the rocks along these shores. Cape of Good Hope. Cape of Storms. Ever the contradictions.

We visited 'comrades' who had returned to South Africa, and the aged Bledin relatives, who had barred themselves into their white suburbs, desperately fearing the mayhem and bloodshed they predicted after the elections.

South Africa had moved on, but so had I. Somewhere, deep down, I knew that my life now was in England – though, god knows, I might still come back to live out my last days here. What I had to do, I thought, was keep alive in England the passion that had inspired me when I was so much younger. Ten, twenty, thirty years before, South Africa had driven out so many of us who were talented, who could have contributed so much. But like the people driven out by the Tsars a century before, and the Nazis mere decades ago, we had some role to play in our adopted countries.

My daughter Thembi – the four-year-old forgotten at school by her father – went to live and work in South Africa in 1994. She stayed for eighteen months and I visited her, staying with her in Cape Town. Together we made a trip into the Western Cape, across the mountains that divide the Peninsula from the interior. I finally shared with her some of the landscapes of my own child-hood, which she had often heard me speak of. We gave lifts to people waiting by the side of the long, empty roads and I found I could still speak and understand Afrikaans, after all those years.

And now, after all these years, just as I had imagined, my children ask me about the time of my exile and how it happened. Forty years on, it turns out much harder to explain, let alone justify, than I ever thought. At the time, it all seemed simple. There was an evil. We were young, strong, intelligent. We had to combat it. *Quod erat demonstrandum,* as we used to say in our maths classes with Win Roux. For nearly forty years, I kept what we had done in South Africa largely to myself, telling only a selective and carefully edited story. When people found out I came from South Africa, they almost always dealt me a dilemma – beautiful country, they would say. You must miss the sun/the sea/the landscape/ the space. Yes I did, I would say noncommittally. There would be those who assumed that, as a white South African, I supported the regime, and they would either offer sickening, collusive approval or express outright hostility towards me personally. Either way I was torn. In the early days, I allowed myself to become extremely upset and sometimes quite aggressive towards the apartheid supporters. Once, I rushed from a drinks party unable to contain my rage at my host's blatant racism. I would dread the dinner parties when I would find myself listening to stereotypes and judgemental remarks about black people – whether in Africa or in England – which were so familiar from my youth. I found myself blanking out, going elsewhere in my head: the old strategy from my adolescence. I learned to choose how to object and argue my case. I realised that in England, too, I needed survival strategies for these social occasions, for it was always me that got wounded; my antagonists seemed neither to change their minds nor to be upset by my objections. Some situations I would simply avoid, knowing I'd be forced into close proximity with people whose views I could not tolerate, but whom I would find myself powerless to argue against. It felt a bit like being a Jew in the casually anti-Semitic atmosphere of my childhood, all over again. Where I could, I tried to talk about economic, political and social exploitation and the negative aftermath of colonialism, and I never allowed anyone to believe I supported the apartheid regime. Against the common white South African rejoinder that people who weren't living there had no place criticising, I went out of my way to say that not only did people in Britain have a perfect right to protest, they *should* support sanctions and boycotts ... and that South Africa was probably worse than they were led to believe.

I was part of the ANC Education Committee in London, and went to the cultural functions and some of the political meetings; but, unlike many of the South African exiles in London, I was determined to 'live forwards': to make myself a life in London as best I could. If this meant deliberately 'forgetting' and denial, at least in public, of who I still was, then so be it. So, I went about my business as a middle-class, respectable (well, moderately!) mother and teacher of young children. An ordinary person, not an outcast or a renegade, I went on the bus or rode my bike to work; I shopped, I made my house and garden as comfortable and attractive as I could. With selected friends – to raise a laugh – my party piece was to mimic various South African accents, which I could switch into as easy as clicking my fingers: my own sad brand of nostalgia for my lost childhood. I taught my children – and later my beloved grandchild – some of my songs. I taught them to harmonise as Africans do whenever they sing, to hold a tune or sing the descant against another voice: the multilayered music that drifted off the streets and from the gatherings in public places as we grew up.

Few people realised that I came from that evil southern land of apartheid. Chameleon that I have always been, my musical ear and my middle-class upbringing meant that within a very short time, I'd adapted my accent – I was 'passing' again. Who would ever think that once I'd been part of a group that made timers for explosive devices in our living room, that I was a banned person and had fled to avoid prison? At the time of the IRA bombings in London, I was even more reluctant to say what I'd been part of, sure that I would encounter only the generalised and palpable hostility against sabotage, the failure to understand the despair and the determination that grows when every legitimate protest hits a roadblock. With Mandela's release, it did become possible and acceptable to admit that one had been a saboteur. Mandela, the hero of our time, had, after all, famously endorsed armed struggle from the dock – as the Western world now discovered, through the many documentaries that tried to tell the story of what had led to his long imprisonment.

But now, in the twenty-first century, with great cities all over the world ripped apart by fundamentalism and terrorism which seem indifferent to human life, it is important to keep the faith; to remember what we were involved in, back in the early sixties. In this attempt to understand the past in the light of the present, our credo, that we would not kill, seems now like some sort of safety net. And so, if my children ask me, all I can say is: 'It was the right thing, the only thing to do at the time. I don't know if it helped anything, really. I don't know if anything went faster because of what we did. Perhaps not. But I am still not ashamed or sorry. You do what you can. Ja–nee.'

The nature of life is change, and there is no real way to save one's life, except through memory and the music to which it sings. The songs of my childhood and my growing up are with me always – the songs I learned from my father, the songs and hymns I learned in my schools in South Africa, the pop songs and the political songs that became so integral to my identity in adolescence, the folk songs that sang my life after I came to England ...

> *I guess some things we bury*
> *Are just bound to rise again*
> *And even if the whole world has forgotten*
> *The song remembers when.*